Game

Roosh Valizadeh

Table Of Contents

Prologue

In early 2006, I started writing my first book *Bang*. I could not have predicted that it would become one of the preeminent resources to help men with their dating lives. Since then, I've tried to surpass its popularity with more than fifteen other books, but with the exception of *Day Bang*, none of them have come remotely close. Parents are told not to show overt favoritism to one particular child, but if my books were my children, *Bang* would be my favorite.

Besides an update in 2010 to cover text messaging game and going out solo, I have not made any additional edits that address the massive changes we've seen in culture and technology. Many men believe that the most damaging change to society has been the widespread adoption of smartphones, which women treat as surrogate boyfriends, but even worse is the normalization of feminism and social justice. These leftist ideas have increased the hostility between the sexes by inventing myths such as rape culture, the wage gap, and gender fluidity. It would not be an exaggeration to state that relations between the sexes are the worst they've ever been, with both women and men developing a genuine animosity for each other. Explaining the cause of this hostility, and why I believe it's a deliberate agenda of the elites, is another subject entirely—this book instead provides men with non-political advice on how to connect with the opposite sex in an era when it's become harder than ever to do so.

I am writing this book for many reasons. The first, to be honest, is pride. There is nothing more rewarding than creating something that elevates your esteem among your fellow man. Second, you have demanded it. A week doesn't pass without me being asked to share updated game advice. *Bang* has withstood the test of time more than I could've expected, but I must admit that it is showing signs of age. My livelihood depends on satisfying the customer—ask and you shall receive.

Lastly, I want to protect you from danger. Women are being trained to believe they have been raped when they weren't, and new laws are making it easier to ruin a man's life with dubious allegations that have zero physical evidence. This rape-obsessed climate did not exist when I wrote *Bang*, so I did not lay out protocols and defense mechanisms to minimize your chance of getting caught in the cultural snares that are elevating women to the status of eternal victims while redefining normal masculinity as "toxic" or even criminal. In this book, I will give you advice that I have given to my college-aged brother, who I have a strong interest in keeping safe.

Regrettably, the best era to be a player has passed. Between 1990 and 2010, sexual norms were loosest *and* there was no feminist or government persecution of men. During this time, feminism was a rising cultural force, but it mostly focused on issues such as abortion, domestic violence, and workplace sexual harassment. Once feminists had achieved their goals in those areas, they moved onto college campuses and promoted "rape culture," which attempted to redefine sex and intimate relationships for everyone. With the help of the media, universities, police departments, courts, and governments, they have successfully given women a rape card to use anytime they feel regretful, sad, or depressed. The player era ended when these ideas started to infect the mainstream. There is now more downside than upside for sleeping with whomever you can.

What a great time it was in 2005 when sex was relatively easy, with zero chance of being accused of rape after a consensual sexual encounter that happened to involve alcohol. False accusations were barely heard of back then. I remember laughing at the crazy online rantings of beastly women claiming that "all sex is rape," failing to see how such a preposterous notion would become a dystopian reality. As the years passed, I started hearing stories from friends about women acting weird after sex and making vague statements about being taken "advantage" of. Soon I received emails from worried men stating that girls were accusing them of rape outright and might go to the police. Then I got a panicked call from a close friend who needed advice on what to do after the police showed up at his door to investigate a rape claim. I believe that all these cases involved consensual sex, but those in power can change the definition of consensual sex. Laws can be altered to make illegal what was once legal, and I have no doubt that they will keep being changed until every single sexual encounter that a man has could be interpreted as rape by the judicial system. This will happen within my lifetime.

Since the judicial system is being subverted, we must rely on our behavior, intelligence, and knowledge to stay safe. The days of racking up notches and banging drunk girls have come to an end. You now have to say "no" to women who want to have sex with you if they've shown signs of derangement or instability. Otherwise, I can almost guarantee that you will have problems if you try to live out a dream of sleeping with hundreds of women. The ideal game plan today is to find a mentally stable girl who has some resistance to feminist ideas, and entering at least a mini relationship with her.

I know that you bought this book to improve your sex life instead of worrying about crazy changes that are happening to the culture, but understand that we can no longer separate the two. I'm confident this book will account for those changes so that you can stay out of harm's way and enjoy pleasant relationships with women, whether for the short or the long term.

Reading *Bang* is not a prerequisite to getting the most out of this book. *Game* is not an "advanced" or upgraded version of *Bang*, but a rebooted game book based on ten years of additional experience. I purposefully did not look at *Bang* before writing *Game*, so if you read something here that you remember from *Bang*, it's an idea or tactic that strongly correlates to sexual success. I will now teach you absolutely everything I know about game and women. Let's begin.

Chapter 1: Introduction To Game

Beautiful girls in big cities are now directly and indirectly offered sex more than 1,000 times a month from men on the internet, in bars, on the streets, and within their social circles. If a girl has a basic internet profile, spends time on social networking, and goes out twice a week, I guarantee that she is offered more cock than even the most famous women of the past. A girl is not interested in 99% of the men who offer her sex, but try to imagine the effect on your psychology if 1,000 women a month were trying to have sex with you. What kind of person would that make you?

I can tell you what I would be like if I were getting over 1,000 sex offers every month: I'd be spoiled rotten, thinking that I deserved all those women just because I existed. I'd be flakey, cancelling dates often, because I'd constantly be unsure whether I was getting the "best" possible girl. I'd be bitchy to women who didn't read my mind and failed to treat me exactly the way I wanted, because don't they know that I could sleep with hundreds of other women any time I wanted? I'd be moody, always dependent on the reactions I get from women. If I received less attention one weekend than usual, I'd throw a temper tantrum and demand immediate satisfaction. I'd also get bored easily. With so many women constantly trying to entertain me, I wouldn't be able to tolerate five minutes with a boring girl who didn't jump through hoops to make me laugh. Lastly, I'd be primed to value novelty more than stability. I'd become addicted to experiencing one new girl after the next, and believe excitement and fun were worth more than stability and commitment. My attention span would morph into that of a small child.

Haven't I just described the modern woman? While a large

part of who we are is shaped by our genetics, environment plays a huge role, and when your environment is getting nonstop attention from thousands of people trying to have sex with you, your personality and even your humanity will become degraded, making it hard for you to connect meaningfully with *anyone.* Trying to find lasting love, comfort, and stability with a modern woman is like trying to have a deep conservation with a cat that just wants to chase after a red laser dot darting around on the floor.

I'm sure you've had the experience of losing a girl's attention in a bar or nightclub and watching her get approached by another man not even ten minutes later. Even girls in small towns are getting hit on a lot. I've met girls from backwater European villages who can describe to me all the local beta orbiters who are trying to sleep with them, the Spanish or British tourists who have approached them in the mall, and men on the internet who are outright offering them gifts and free travel just for the chance of landing a date. Understand that the amount of dating choice a woman has is the *primary driver* that determines how we must structure our game. The more choice a woman has, the more methodical our game has to be.

Girls have become so used to having ample choice in men that they believe things have always been like this, not aware that just a few generations ago, they would've been lucky to have only two good men a year knocking on their door. Most of this choice is a result of technology, which allows women to access and "meet" more men in one day for sex than they could have in an earlier lifetime. Since technology is continuing to advance rapidly, I don't envision a return to the old ways. If anything, it will soon become impossible for a man who doesn't use some sort of game strategy to even get a date.

Paradoxically, we are living in both the best and worst time for sexual relations. It's the best because sexual norms are still loose enough where you can have sex with a girl without committing to her, even traveling around the world to do so, but it's also the worst because women have far more choice than you, which allows them to demand men of the highest standard while the culture gives them a free pass to attack men if they feel bad or upset at any moment. Since we don't have the power to change the culture, the best plan is to mitigate the bad while maximizing the benefits that we can receive. With the stage set, let's start talking about what game is and how it can enable us to get what we want.

What Is Game?

Game is a collection of beliefs, behaviors, strategies, and tactics that make women more attracted to you while increasing your likelihood of experiencing intimacy. It's often based on cold approaching, an active strategy where you walk up to a girl you don't know and present yourself in the best way possible so that she decides, at some point, to have sex with you. Game can also be used on girls within your social circle, a more passive strategy where you have to be less aggressive, because a hard rejection may lower your status within the group. It doesn't matter if you are rejected a dozen times a day when cold approaching, because you probably won't ever see those girls again, but within a specific social circle it's best not to work on more than one or two girls at the same time to keep conflict and drama at bay.

The popular misconception about game is that it's simply a collection of pick-up lines where you walk up to a girl and say something cheesy while wearing an outlandish hat. Not only is it more strategic than that, but game has evolved into a more holistic program of changing your appearance, behavior, and living habits. I remember the days when boldly approaching a girl was enough for her to think you were confident and attractive, but now that girls are approached so frequently, how bold is she going to think you are when you're the third guy to speak to her that day? As time passes, higher levels of game are required to accomplish the same result.

Back in 2002, the game I needed consisted of rubbing my crotch against a girl's ass while dancing, asking "What is your name?" after a few songs, having a short, banal conversation before resuming crotch-on-ass dancing, and eventually getting her number. Not only is that type of game insufficient today, but it may get you kicked out of the nightclub.

When I got a girl on a date, I would use the "roller coaster" routine that I found on the internet. I'd tell her about the experience of going on a wild roller-coaster ride, up and down, up and down, and how thrilling and exciting the ride was, and how I wanted to go on this ride again and again. The goal of this sexual metaphor was to make the girl horny, and although I'm not sure if it ever did, I never received a bad response. If I tried this routine today, the girl would stare at her iPhone before announcing that she has to leave.

I used countless other awkward moves successfully, but now girls expect much more. If you're living in a hyper-competitive city that has as many men as women, your game has to be above average just to pull a cute girl, and once you find an effective game strategy, you'll continually have to improve it so that the tens of thousands of men who are working on their game don't surpass you.

On the surface, it seems crazy that a man has to put in massive amounts of work in order to have sex with the women he wants, but men who don't use game, who toil in jobs or businesses to accumulate money and fancy cars in order to impress women, are doing the same thing. They're just relying on "provider" game that used to work before women made their own money or had a wide choice of who to date. Because having a good job or car is no longer a reliable way to secure the affections of a pretty girl, a more direct method in the form of modern game was developed, which has a far higher return on investment than trying to impress a girl with your career or material possessions.

All around you, men are working hard to get sex, from learning game, opening bars, incurring massive debt to appear rich, or trying to become famous. I'm in my late thirties and can go an entire day without thinking about sex, but I remember when I was in my twenties and couldn't go an hour. I won't ever shame a man for moving mountains in order to get laid, because I know that when your hormones are at their peak, you don't want to hear rational explanations or embrace Buddhist ideas about not desiring pleasure. You want sex and you want it now. My job is to help you meet that need in the healthiest way possible while preventing it from ruining your life.

The bad news is that it was easier to help you move that mountain years ago when few men were game-aware and only a small percentage of the female population were lesbians, morbidly obese, or green-haired man-haters. There are more men eager for sex with attractive girls than there are attractive girls. This crisis of supply and demand means you will have to work harder to get even less than I did when I was running game full time in the early 2000s, and young boys today will face an even greater struggle than you when they grow up and become men.

I fondly remember one of my first successful nightclub pick-ups back in 2001. It was my third or so visit to the club after graduating from college. I had no idea what I was doing, but I wanted sex badly. I tried my crotch-on-ass dancing move and it worked on a cute Filipino virgin. She gave me her number and I called her. I managed to get her out on a date where I essentially rehearsed memorized routines I had read on the internet. I guess they worked because she allowed me to kiss her. On the second date, I invited her to my apartment. She put up heavy resistance when I tried to take off her clothes, so I did the first thing that came into my mind: I put on a VHS tape of hardcore pornography. It didn't work at getting off her clothes. Do you know what I did next? I gave up! I just stopped calling her because I didn't know what else to do.

It's a miracle that I got as far as I did, and I wonder whether today an attractive Filipino girl of her age would respond to my moves in the same way as the virgin did more than fifteen years ago. Chances are she'd have over 1,000 thirsty male followers on Instagram and get approached in the club by guys who have a more refined technique than my crotch-on-ass move. Back then, the Filipino girl didn't have many options, so my awkward self was enough to get her out on a date, but today she could pick and choose from a greater supply of men.

A low level of game used to get you dates with attractive women, but advances in technology—particularly the invention of the smartphone—have turned game into an arms race, where every year the level of game that women expect rises in tandem with their options. I experienced this directly in Toronto when I visited in 2013. From the girls I talked to, I noticed that I was being evaluated on *every* joke I told. They would actually complain if a joke wasn't great, and suggest that I was "losing" them because of it. Instead of wanting to connect with men, the girls acted like they were attending a comedy show, eggs in hand, ready to throw them at the comedian if he didn't make them laugh hard enough. It's no surprise that a substantial percentage of my readers come from the Toronto area.

Another reason for the game arms race is the existence of teachers like me. My websites and books are training a large number of men to use game. The more men who know how to use game, the harder things get for every man, because the standard of game that women expect rises. Fortunately, I'm finding that game is becoming *less* popular than before. The younger generation of men is becoming lazier and softer than men of previous generations, mostly because they are addicted to video games, porn, estrogenic soy products, or social networking. This tells me that the technology which allows women to have more dating options is a far greater contributor to the need for higher levels of game than the availability of game knowledge alone. Whatever the reason for the game arms race, the reality is that you have to become like a doctor who must keep up with the latest medical advances to try improved treatments on your "patients." Thankfully, once you have a basic foundation of game, it's quite simple to maintain it at an optimal level, and by then it's likely that you'll have discovered a niche or two that reduces the amount of work you have to do.

An additional factor that makes game necessary is that the ratio of men compared to women in the population is far higher compared with the past, when frequent wars killed men almost exclusively. Although I do not wish for a huge war to make my sex life easier, the period of peace and stability we're living in is one of the factors that led to the creation of game in the first place. If there were two women for every one able-bodied man, a book like this wouldn't even be necessary. Instead, *women* would need books on how to compete for the few available men.

Game ends up becoming a scavenger strategy in any environment where there is a decreasing supply of quality females who have unlimited choice on who to date. It works in any society with loose sexual norms and declining birth rates, factors that signify the breakdown of the family unit and the promotion of "free love," where people have sex just for fun. There is a reason that my books don't sell well in countries with high birth rates, such as those in Africa, or where the traditional family is strong, such as those in the Middle East. The more fractured a society is, the greater the opportunity for game tactics to be useful for men who desire sexual relationships, as long as they continually upgrade their game or find niches that enable them to achieve consistent results among a fickle and bored female population.

The biological justification for game is strong: most women crave alpha males who display strength, confidence, and power, but game is not effective in a Muslim country, for example, where pre-marital sex is forbidden and women are not allowed to choose their marriage partner. The only reason you can use game is because your society is firmly on a path that will lead to a declining population and its eventual death. The relatively easy sex we can get with game is a symptom of this decline, but since time immemorial men have powerfully desired sex and will do almost anything to get it, whether it's marrying at a young age, as they did in the past, or approaching twenty women a week, as they may do today. Game, however, is of little help when you start to demand more from a woman in a long-term relationship, such as honesty, loyalty, and character. Game is a great tool for initiating a sexual relationship with a woman within a society that's declining, and for *identifying* the few good women left, but it does not create good women.

I have many critics who argue that I'm making society worse by teaching game to men, or that I'm corrupting "innocent" women, but a woman who sleeps with a man relatively quickly because of his game is far from innocent. Society, thanks largely to liberalism and technology, has made women promiscuous, and now we are using game to have the sex they've already decided they want, and which society has trained them to feel empowered for having. Every slut used to be an innocent and socially awkward virgin, and if you look at how high-school girls behave today, and who their role models are, you don't have to be Nostradamus to predict that the situation will continue to get worse.

The decline of Western society is out of our hands, but at least we can use the experience of getting sex to build our confidence and become stronger, more satisfied men. Along the way, you will have to overcome many insecurities and personal demons to go from a man who isn't getting laid frequently or meeting attractive women to one who is. Game has the potential to bring out the best in men, more than any other modern behavior available to them, because getting laid in a competitive environment unlocks your most masculine qualities.

Consider the type of game your grandfathers had to use on your grandmothers. In all likelihood, it was to be good men, get involved with the church, line up stable jobs, and be friendly. They didn't have to sleep with a dozen or more girls to enter a relationship that would last less than a year. There was no conscious effort on their part to try to be an alpha male or not to appear needy. When "grandfather game" becomes the best game to land a great woman, I will be the first to get excited, but we have to admit that your grandfathers may not have reproduced today if they had been forced to meet your grandmothers in the kind of climate we have to face.

Since game is a scavenger tool in a rapidly changing environment, we constantly have to be ready to adjust our tactics. Although the core principles of game remain the same, shifting trends and demographics may affect what works, and you'll have to stay on top of them to maintain results. For example, cities in Eastern Europe and Asia are starting to see a large increase in the number of male tourists and immigrants. I'm hearing complaints from men visiting Southeast Asia, one of the easiest places in the world for Western men, that things are not as good as in the past because the local women are getting spoiled. A time will come when a strategy or tool that worked well stops working, forcing you to adapt. The advice I share in this book assumes that things will continue to get worse for many decades into the future.

Adaptation is a concept you may be familiar with when it comes to doing business. Hundreds of years ago, a shoemaker would set up shop in a little store and make shoes for his entire life, with little change in how he did things. Today, technology and globalization mean that a shoemaker has to change his tactics every six or twelve months to maintain a consistent level of business. He has to compete not only with every shoemaker in his city, but also with every shoemaker with a website in the next city, and every shoemaker in China who can make shoes for half the price he does. If the shoemaker doesn't match or beat the advantages offered by his global competitors, he will go out of business. You have to keep an eye on what your potential customers want and what is working for your competitors. If you don't, you won't make any sales.

Modern dating is not much different. It has become a system of commerce where men and women can seek partners around the world, often without even leaving their couches. It's great that you can try to date beautiful women in Europe through the internet, but the downside is that these women can meet high-status men worldwide with even greater ease than you. It used to be that you had to compete only with the men in the bar you were visiting, or perhaps the men a woman interacted with that day at work, but now you're effectively competing with men from *the entire world*. You may be the top guy in the bar right now, but you're definitely not the top guy in the world, and she knows this because many of them are messaging her daily through internet sites and apps. Meanwhile, cheap air travel allows "exotic" men who are sexier than you to fly in and impress her with their foreign accents.

The globalization of male-female bonding has transformed it from traditional monogamy to a free-for-all sexual marketplace.

As with any other marketplace, the Pareto principle is at play where the top 20% of goods (men) attract the top 80% of shoppers (women). In the past, women had fewer choices and were constrained from acting on their desire to secure a top-tier man. Today, they are encouraged to spend years finding high-status men (and to get fat and tatted up while they're at it). The end result is fewer monogamous relationships, families, and children.

I hope you can see how the modern sexual marketplace creates fierce competition where a man has to increase his value as much as possible simply to have sex, with no guarantee that he will enter a monogamous relationship that leads to establishing a family, a prospect that many men come to see as negative or even harmful after having to deal with the amoral and promiscuous modern woman.

For many men, game is a strategy to have a bit of fun and get a girlfriend. After all, it's difficult to invest your time, year after year, into adapting to constantly changing conditions that are pushing down the quality of women, all for sex that becomes less novel with experience. Many men who thought they had solved their problems by hopping on a plane to South America, Southeast Asia, or Eastern Europe have seen the women in foreign countries degrade as well, while the march of technological progress continues to make it easier for thousands of men to hit on a single woman. An app such as Tinder was well received by men when it first came out, because of how easy it was to get a date, but now those same men are complaining that it benefits mainly women.

Things are not going to get any better if technology continues to supplant face-to-face communication, traditional monogamy is not promoted, and the male-to-female ratio remains high. This means that game will be absolutely necessary just to get laid, and this game must always be refreshed, upgraded, and adjusted to produce results over the long term.

It's hard to continue committing your time to something that you value less with every passing year, so for most men game has a definite lifespan, even if that span may be as long as twenty years. When I first got into game, I valued nothing more than getting a new girl in my bed for sex, but as time went on, I started to value other things such as a good night's sleep, not being hungover the next day, and getting work done. Since how you value sex today will change tomorrow, think about how you will exit the game once you've had your fill by keeping an eye out for the type of girl who you'd consider suitable for a long-term relationship. If you're sure that you don't want any sort of relationship, you should focus on continually adapting your game over time to suit changing conditions and your advancing age.

The Nature Of Game

The goal of game for me was to lose my virginity and get a girlfriend. I was a late bloomer and didn't even start puberty until I was 18, so I looked like a child next to guys who were the same age as me. In college, I attempted to use the strategy of being friends with a girl to get sex from her, but of course that didn't work. After learning game and losing my virginity, I experienced such a great thrill from sleeping with a *new* girl that I kept going instead of focusing on relationships. Game became more about conquest and excitement than intimate connection, until the novelty of it all wore off and my energy declined.

Your game goals will primarily depend on the quality of women around you and how suitable they are for long-term relationships. The lower the quality and the less suitable they are, the more likely you will decide—consciously or subconsciously—that banging a lot of them is the best outcome, but if you're surrounded by virgins who want to be honorable and traditional wives, you are unlikely to conclude that going on a decade-long bang mission is the best course of action.

If I had asked you in the 1950s what the purpose of game was, you'd have said that it was to find a wife so that you could create a family. Back then, there was little playing around because the infrastructure of bars, shopping malls, and internet, which allow you to meet random women easily, did not exist. You would meet one good woman, marry her, and spend the rest of your life with her. It also helped that it was harder for her to cheat since there was no social networking that enabled other men to invite her out for "coffee."

If I had asked you in the late 1980s what the purpose of game was, you'd probably have said that it was to have a bit of fun before finding a wife. After the sexual revolution of the 1970s, women were starting to enjoy random sexual attention while their resistance to sleeping with a man they barely knew decreased. Night venues were being constructed to make it easier for men and women to meet for the purpose of having sex. The divorce rate started to climb, partially thanks to no-fault divorce laws, and men started to become more skeptical of marriage.

If I had to ask you today what your game goals are, what would be your answer? My guess is that it would fall on one of two extremes. Either you are looking for one special girl to have a family with or you want to simulate a rock-star lifestyle and sleep with a lot of girls for fun. Few men would say they are looking for a wife, even though having a family may be at the back of their minds, because wife-worthy women are disappearing, the likelihood of a successful marriage is decreasing, and the punishments sustained by men—but not women—for a failed marriage are severe. In the past, a man who just wanted to sleep around was looked on as crazy, because there were so many potential wives around, but today the man who wants to get married is seen as crazy, because marriage has become such a bad deal for men.

Over the decades, the goals of men have shifted from family to fun because of changes in the environment. If you are entering the game with the goal of starting a long-term relationship, your experience in the unregulated sexual marketplace may change that notion, because you will see firsthand how women flake, lie, cheat on their boyfriends to sleep with you, disappear without explanation, and refuse to assume the traditional female role of taking care of the home and her man. In your darkest hours, you will begin to doubt that "good" girls exist at all, making you more cynical that a long-term relationship can be sustained in an environment that seems to be doing everything possible to prevent family formation. You may even completely write off long-term relationships and decide that you want to bang a rotating supply of sluts indefinitely, turning your game goal into one of hedonistic entertainment.

Do you remember having a favorite movie when you were young? You probably watched it ten times until finally you got tired of it and moved on to something else. Today, you'd watch that movie only to feel nostalgic. If you use game for purely hedonistic purposes, it will be self-limiting, not unlike watching the same movie over and over again. Humans are resistant to putting in time and work for decreasing rewards.

Without having a goal of securing a long-term relationship, game will likely be a phase of your life to satisfy you sexually, occupy your free time, and challenge you in a way that results in an enhancement to your masculinity. If a man playing the game doesn't have an exit strategy of a lasting relationship, there is a high chance he will become jaded and be less interested in women at the end of his journey than he was at the beginning, because he will have repeatedly encountered their most negative traits. The secret to being a success story with game instead of a burn-out case is to extract the self-improvement benefits that encourage your development as a man while having a general idea of what you'll do when your desires change and your willingness to put in work for sex declines.

In spite of the potential for game burn-out, a man who is tired of women suffers less than a man who can't sleep with them. With game, you may experience a variety of middling outcomes down the line, but without game, you get no sex. Even if you have good looks, or a niche in life where random women become attracted to you, a lack of game will prevent you from closing the deal. Simply reading this book once, and remembering a handful of random details about what to do in the presence of women, or remembering details on what *not* to do, will do more to increase your lifelong success with women than doing nothing at all.

Just like how every man needs to own a set of basic tools to repair his car or home, every man needs to possess the basics of game, which at a minimum require a part-time commitment during the phase of his life when he is most motivated to meet women. If you want sex at all, even the shallowest sex that doesn't begin to satisfy your emotional needs, you'll need game, unless you want to pay for hookers or become celibate, neither of which require you to read a book such as this.

Achieving Competent Game

When I wrote *Bang*, I imagined in the future writing an "Advanced Bang" that included more complex game methods to achieve even higher rewards, but I've learned that extra game past a certain point won't bring you better results. The reality of diminishing returns means that having three times better game when you're already competent won't bring you three times the quantity of women, or women who are three times hotter. Once you've achieved competent game, which I define as having the ability to cold approach attractive women in a specific environment with reasonable odds of getting one into bed before exhausting yourself, your time is better spent doing things other than dedicating it to women.

Your game should be strong enough so that, if you're able to find or identify a girl who is attracted to you, you know how to take her to bed without making huge mistakes that cost you the lay. To reach that goal, you will need to accumulate a notch count of about ten, with at least half of them coming from cold approaches, where you walk up to a woman you don't know and try to start a conversation with her.

Looking back at my game history, after I had been with ten women (mostly from cold approaches), I had a solid enough understanding of the game process from beginning to end that I could adapt it to any environment. Most of the game skills I learned after my tenth lay were more necessary to *teach* game to other men and become a respected "game guru" than to benefit me personally.

You can aim for more than ten lays, but the danger of doing

so is that it can turn you into an addict who uses women to achieve an emotional or ego high, where the experience of laying girls you don't particularly care for becomes the purpose of your life. If you're unable to lay a girl, you remain sad and depressed. In my case, if I didn't have sex with a girl soon after I had arrived in a foreign country, I became upset and wondered whether I was some sort of failure. When your existence becomes bound up with how women respond to you, you become a slave to getting laid, just like how a cocaine addict structures his entire life around his drug use.

The ten-lay guideline ensures that you learn enough skills to become competent at game without it becoming an addiction. The signs that you're addicted to game include pursuing girls you're not really interested in, immediately wanting to text a buddy after a new lay to brag about your achievement, maintaining a detailed record of your lays with the intention of adding to your count, and setting random time-based goals such as sleeping with a certain number of girls in a weekend. If you start doing any of these things, you're using game for ego gratification or entertainment rather than to establish healthy relations with women. Not surprisingly, I did all of these things at my game peak.

I wish I could tell you that if you sleep with 100 girls, you'll be enveloped by a magic aura and never stop feeling happy, masculine, and strong, but that hasn't been the case for me or the men I've known. Once you hit 100 notches, you'll start hearing about men who have counts of 200, 300, or even higher, and suddenly your achievement won't seem all that significant. In fact, you'll feel *less* happy and secure with 100 notches than when you hit ten. And guess how many of those 100 girls you'll actually remember? Unless you save their photos or maintain a detailed record, you'll be able to recall only the top three or four girls you were with. Ask an addict about his most memorable drug experiences and he'll tell you about his first high and a few others that had a novel feature attached, but he won't remember them all.

If your goal is to sleep with 100 or more women then so be it, but don't overestimate what those notches will do for your life. I thought that once I hit that number, I would feel eternally happy and confident, but just one day after this grand achievement, I felt no different than before. It was like having a great birthday party and then going back to normal life the following day. The journey I took to get those notches definitely changed me, but the 100th girl I had sex with did not. I don't even remember her name.

I imagine that I felt similar to men who climb high mountains. When a man makes it to the top of Mount Everest, he feels intensely happy and has a sense of accomplishment that lasts for days, but once that feeling fades he's the same person with the same problems as before. His achievement becomes a pleasant memory that fades over time. The problem with some goals is that upon achieving them, you immediately want more to keep getting higher highs. A more sustainable goal is one that, once you've attained it, you don't necessarily want more of it, and are instead content with your accomplishment and what it gave you, ready to move on to life's next challenge.

The healthiest way to approach game is to see it as a tool, not a lifestyle. Aim to attain a level of competency where you feel confident in your ability to meet an attractive girl in order to have a relationship of some kind. You should be able to do this without feeling the need to compare your results to those of other men for the sake of alleviating an insecurity. Game should be a tool you can use whenever you need it, not a ball and chain that you have to drag around.

If I'm seeing a girl and she satisfies my needs for sex and intimacy, I don't approach other girls. If I'm not seeing a girl *and* I'm developing a strong urge for sex or intimacy, I will start a new campaign and approach nearly every day. My first few approaches when re-entering the game are rusty, but my training will kick in and put me back in the groove. After getting a girl who satisfies my needs, I stop approaching and enjoy the relationship as long as it lasts. If the relationship ends, I wait until I strongly crave another woman and then start a new campaign. It took me over a decade to adopt this simple habit of pursuing women only when I need to. It's the healthiest and most balanced way to run game, because it ensures that game is your slave rather than you becoming a slave to game.

To achieve competent game, focus on the modest goal of ten lays (or even fewer if you consider yourself a fast learner), and maintain a high level of awareness during the learning process so that you can extract valuable lessons that will help you in your future dealings with women, even if the environment changes drastically.

How many approaches does it take to get one lay? What is a good number? It depends on where you live, your overall value, the value of the girls you approach, the style of game you use, your personality, and the venues you approach in. If you're using internet game, you may have to contact more than 200 girls to get one lay. If you're running game during a ladies' night at a club, where it's likely there'll be far more girls than guys, you may need to do only five approaches to get one lay.

What matters is not whether your bang number compares favorably with that of other men, but whether it's a number you can achieve in a reasonable amount of time without getting so frustrated that you quit. If the number is 60, and you're fine with doing two approaches a day for one month until you get lucky, it doesn't matter if another man claims to get laid with every few girls he approaches.

When you start your training, you'll be very conscious of how much effort you're putting in, such as doing a certain number of approaches per week, but once you become more competent you can tailor your workload to fit the circumstances. For example, while training you may have to approach when you're not in the mood, but once you've completed your training you can take long breaks from game and focus on other things, because you will have internalized important concepts that can be activated if an attractive girl you want to meet happens to cross your path. After training, you can also pursue niches or experiments that won't necessarily have a high chance of helping your game. For example, you may want to see what happens to your game when you grow a one-foot-long beard that makes you look like a

Muslim terrorist, something that I've done in the past.

At this point, if your need for sex is not strong, you may be thinking, "Why bother? This is too much work, and it sounds difficult." It is indeed a lot of work, definitely more than our male ancestors had to put in. If you're not convinced that you need game to get laid, you won't put in the effort required to become competent at it. I suspect that you're reading this book because you already have such a burning desire to get laid that putting in work is the least of your concerns, but if having sex with women is not one of your top priorities, I don't have any argument that will change your mind.

The main danger facing men when they start out in the game is becoming discouraged and giving up on women entirely, or taking the shortcut of using prostitutes. The problem with paying for sex is that it affects your mentality over time in such a way that it can prevent you from ever using normal game again. It's hard to turn back from handing over cash to women you want to have sex with to doing, say, five approaches in a park. Once your brain associates sex with cash payments, and you interact with enough prostitutes to develop the impression that all women are "whores," your ability to have standard relationships is compromised.

At the same time, men who have not had sex for a year or longer should not be denied a way to alleviate their suffering. This is likely to apply to the 10% of men who are at the bottom of the attractiveness and social scale. Even in this case, men should use prostitutes only as emergency relief, perhaps once or twice a year.

For men who want to have a normal sex life while learning enough about female nature to ensure strong long-term relationships, a goal of ten notches within three years is reasonable, assuming that many of these notches will lead to at least a short-term relationship. If you're having sex with a girl only once, three sex acts a year won't give you much satisfaction.

Ten notches in three years will keep you involved in the game, teach you the true nature of women, and give you the sexual and emotional experience to maintain longer relationships, all while keeping you away from the more addictive aspects of wanting to sleep with a lot of women simply for physical pleasure or to boost your ego. If you're a complete newbie who has never even kissed a girl, it will help if you add intermediary goals to keep you motivated. This may mean setting a goal of getting a certain number of phone numbers, and then a certain number of kisses.

Once you hit ten notches, or if you've already hit it, you can set your own goals based on your needs and what you've learned. For many men, this means refining their game further to get more with less effort, or going deeper with more fulfilling relationships. This book will help with both, but understand that the more experience you accumulate, the more soul-searching and careful thinking you'll have to do in order to determine exactly how you should proceed, particularly in a rapidly changing culture where a fun goal yesterday, such as hitting a hundred notches, may be a bad goal today because of relentless "rape culture" hysteria. Once you've gained a certain amount of experience, the only man who will be able to give you advice on how to proceed will be yourself, simply because it will be hard to find anyone else who has a similar life and game trajectory as you.

That's the situation I'm in. I'm 39 and have worn myself out from sleeping with promiscuous girls, and think more about experiencing fatherhood. What man out there can give me a clear recipe for what to do next? If I seek advice from men who haven't been through what I've experienced, what can they say that will be worth listening to? The more you are in a later stage of the game, the more you're on your own.

I'll be able to hold your hand for part of the journey, but at some point you'll have to decide the best path to take. Whatever path you choose, and whether you want to be a player for life or a faithful husband and father, you cannot avoid having to understand women and how game works on them. This book is for the modern man, young or old, in whatever stage of life he finds himself in.

Chapter 2: Internal Game

What does it really take to succeed at the game? Effort. You need to put in the work by placing yourself in the company of women and speaking to them. Knowledge is also important. Unless you want to reinvent game from scratch by doing 10,000 approaches, you need to have a good idea of what to do. Being motivated, living in a city with lots of girls, and having a favorable living situation (logistics) will also help, but the most important factor for game success is something you cannot see or touch. It's an invisible force embedded in your mind that controls you every second of the day. It's your belief system.

Your beliefs determine your behavior. Tell me what a man thinks, and I'll tell you what he fears and what he desires. I'll tell you his past, describe his present, and predict his future. Tell me a man's beliefs and I'll tell you *who that man is*. Beliefs are the fuel that propel a man in this direction or that, which is why if you have the power to shape a man's beliefs, you have the power to shape the world. This is why governments have mastered the art of propaganda, to mold the beliefs of citizens who will then obey laws and authority.

Our goal is not to dominate the world but the self. Either we allow external forces to install beliefs into our heads, without us even knowing it, or we consciously install beliefs that will allow us to accomplish our personal goals.

If you're hopeless when it comes to women, chances are you believe the opposite of what you should. If you have achieved varying success with women, you may possess some, or most, of the correct beliefs. These beliefs not only include what you think about women, but also what you think about yourself. It is often the case that the biggest obstacle to success in any area of life is having negative beliefs, often called "self-limiting" beliefs. Without even knowing it, men sabotage their lives by nurturing beliefs that lead them away from their goals.

Adopting a belief is not a simple matter of reading it in a book, agreeing with it, and then getting on with your day. A belief is like a seed that must be sown and nurtured so that it will develop into a sturdy plant that will one day bear fruit.

There are two ways to implant beliefs. The first is through regular study. After learning a belief, make notes on it and revisit the notes often. Another option, and one that I recommend, is to have a daily or weekly affirmation session where you repeat each belief to yourself between five to ten times, preferably out loud. Affirmations can also include motivational statements that encourage your work ethic and persistence, or any other area of your life that you want to improve. I'll share more about affirmation sessions after discussing the beliefs.

The following seven beliefs are essential to being good with women. Don't worry about memorizing them now—you'll have plenty of opportunities to tackle them later, one or two at a time, as you ramp up your game efforts.

"I don't care if I get laid with *her*, but I do care about getting laid."

This belief is related to the expression "Don't put pussy on the pedestal," which you've probably heard in the context of advice that women don't like needy men who drool over them. The second you show intense interest in a girl, at a level *above* the interest she is showing in you, it's nearly guaranteed that you won't ever sleep with her. That near guarantee becomes unbreakable when you are rejected outright but continue to fawn over a girl in the hope of convincing her that she should be with a needy man.

I still get a lot of emails from men who want to know how they can get that one special, amazing, beautiful, perfect girl who *already* rejected them. These men think that if they don't get her, they will never meet another great girl. This scenario forms the premise of many Hollywood movies, which train men to be spineless glops of emotion when it comes to romance. The reality is that being "romantic," needy, and desperate doesn't work today, so you must be convinced that you don't care whether or not you succeed with an *individual* girl, even if you develop feelings for her.

On the other hand, it takes genuine effort and time to meet a desirable woman and date her. If we take "Don't put pussy on the pedestal" to its logical conclusion, we will be monks living in caves who don't care about being with any woman. The correct belief is not to care whether or not you lay a specific girl, but to care strongly about getting laid in general. You want to be the guy who steps into the bar wanting to get laid more than any other man, but who absolutely does not care if your top choice rejects you. You're sufficiently motivated to do what it takes to succeed, but you won't let one girl impede your overall progress.

Although you don't want to fawn over a girl, you should try to escalate an interaction instead of waiting for her to put the moves on you. A girl is turned off when you like her more than she likes you, but she is turned *on* when she likes you and you show her that you're not afraid to go after what you want. This is why we don't give our attention to girls who treat us poorly, don't return our text messages, or cancel dates. The ideal is to have a strong need to get laid with women in general, but zero hesitation to dump any girl who rejects you or doesn't treat you in the way you want. *I don't care if I get laid by her, but I do care about getting laid.*

"A girl primarily evaluates my value based on how I treat her."

Many men get hung up on looks as the main factor that determines how girls will respond to them. While looks are definitely an important factor, and something you should optimize as girls become increasingly superficial, it's only *one* of many factors that girls use to judge our overall value. After you've maximized your physical attractiveness, you'll notice that what really determines your value to a girl is how you present yourself to her, which is something you can control, unlike your height or facial structure.

A woman does not want to be with a man she *thinks* possesses lower value than her. She is hard-wired to date men who have a higher status level, but as you can imagine, it's not easy for a woman to judge a man's overall worth. They are forced to take shortcuts when determining value. If you know what their shortcuts are, you can hijack their value-judging system to achieve your desired result.

Let's imagine you are looking at two men and you want to know which one is richer. You'll probably examine their homes or cars since you don't have access to their bank statements. These are indirect ways of judging a man's net worth, but because of credit and bank loans, the man with the bigger house and fancier car may, in fact, be poorer.

How about if you wanted to judge the quality of a nightclub? You would look at reviews online or walk by on a weekend night. If you noticed a long line outside, you would assume that the party must be amazing for people to be willing to wait, but it's possible that the bouncers were holding the line to give the appearance of popularity.

We're always looking for shortcuts to judge value, but they are far from reliable, and if I know what shortcut you are using to judge me by, I can fake it so that you think my value is higher than it actually is.

Women also look for shortcuts to judge the overall worth of a man. Social proof is one, where they note whether other women are giving you their attention. Being interesting or funny is another, because they are signs of intelligence and therefore a high income. A far more important shortcut is how a woman evaluates your *treatment* of her.

If a man does not treat a woman well, she concludes it's because he knows his value is much higher than hers. He's treating her poorly because he believes she's "beneath" him. Therefore, a woman will be more attracted to a man who doesn't constantly give her favorable attention. On the other hand, if a woman interacts with a man who is always complimenting her, doing favors, and buying gifts, she will conclude (rightly) that he must have lower value than her: "He prizes me and is constantly doing nice things for me because I'm too good for him." She will then make the logical decision not to pursue a relationship with him.

Even men use this shortcut. If there is a girl who is showing you a lot of affection, much more than average, you will wonder why she's so desperate, or whether there's something wrong with her. Not only will you be hesitant to pursue her, but it's also more likely that you'll treat her poorly. You will skip out on replying to some of her texts, be slower to please her with stories or jokes, and be quicker to say no if she asks you for a favor. Without consciously thinking about it, your mind assigns a value to her and you treat her accordingly.

Here's the fascinating part: you get to *choose* what your value is when you interact with a girl who doesn't know you. Unless she has heard of you from others, she has no idea what your value is before you start talking to her. Depending on how you treat her, and how you present yourself through your body language, you have an incredible amount of control to shape her value judgment.

If I walk up to a girl in a bar with my shoulders hunched, and I start telling her how I want to buy her gifts because she's so beautiful, she'll judge my worth as lower than hers, but if I walk up to that same girl with my body erect and show that her beauty doesn't have an effect on me, while throwing in a joke that girls usually buy me drinks, she may judge my worth to be at least equal to hers. In both approaches, I'm technically the same man, but I'll receive two completely different responses, only one of which will open the possibility of taking her to bed. The catch is that it's not easy to be aloof when approaching a beautiful girl if you're inexperienced around women or have low confidence. This belief can become a reality only once you begin to succeed with prettier women as your game progresses.

When a woman allows you to converse with her after a successful opener, how she judges your value is mostly in your hands. If you believe that your value is higher than hers, even if it objectively isn't, how will she know otherwise? *A girl primarily evaluates my value based on how I treat her.*

"Every time I fail, I take one big step towards success."

Failure is a subjective phenomenon that, like the previous belief, lies mostly within your realm of control. For anything that is a "failure," you can easily identify lessons that will not only make you stronger, but also increase the chances that you'll succeed in the future.

Let's say that I get rejected by a girl in an embarrassing way. Automatically, I start feeling bad by dwelling on negative thoughts. "She thinks I'm a loser… I'm so ugly that she doesn't want to have anything to do with me… She thinks I'm scum of the Earth." Even if these thoughts are mostly accurate, a universal fact is that it takes an unknown amount of failures to achieve a single success. Statistically, being rejected actually makes success more likely, *as long as you keep going.*

Once you realize that you've probably learned something new from a failed approach, you can clearly see that rejection and failure are absolutely necessary to succeed. No one succeeds on their first try, and if they did, they'd have no idea what they did right to duplicate it in the future. In order for you to be consistently good with women, you must be rejected enough times until you learn what works for you and what doesn't while shedding the fear of rejection that all humans are born with.

The best strategy is to embrace rejection as an essential step on the road to success. If you don't accept this, you won't succeed with women. Having a goal of never being rejected is not only unreasonable, but will lead to *total failure*. You may see rejection as uncomfortable and painful, but you have full control over how to interpret that rejection. Why not interpret it as an essential ingredient to accomplishing your goals? Rejection is a natural barrier to separate the men who truly want to succeed from those who don't.

With each interaction, try your best to nudge a woman as far as she will go until it's absolutely clear that she's not interested, because if you exit too early, before the real rejection comes, you're not experiencing rejection at all. The rejection must be real for it to put you closer to success.

I've talked to many girls who didn't have sex with me. Instead of being upset, I'm thankful they were part of the number of failures the universe required from me before I could experience a sexual success. Another benefit is that every time a girl rejects you, you learn a vital piece of the puzzle to becoming a stronger man. While I wouldn't go so far as to say that you should experience a life of rejection, only adversity and rejection can strengthen a man, not success and comfort. The more setbacks you have suffered in life, the stronger you are and the more you're able to deal with difficult situations and problems. It's when life is a bit too easy, when I'm not experiencing difficulties, that I know I'm getting weaker.

When you get rejected enough times, you start to build a solid data set of what works and what doesn't for your unique personality, vibe, and environment. If you're failing soon after the approach, you know that you have to adjust your look, opener, or the type of girl you're approaching. If you can get a lot of phone numbers, but girls don't respond to your first message, you know that you have to strengthen the connection you make when meeting them. If you're getting girls back to your apartment, but they won't sleep with you, you know that you have to raise a girl's level of comfort and trust at the key moment of intimacy. Rejection provides you with feedback about where specifically you need to improve so that you can move forward.

Failure is like a trail of bread crumbs that tells you where to focus your efforts, but sometimes it's hard to know exactly where the trail is leading, because we can't isolate for variables as in a laboratory experiment. When we're running game, it's not always clear whether there is one *big* thing we're doing wrong or several things we're doing *slightly* wrong. There will also be cases where you're not doing anything wrong at all, but your standards are just too high.

Even if you can't find anything specific to learn from a rejection, the fact that you did get rejected desensitizes you from future rejections, strengthening your mental core. This is why some psychologists recommend "rejection therapy" to clients with self-esteem problems. Paradoxically, getting rejected builds your confidence, because you learn that you're not made of glass that will shatter when something doesn't go your way. Failure is an important step on the road to success, and something you should embrace and learn from. *Every time I fail, I take a big step towards success.*

"It's fun to try new things just to see what happens."

This is one of my favorite beliefs, because it instills a playful and curious mindset that allows you to develop a game that is tailor-made for you. Having the belief that you want to see what will happen if you try something new is the only way you can customize your game.

When I was about 12 years old, I bought a science kit and started doing experiments with chemicals in my bedroom. I so enjoyed mixing the chemicals to see what the result would be that I eventually chose a career of microbiology. That career didn't quite work out, because it was more about sitting in meetings and following orders than discovering new things, but the curiosity mindset has stayed with me. If I do this thing, what will be the result? How will a beautiful girl respond if I ask her, "Can you even read?" How will my body respond if I don't eat for twenty-four hours straight? If I change one ingredient in a bread recipe, how will it affect the taste?

Curiosity leads to experimentation. For example, I may be curious whether a certain opening line will work, so I try it out on several different girls. If the line gets a more favorable response than one I've used before, or it gets the same response but I'm way more motivated to use it, I now have a new line in my game repertoire. The process will repeat as I get curious about trying other lines, moves, or changes to my appearance that may improve my results.

I'm sure I have some genetic wiring that makes me naturally curious, but if you don't, you'll have to implant the curiosity belief in your mind to encourage experimentation. If you're not curious, you will get stuck when you encounter problems. You'll be a mini-Roosh when you start out using the foundational game I teach, but very soon thereafter you can adapt that foundation to make it work better for you. A lack of curiosity will prevent you from doing so.

Mimicking another guy's game can get you started, but it won't allow you to match his results. When I was living in Odessa, Ukraine, I met a man who was doing very well with online dating. He showed me his lines and I copied them word-for-word to use on girls, but I got less than 20% of the positive responses he did. The reason is that those lines were optimized for his pictures, personality, and taste in women. I'm not a fan of internet game, but if I truly wanted to get good at it, I'd use existing material as a starting point and adapt it over time to fit my look, vibe, body language, humor, taste, and so on.

While there are universal game strategies that will work for all men, that universality decreases as you get more granular into word-for-word lines and routines. The ones I teach are more universal than most, but understand that the words you use must eventually suit your personality and the environment you're in. Whenever a guru teaches you how to do anything, what he's really teaching you is what worked for *him*. You must possess the curious mindset to adapt my teachings to your situation as you gain more experience.

Unfortunately, modern culture has launched a war on curiosity and experimentation. Corporations are eager to provide you with ready-made solutions to your problems that don't require thinking or customization. Many people enjoy shiny gadgets and porn that meet their need for entertainment and sex without having to expend any effort. The culture has not given you the tools to overcome the challenge of getting laid, and has allowed your curiosity to atrophy. We have to activate it, which won't be hard, because most humans are naturally curious. Be curious, because *it's fun to try new things just to see what happens.* Your sex life will thank you for it.

"I will invest my time only in girls who add value to my life."

Men who don't have much experience with women, and whose views on them have been shaped by movies and television, may have the misconception that women are capable of making them happy. To understand what role women play in our happiness, we must first define what happiness is.

As defined by mainstream culture, happiness is a feeling of bliss where life is great, nothing bad is happening to you, your consumer products are functioning as they should, and you are pleased with your body, job, apartment, social interactions, friends and family, love life, hobbies, and the restaurants near your home. When someone asks us "Are you happy?" we're supposed to either answer that every part of our lives is wonderful or that everything is not great, we're not happy, and because we're not happy, we're suffering in some way and must immediately make a change so that, when the next person asks us whether we're happy, we can enthusiastically say "Yes."

The problem with this idea of happiness is that it doesn't correctly identify happiness as a transient emotion that depends on external conditions. The first day you're in your brand-new luxury car, you feel a rush of happiness. The 180th day you're in the same car, you don't even notice you have a luxury car, and simply want to make it to work on time. The first night you move into your loft penthouse, you imagine all the parties you will throw in it. The 180th day you're in the penthouse, you see it merely as a comfortable place to live.

While the car and the penthouse make you content in that you would rather have them than not, they eventually stop providing you with a positive emotional feeling. The result is something more like satisfaction. Once happiness subsides, your mind returns to focusing on your insecurities and troubles, and you start aching for something new to alleviate them. New and exciting things will make you happy only for the short term.

I see this phenomenon when I'm in Eastern Europe and meet male travelers who are there for the first time. I already know what they're going to say to me after their first week: "There are hot girls everywhere—this is amazing!" I smile and remember my first time in Eastern Europe when I felt like a kid in a candy store, but years later I barely notice the beautiful women all around me. The reason is that I've adapted, and you cannot get happiness from something you've adapted to, only contentment. The problem is that humans are designed to adapt to everything, so shaping your life around something that you think makes you happy, without considering its cost or the process of adaptation, will put you on a never-ending roller-coaster ride of happy peaks and frustrating dips.

If I give you a great girl today, you will experience high levels of happiness because of the pleasant novelty, but soon you'll be reminded of all the other things that make you unhappy, because a great girl cannot put you in a state of permanent happiness where you don't experience problems, insecurities, desires, or worries. A girl can make you temporarily forget all the things you're unhappy about, but often you will bring your existing problems into a new relationship. The best sign that you'll be happy in any relationship is that you're happy while not in a relationship.

This is not to say that a girl can't add value to your life. She can add companionship, intimacy, sex, humor, and children, all while reducing boredom. You can have experiences with a girl that you can't have while alone, and some of these are pleasant and make life fun. A girl is certainly capable of improving your overall contentment, but there's a catch: not every girl out there can provide you with positive value. Many girls, because of their own problems, yield negative value, and will make your life worse if you get into a long-term relationship with them.

Consider that girls have *more* mental issues and insecurities than you, and think far more illogically. Whatever benefits they provide must be weighed up against the fact that they are the weaker sex and need additional care, monitoring, and maintenance. While your standards shouldn't be sky high if you only want to have sex with a girl, you should be careful of which girl you choose for a monogamous long-term relationship, because the wrong girl can make your life worse. Only a man who understands what happiness is, and how transient it can be, will not rush into a relationship with a girl who is not right for him.

I'll have sex with the most attractive girl I can find, but I'll only pursue a relationship with a girl who adds value to my life in a tangible way. Does she treat me with respect? Does she not create constant problems? Does she satisfy me sexually? Does she have good family values? Does she have homemaking skills? Unless I can answer yes to all of these questions, I won't pursue more than a sexual fling. If she is the right match, I will enter a relationship with the understanding that whatever mental or other problems I had before the relationship will be brought into the relationship. A girl, even a great one, is not a magical cure for my issues, so I *will invest my time only in girls who add value to my life,* and stay away from the ones who don't.

"I ultimately choose how a girl treats me."

No girl can treat you in a way that you don't accept. The only way a girl can disrespect you, cause drama, or abuse you is if you give her permission to do so. This starts early in the interaction. Think back to the last time a girl canceled a date on you at the last minute. Did you make a comment about her wasting your time, or did you show that the cancelation was no big deal to you? If you did the latter, you indirectly told her that it's okay for her not to value your time, and that if she disrespects you again in the future, she will not be punished for it.

A man may wonder why a girl keeps canceling on him without realizing that he's *allowing* her to do it. Little acts of disrespect, if not squashed early on, will morph into bigger acts of disrespect later. This is why it's so important that you insist on being treated properly from the very beginning, even if this may cause you to lose out on sex.

The hornier you are, the more likely you will accept disrespect from a woman, because you're allowing your phallus to overpower decisions that your mind wants to make. When I was thirstier for sex, I accepted all manner of flaking, sarcastic jokes, and inane feminist comments from girls, hoping I'd get laid anyway. If I didn't get the lay, I'd feel like crap because I had let a girl treat me poorly and got nothing out of it. If I did get the lay, I'd still feel slightly like crap because I had sacrificed my self-respect to get an orgasm or two. As long as you're not strict like an army drill master and freak out if a girl merely looks at her phone on a date, you should walk away from girls who are treating you in a way that you don't deserve. If you don't, you'll feel degraded.

If I had listened to the advice I'm giving you now, I'd have gained fewer notches with girls who provided me with nothing but forgettable sex. I now stop girls when they behave disrespectfully, and firmly but politely tell them that I do not accept being spoken to or treated in a negative way. If they don't stop, the interaction ends. If they do stop, we can continue to build our connection.

It's tempting to lament that a girl is not behaving in the way you want, but as long as you choose to continue interacting with her, you have only yourself to blame. If a girl walks away from you after you've told her to stop her demeaning behavior, I guarantee that you have been saved from a lot of headache in the future from someone who is more likely to subtract value from your life than add to it. *I ultimately choose how a girl treats me.*

"If she pushes me away, I must pull away."

If there is one consistent way to kill any attraction a girl has for you, it's to respond to her actions that push you away by giving her even more attention. Girls are far more sensitive than men when it comes to knowing where the power resides in an interaction, which means that you must never respond to her apathy or disinterest with attention or affection. You must match her apathy with greater apathy. You must match her long text reply times with even longer reply times. You must match her disinterest with even greater disinterest.

By pulling away when she increases her distance from you, you'll pass all the tests a girl does to see whether or not the man she's interacting with is weak. Girls take small, barely perceptible steps away from you during an interaction to see whether or not she has you firmly in her pocket. When you respond by taking a step away yourself, you "pass" the test. As a result, she recognizes that you have genuine value.

Remember that it's very difficult for a girl to judge a man's true value, so she has to see how he will treat her to get an assessment she can act on. If a man has high value, and a girl beneath his value pushes him away, what do you think he will do? He will begin looking at other girls. If he leans into her instead, she will perceive that his value is low and decide she is too good for him.

Pulling away from a girl who is being cold helps to train your subconscious that your value is high, because only a high-value man can walk away from an attractive girl. You also save a ton of time, because girls who pull away tend to have lower interest in you than girls who don't. You will have better experiences with girls who don't play many games before they allow you to bed them.

If a girl pushes you away, and she doesn't respond positively after you pull away in response, she's not testing you: she's really not interested. If a girl likes a man, she won't do too many things that will cause him to lose hope of getting her. She will play "hard to get" mainly in the bedroom when you want to seal the deal, but usually not before that when you're having a conversation, getting her phone number, or setting up the first date.

A girl who is interested in you will not want to lose you, so she will continually give out encouragement and positive signs. If you're not getting these signs, and she doesn't dive back into you after you pull away in response to her cold behavior, she simply isn't interested. *If she pushes me away, I must pull away.*

Implanting Beliefs Through Auto-Suggestion

The seven beliefs above will help you to internalize the mindset you need to be successful with women, not only in casual relationships, but also in long-term relationships with women you want to have a family with. Even if you stop reading this book right now, as long as these beliefs become fixed in your mind, you will be able to develop behaviors for attracting and managing women. The problem is getting them into your brain and keeping them there, particularly if you've believed their opposites for most of your life.

When I started with game, I approached girls at least three times a week. I was so obsessed with game that it became my career, making it easy for the right beliefs to stay in my head. Most men, however, are unable or unwilling to dedicate the same amount of time to game as I have, so they need a technique that takes into account the limited amount of time they practice game each week. If you see a girl you like but haven't run game in a while, the beliefs must be fresh in your mind so you can approach competently with only a slight amount of hesitation. One strategy to accomplish this is auto-suggestion.

Auto-suggestion is a method of repeating statements to yourself regularly so that they become implanted in your subconscious. The easiest way to do this is to repeat a handful of beliefs or affirmations daily or weekly, and then add or remove beliefs when necessary. For example, imagine that you are an athlete who wants to compete in the Olympics. You may repeat these three auto-suggestions every day before training:

1. Your daily work will make you a champion. You will work harder today than anyone else.

2. The difficulties you face today make you stronger, while any comfort you choose makes you weaker.

3. If it were easy, everyone would be doing it. You will avoid what is easy and push to your genetic limits of endurance.

These three auto-suggestions are designed to motivate the athlete to embrace a rigorous training regimen. A starter program can include one session a day where you repeat each auto-suggestion five to ten times (preferably out loud) while in a relaxed state. To not overload your brain, I recommend a maximum of eight auto-suggestions (an ideal number for me is closer to five).

Let's say I'm a reader of this book and want to program my mind with the seven game beliefs. The first step is to write the beliefs I need to embrace on a piece of paper or type them up in a computer file. Find a quiet space and breathe deeply ten times. Take the first belief and read it out loud between five to ten times. Then breathe deeply five times while imagining yourself executing the belief in a particular scenario. Repeat these steps with the other beliefs. When you've gone through the entire list, breathe deeply ten more times.

The whole exercise will take only a few minutes. If you're feeling relaxed and loose after the session, it's because you've put yourself in a mildly hypnotic state that accelerated the incorporation of the beliefs into your subconscious.

You're probably thinking, "Does this really work?" At a minimum, it will prevent you from forgetting the most important concepts that you want to focus on. When you encounter a situation that is related to one of the beliefs, you will react more quickly with the correct behavior. Other signs that it's working are that thoughts about a belief pop into your mind during the course of the day or you start dreaming about putting a belief into action.

Once you've incorporated a belief into your thinking, take it off your list. You can add it back later if the bad behavioral pattern it was supposed to correct reappears. Your auto-suggestion list will be continually updated by adding or removing beliefs and affirmations depending on the challenges you need to overcome. For example, at the time of this writing, my auto-suggestion list is based on the fact that I am re-entering the game after a long relationship. The problem is that I've lost my killer instinct because I haven't had to approach women for so long. Here are the three auto-suggestions I've been using:

1. The best thing you can do today is get brutally rejected by at least one girl.

2. You are a hunter with a track record of consistent success. Now go do what a successful hunter must do.

3. You're not in a relationship anymore, so stop being a pussy. It's time to be masculine again.

The first auto-suggestion is tied to my commitment to approach one girl a day, a tactic I will discuss later. I included the word "brutally" because I want to do high-risk approaches that may have a high reward. The second one is meant to give me confidence by reminding me of my past success. It also encourages me to embrace a "hunter" identity that I want to see myself as. The final auto-suggestion is aimed at getting me out of relationship mode, where I was bathed in comfort and took no risks.

These three auto-suggestions have been customized to suit me, my current situation, and the goals I want to achieve in the short term. They will change within a few weeks as I progress. I'm always ready to update my list whenever I hit a new obstacle that is hindering me. I suggest that you start with broad beliefs that are new to you, and then add customized auto-suggestions over time that motivate you to take action daily.

Chapter Conclusion

As effective as auto-suggestions are, they aren't enough on their own to elicit the desired behavior. You need to *act* to forge connections between the beliefs and reality. Since the proper beliefs will come anyway from experience alone, the purpose of using auto-suggestions is to speed the process along, motivate you, and give you the feeling that you know what you're doing. Even if you can do only one auto-suggestion session a week instead of every day, your mind will absorb the beliefs faster than if you didn't do any sessions at all. When you're satisfied with the results of your game work and how your relationships are going, you can drop the sessions entirely, and do them only if you need a minor check-up to address a specific problem.

In the past, I believed that internal game wasn't important, and that a man should simply dive in and approach a lot of girls. There's nothing wrong with that, but I now believe that giving your mind a "tune up" before you start will improve your results.

Remember: your beliefs drive your behavior. You cannot behave in an optimal or ideal way if you have the wrong beliefs. Once you get your mind fully on board with the game work you want to do, you'll have a much easier time. Study the correct beliefs, understand why you should believe them, and make up your own auto-suggestions that are tailored to your environment and help motivate you to act correctly.

With internal game out of the way, we can now focus on the concrete physical changes we make to ourselves that have a direct impact on attracting girls.

Chapter 3: Pre-Game

Many men mistakenly think that game is simply about walking outside, finding the first attractive girl, and saying a handful of lines that will make her panties wet, but your lines are only a small part of what girls use when assessing your value.

In the past, I focused more on my approach frequency and the quality of my lines, but now I see the benefit of improving myself to the extent that I can use *less* game. If you make the most of your genetic potential in a way that is attractive to girls, you may need only a touch of game to get the girls you want. The areas that are most worth improving are your physical health, appearance, and hygiene.

Biological Functioning

Are you healthy? Is your weight under control? How are your energy levels and vitality? With so many harmful chemicals in the environment, it's likely that your physical well-being, particularly your testosterone levels, is being negatively affected. Do a web search on "testosterone decline" and you will see that this hormone, which is the most important one for peak male performance, is on a worldwide decline thanks to estrogenic compounds in our food and other consumer products. Another reason for the decrease is unhealthy lifestyle choices that stem from sitting for extended periods, eating badly, not getting enough sleep, and forgoing weight resistance training.

Testosterone is the main reason you're a man. It is what makes men *men*. Your aggression, strength, energy, and mood are tied to having the appropriate concentration of this hormone.

Low testosterone can result in a lower sex drive and mood disorders that make you feel like you're going through menopause. Your game success rate depends largely on you having a normal amount of testosterone. Starting a game program with inadequate testosterone is similar to a runner starting a marathon with asthma or a leg injury.

Even if you're relatively young, I recommend that you have your testosterone level checked, either by visiting your physician or by contacting a laboratory. This will enable you to establish a baseline testosterone value. If, in a few years, you're starting to experience symptoms that suggest a decline, you can get retested and compare the new value to your baseline. I regret that I was 35 when I had my testosterone checked for the first time. While the result was normal, I don't know whether it has remained stable or has been decreasing since my twenties.

Low testosterone can also cause a lack of interest in women. I remember how insanely motivated I was to approach girls when I first started using game, even though I didn't know what I was doing. The hornier you are, the less anxious you'll be about rejection, simply because you're so energized to get laid.

I suspect that men who have above-average levels of anxiety, and who can't make themselves do an approach after weeks of trying, have low testosterone. If a test confirms that this is the case, these men can start to remedy the problem through exercise, a correct diet, vitamin and mineral supplementation, adequate sleep, and other lifestyle changes. I don't recommend testosterone replacement therapy except in extreme cases, because it results in pharmaceutical dependency and won't solve the root of the problem.

Testosterone levels may also be falling because few men engage in activities that require the hormone in the first place. We don't hunt for our food, sire numerous children, conquer new lands, physically exert ourselves on farms, defend our family from barbarians, or face life-threatening situations. Why should our body send a signal to produce testosterone if we're sitting on our butts all day staring at computer screens and walking a few feet to the refrigerator to retrieve prepared food?

Men report that the most improvement to their horniness and energy results from lifting weights, probably because it mirrors the physical exertion our ancestors had to do. This suggests you must adopt behaviors that convince your mind the body needs testosterone. Trying to lay new girls helps, but it may not be enough. Once you've removed estrogen from your diet and environment, and adopted a more active lifestyle, convince your mind that you intend to *reproduce* with women and need help in the form of a testosterone boost, even if you don't want to be a father right now.

Apart from boosting your testosterone, treat any lingering health problems that affect your energy level or ability to talk to girls. We all have untreatable flaws that we wish we didn't have, but if something is treatable, you should start putting the time into fixing it right now. Consider yourself a sort of athlete. Before you step on the field, make sure you have no "injuries" or excess fat that may hamper your motivation or performance.

Physical Appearance

How you look has become more important over the years because girls are being culturally programmed to go for "sexy" and "hot" men who instantly turn them on. This programming starts when a girl is barely a teenager and is fed a nonstop stream of attractive male stars who are supposed to represent the archetype of the ideal man. In the past, simply making a bold display of confidence was enough to create attraction, but this is no longer the case. We have to compensate by allowing our physical appearance to create much of the attraction.

I know that a lot of men are insecure about how they look. Even men I would describe as handsome think they're ugly. It doesn't help that certain dating apps force girls to evaluate you *only* on your looks, which has the effect of rewarding the top 10% of good-looking men—a group to which I do not belong. So yes, if you use the shallowest dating app, and you're a six out of ten or worse on the looks scale, and you don't put any effort into optimizing your appearance, you will see poor results that cause you to become discouraged and swear off game and women entirely. Once you step out of the looks-centered internet fishbowl, however, you will receive much better feedback from women.

The correct strategy is to optimize your physical appearance as much as you can and then start talking to girls in venues where appearance is not the most important feature that determines your value. Instead of worrying about your physical flaws, focus on improving your overall look. Not only will you gain one or two points on the looks scale, but you'll gain something far more important: confidence. It's confidence that will ensure you do the required number of approaches, without which you won't succeed.

We all have our insecurities when it comes to how we look. When I look in the mirror, I see that my chin is uneven, my ears are huge, and one of my eyes is open wider than the other, but these flaws haven't prevented me from having sexual relationships with attractive women. Based on the amount of sex I've had, whatever problems I've perceived with my appearance existed primarily in my mind. My appearance was less of a problem than low self-esteem. When you don't think highly of yourself, you search for excuses to prevent yourself from taking risks that may confirm the low opinion you've created.

You are your own worst critic. It won't take more than 25 approaches for you to realize that your negative fantasies of how you'll be treated by women don't match reality. Experience is the only reliable cure to smashing low self-esteem, because your mind will be forced to modify its incorrect beliefs.

Your mind is both your friend and your enemy, because while it gives you the cognitive ability to fulfill your goals, it also tells you that you are ugly and will experience nonstop rejection. The first step is to get over your physical flaws and work on improving your overall appearance.

Imagine for a second how a warrior in the ancient past must have appeared. You may have in your mind a man who is strong, big, and mean looking, but I guarantee he was also dirty, smelly, and hairy. While girls today want a strong man, they also want one who smells good and brushes his teeth daily, unlike an ancient warrior. Most girls now prefer a man who is somewhat like a cat: clean, hygienic, and well groomed. In other words, girls want men who are like gay men of a few decades ago when it comes to grooming habits. Girls generally want masculine men, but ones who don't stink or have forests growing on the back of their necks. To present yourself as attractive to the modern girl, you'll have to groom at a level that is more feminine than masculine, but this is what gets the best responses.

Many of the men I've met who have had great success with women don't appear hyper-masculine. They pay close attention to their appearance and have a chatty personality where they're able to talk to girls endlessly about any topic. Of course, a hyper-masculine man doesn't have trouble getting girls (imagine a confident body builder), but a lot of girls simply want a well-groomed man who knows how to arouse her emotionally with language. This is particularly true in large, cosmopolitan cities, where the gap between masculine and feminine is much narrower than it is in rural or traditional areas. A girl in New York City, for example, is going to demand men who are more groomed compared to a girl who lives on a farm in Russia. The more urban and modern your environment, the more likely women will prefer a man who puts extra care into his appearance.

If a grooming task is making you feel weird, it could be a sign that you should skip it. Everything you do to improve your appearance should also make you more energized to talk to women. If you feel a decrease in confidence upon doing an optimization step, pass on it for the time being.

Managing Your Body Hair

Hairy men used to rule the world, but not anymore. Most women now prefer men who are nearly as hairless as they are. This has made my life slightly challenging, because I'm one of the hairiest men I know. I have nose hair, ear hair, neck hair, shoulder hair, back hair, butt hair, and even toe hair. Your goal should not be to remove all the hair from your body, but to get rid of the most objectionable hair that is visible before intimacy occurs. In the case of the areas where it's not bad to have hair, such as our face and chest, we only need to maintain a desirable length.

Nose hair is the first area to examine. When looking in the mirror, can you see any hair that is trying to escape your nasal cavity? If you can, get rid of it with a nose trimmer. Then look at your ears. Is any hair growing on your earlobes, or in the ear canal? You can use your nose trimmer to remove it.

Eyebrows are next. If you have a long, caterpillar-like unibrow, you should remove the hair in the middle to ensure you have two eyebrows. I tend to have extra-long eyebrow hairs that are like the consistency of electric wire. They float beyond the boundary of the eyebrow and sometimes even encroach on my vision. I yank these out with tweezers every week or so. I do not recommend you shape or thin your eyebrows, because girls may think you're gay. Thick eyebrows are fine, but make sure individual hairs don't escape the eyebrow zone.

The next area to target is the back of your neck between your hair line and the top of your shirt collar. There should be no noticeable hair. I shave my neck once a week. All you need is a small mirror so you can see what you're doing.

Next is upper arm hair. There is nothing wrong with leg and arm hair in general, but if you have extra *upper* arm hair that connects with your shoulders and back, you should ensure it doesn't get so long that it's immediately noticeable while wearing a t-shirt. When it comes to body hair below your neck, I do not recommend shaving with a razor because it will look weird if some areas of your body have hair and others don't. Instead, use a beard trimmer so that all the hair is of a consistent length.

Next is back and shoulder hair. I use my beard trimmer at a short setting and mow it every month or two. Back hair is not attractive to women, but they won't see it until they've already decided to have sex with you, which is why shaving your neck is more important.

I don't touch my butt or leg hair. I often trim my underarm and pubic hair, but that is for controlling odor as much as appearance. Definitely trim your underarm hair if there is a huge bush sticking out when your arms hang down from your sides.

Next up is chest and stomach hair. Many girls like chest hair, but once you start getting long, straggly hairs protruding from your shirt collar, it's time for a trim. Don't trim your chest hair too short, because girls might notice that you're aggressive with your body-hair program. If a girl ever asks you, "Do you shave your chest?" you've probably gone too far. I keep my stomach hair the same length as my chest hair. It could look weird if you vary the lengths within the same general zone.

I adjust how aggressive I am with trimming depending on the season. In summer, when more of my skin is more visible, I am more aggressive, particularly if I will be shirtless on a beach. In winter, when far less is visible, I'm a bit lazier.

You may be resistant to the idea of managing your body hair and think it's gay. I fully understand your concern. I don't enjoy trimming my body hair, but at the same time, competition for the best women is intense, and it's clear that they've been trained by the culture to want clean, hygienic, and properly groomed men who aren't too hairy. There's nothing wrong with being hairy, and I cherish the fact that I come from a beastly male lineage, but the type of women I want to attract should not find my hair objectionable.

Optimizing Your Head Hair And Beard

I bet right now that you have a hair and beard configuration that is far from optimal. I know this because for a long time I maintained configurations that—on hindsight—were ugly. I went through a soul-patch phase, a pony-tail phase, and judging from old photos, a homeless man phase, all because of how I shaped my hair and beard.

I encourage you to be your own man and not change yourself completely just to get laid, but you should be working on improving your look to entice women. Optimize it to the point where you start to feel you're no longer "you." You'll have to discover this point for yourself. At the end of the day, you should be able to look in the mirror and be satisfied with what you see. If you aren't, it won't matter how good you look—you'll feel uncomfortable in your own skin, and that will come through in your game. Instead of a rapid transformation, it's fine to make improvements over the course of a year or longer.

Let's start with facial hair. Having a dense beard shows masculine virility, but many men have beards that are not full, don't grow to a proper length, or have bald patches. If your beard suffers from these problems, it's unlikely to look good when you grow it out, and you're better off clean-shaven. You could try having a few days of stubble growth or a goatee, though the latter hasn't been in fashion for some time. It's not necessary to have a beard to be attractive to women, but it is worth experimenting with one to see how they respond.

Whenever you make a physical change, run with it for a while to see whether it makes a noticeable difference to how girls respond to you. Typically, you won't be able to sense a change in how girls treat you, so you'll decide to keep a change more on how it feels to you rather than the reactions you're getting from women.

If you have three days of stubble and it makes you *think* you look more attractive, you'll be motivated to approach girls and be more confident during those approaches. At some point, you'll realize that when you optimize your look, what you're really doing is optimizing your motivation and confidence. Even if a girl hates my gigantic beard, looking like Rasputin makes me feel so damn confident that I'm more energized to interact with girls than when I don't have it. This renewed energy overrides any negative hits I may sustain because of my appearance, pushing my results higher.

Is it more important for a change in your appearance to satisfy a girl or you? You are the one who has to have the courage and energy to do approaches, go on dates, and make moves in the bedroom to secure sex. While you don't want to look like a bum, you'll achieve your best results when you look better in the eyes of women *and* yourself. Some of the changes you make will be solely to increase attention from women, while others will be solely to energize your efforts.

The amount of facial hair you have will dictate the type of clothes you can wear. A big beard means you can pull off a rustic, lumberjack style. Being clean-shaven means you can dress more preppy and classy. Generally, a clean-shaven man will complement his look by dressing up, and a bearded man will complement his look by dressing slightly hipster.

As for haircuts, I'm going to keep it easy and advise you get what's called an undercut, a classic European style that looks good on just about all men. If you do a web search on "undercut," you'll see that it's simply long on the top and short on the sides. Take a picture or two to a competent hair stylist or barber who can do it for you.

If you're balding, and are trying to cover it up with a comb-over style, I recommend you shave off all your hair, mentally adjust to your new look, and try approaching girls to prove to yourself that they won't treat you worse than before. I had a friend who was rather insecure about going bald and tried various haircuts to hide his thinning hair. He finally decided to shave it all off, and after one month, he got used to his new look and went on to maintain his success with girls. His game was even more confident, because he stopped worrying about whether or not girls could notice his thinning hair.

This example shows that how you perceive yourself is not the same as how a girl perceives you. A balding man will insist that he would look better if he had hair, but a girl may link baldness with positive values such as maturity and stability. I've seen this with friends who went bald over time. Their catastrophic predictions about never getting laid again didn't come true, and after a small period of adjustment, their results remained the same. A single change to your look will not make a major difference to your success rate as much as the amount of effort you put into your game. If you do ten approaches with hair, and 100 when you're bald, you will certainly get better results while bald.

Browse magazines and websites for photos of men who have a similar appearance, build, and facial structure as you. Take note of what they're doing and copy what you think will work. During my many experiments, I have taken pictures of celebrities to the hair salon to see if their hair styles would look good on me. Sometimes they worked out well and other times they didn't, but I learned along the way and got closer to realizing my potential.

Your overall goal when it comes to your body hair, beard, and head hair is to look masculine and feel confident while minimizing any flaws, a prescription that will get you out the door and ready to talk to girls who will enjoy your appearance.

Fixing Hygiene Problems

The first body problem we need to address is acne or other visible skin conditions. As a past acne sufferer, I can testify that acne is less damaging from a physical standpoint than how it affects your motivation to approach women.

Acne can be difficult to treat, because there are many drugs on the market and it takes time to find out which drug will work. I remember trying various antibiotics and creams to no effect. Ironically, the drug that eventually worked for me, 5% benzoyl peroxide, can be bought without a prescription. I still have blackheads on my nose, but nothing that is visible to anyone talking to me from three feet away.

The next concern is bad breath. You may have bad breath but not know it, because it's awkward for someone to tell you that your breath smells. I remember going through a bad breath phase and not finding out for a few months. I asked my close friend why he didn't tell me. He said, "Because I saw you doing so well with girls that I didn't think it was a problem." Who knows how many girls I *didn't* get because of it!

The best way to find out if you have bad breath is to ask a friend or relative, or just tell them, "If I ever have bad breath, let me know." You're giving them permission to tell you without feeling awkward about it.

There are three types of bad breath. The first is because of poor oral hygiene where you don't floss and brush often, a common problem in the third world. The second type of bad breath stems from the things you most recently put in your mouth, such as coffee, dairy, garlic, onions, or cigarettes. This is usually the least smelly and can be eliminated by a quick brush, if not a piece of gum. The third type of bad breath, and the most common, is from your tongue.

If you stick out your tongue and look towards the back, you'll see hair-like protrusions that are home to billions of bacteria. If you're unfortunate enough to have "bad" bacteria colonize that area, their waste products will emit from the surface of your tongue, get picked up by air whenever you talk, and be delivered to the face of the person you're speaking to. Saliva helps to reduce the concentration of bad bacteria, but it doesn't kill them outright, and technically nothing can completely eliminate the problem. If you're stuck with bad bacteria on your tongue, you will join a huge percentage of the population who has the same problem. The goal is not to "cure" yourself of these bacteria, because you'll never be able to kill every bad bacterial cell in your mouth, but to reduce them so that people you're talking to can't detect a foul odor.

The best way to minimize the bacteria on your tongue is with a tongue scraper, which is often sold next to toothbrushes in a pharmacy. If you can't find one, you can use an inverted metal spoon. Simply stick out your tongue and scrape from back to front. A film will develop on the scraper. Smell it. If it smells really bad, you'll have to scrape your tongue regularly. If there is no obvious smell, even when you put your nose close to the film, you should be alright. When my friend told me my breath was bad, I scraped my tongue with a metal spoon and smelled a vicious odor, confirming that I had a problem.

The most reliable rinse that has kept the problem manageable for me is 1.5% hydrogen peroxide (I dilute 3% hydrogen peroxide that is sold in stores). After eating my first meal of the day, I floss, brush, scrape my tongue, and do a 30-second gargle with 1.5% hydrogen peroxide. I find that diluted hydrogen peroxide is superior to store-bought rinses such as Listerine, because it's softer on my mouth and doesn't cause excessive dryness, which can make the problem worse. At night, I floss, brush, and scrape my tongue. I do a second daily rinse only if I will be talking to girls in close quarters. I also avoid milk, because lactose is the preferred food of the bad bacteria that live in my mouth. This may be different for you.

If you discover that you have bad breath, it's easy to go overboard and start checking your breath constantly. No one has perfect breath all the time (most people have morning breath), and you'll encounter many women with bad breath. The goal is to minimize the problem with tongue scraping and rinses.

If a girl really likes you, having bad breath may not hurt your chances, because she can rationalize that you just ate a stinky meal or drank a glass of milk, but if a girl is only mildly attracted to you, bad breath can kill the interaction, and the worst part is that you would have no idea it was the reason. In the past, it wasn't worth worrying about this problem, but in an age when competition for the best girls is getting more intense, you want to eliminate all roadblocks that could be hampering your success. Bad breath is one of them.

The next issue is underarm odor. As with bad breath, you may not know that you have smelly armpits, so ask someone you trust to take a whiff. Commercial products use aluminum to decrease your sweating or a chemical fragrance to temporarily mask the odor. The best product I've found to combat armpit odor is baking soda, a powerful deodorizer. I've been using it under my arms for nearly a decade.

After showering, dab a wet fingertip into a container of baking soda and spread it under one of your armpits. Then dab the fingertip again and apply to the other armpit. The less hairy you are, the less you'll need. You'll be odor-free for at least twenty hours. Since baking soda is a strong base, your skin will become red if you use too much. Reduce the dose if you're experiencing irritation.

Baking soda can also remove odors coming from your crotch. Since the skin on your scrotum and phallus is much thinner than your armpit, it can't handle a full dose of baking soda. Create a 50-50 mixture of baking soda and corn starch (or baby powder), and apply it at the base of your phallus and testicles using the wet finger technique. If you experience irritation, reduce the amount of baking soda in your mixture.

Your feet are another area where baking soda works. Simply apply wet baking soda between your toes. If your skin starts to peel, try a 50-50 mixture.

The next thing to fix is butt smell. You may think I'm joking, but my experiences in the changing room at the gym prove that many men have this problem. If you take off your pants in the presence of a girl and she's hit with a fierce butt odor, it could be game over. Wiping with dry toilet paper may not be sufficient, particularly if you're hairy. Either wipe carefully or consider using a moist cleansing product.

Lastly, you may want to experiment with cologne. I use cologne often, although I can't prove that it helps me get a better response from women. If you think that using cologne will make you feel more confident, it's worth a try, and if girls compliment your scent, it's definitely helping you out.

My intention with this section is not to make you neurotic about whether or not you're emitting odors. Human beings are biological organisms that will emit odors even when they're perfectly clean and healthy. The problem is that modern society has launched a war on odors and trained women to be disgusted by them, to the point where smells are on their list of deal breakers when it comes to men. We can blame the first men who decided to eliminate all their odors, because once women could select men who didn't smell, all other men had to manage their odors in order to compete. The hygiene race will continue until the day urban men have to spend as much time on personal care as women.

The list of grooming and odor concerns I've shared is as far as I'll go to get laid. If one day girls demand men with perfectly shaped eyebrows or shaved legs, I'm quitting the game, because this would affect my core value of wanting to feel like a man. I'll scrape my tongue, trim my back hair, and ensure my balls smell fresh, but I won't go much further.

How You Dress

I'm going to go against the advice of most game gurus and say that style doesn't matter that much. I've been much more successful at picking up when dressed in a snug v-neck and jeans than in a "stylish" suit with a pocket square. The reason that dressing up doesn't work for me is that I feel "too cool for school" in fancy outfits and approach way less than if I'm wearing something more comfortable. Wearing fancy outfits puts the idea in my head that girls should approach me, which rarely happens, so I end up doing less of what really determines my success rate: approaching.

You should adopt a style that gets you out of the door feeling good about talking to women. If that occurs when you're suited up and looking like a million bucks then great. If it's when you are wearing a cheap t-shirt and jeans with holes in them, as I've done in the past, so be it. Most men feel more confident talking to girls when they dress up than down, so it's at least worth trying to see how you fare with an upgrade in style. I know what my results are, because I've experimented with wearing suits and other outfits, but if you haven't done this, you won't know for sure.

The first thing you can do is to buy two trendy outfits that are different in style. Wear each of these outfits during at least five approach sessions, and measure your motivation and game results. There are a few options when it comes to deciding what to buy. The first is to copy men you see doing well with women and who have a similar vibe as you. It could be that they have unconsciously tapped into the style that works best with their vibe—hack into that by duplicating them. Second, buy outfits you see on fashion websites, or on mannequins in the trendiest clothing stores in your city. These outfits are designed to be "in style."

An essential guideline is to wear fitted clothing. Pick shirts, jackets, pants, and suits that fit your body snugly and show your frame, which should be thin or athletic (you may need to lose weight to get rid of excess fat). This allows girls to more readily put you in the "sexy" category to begin imagining having sex with you. Loose or baggy clothing will not do you any favors, because they prevent girls from going through the imagination process. If you're older and insist on wearing loose clothing, they may even put you in the "dad" category. Regardless of your age, wearing a cheap fitted v-neck that highlights your chest and biceps will do far more at building attraction than a loose $1,000 suit that looks like a curtain draped over you.

Keep your style goals simple until you develop a finer taste that allows you to try riskier outfits. If you're completely clueless, ask girls for help, particularly those who work in the clothing stores where you shop. Don't be afraid to show them pictures of outfits you saw online. You don't have to re-invent the wheel when it comes to finding the right outfits to wear, and you definitely don't have to spend a lot of money. For every girl who knows the brand name of every item of clothing you're wearing, a dozen have no idea, and if a girl is evaluating your clothing down to the last fiber, you probably want to avoid her for being overly materialistic.

When you try a new beard or hair configuration, it may not be immediately obvious whether girls dig your new look. If you can't tell when an outfit is changing your results, focus on how it makes you feel. If you like how you look and enjoy talking to girls while wearing that outfit, keep wearing it.

Your style is one of the first things that a girl uses to categorize you. If you have big muscles, and you're showing them off with a snug shirt, the qualities you bring to the forefront are youth, strength, and sexiness. If you're wearing a plaid shirt and have a long beard, you're displaying that you're trendy, artistic, and cool. If you're wearing a suit or expensive threads, you're displaying success, ambition, and status. A girl who is turned off when you're wearing one style of clothing could be interested if you wore another, but it helps if your style matches your strengths. If you're a Wall Street banker type, dressing like a hipster will initially create interest in hipster girls, but you may lose them when your Wall Street personality emerges. It's worth experimenting with new styles to see how girls react, but make sure you see an aspect of your personality in whatever it is you're wearing.

Another simple method is to tailor your outfits for venues that attract a certain type of girl. If I'm going to a nightclub on a college night, I'll wear a v-neck. If I'm going to a mega club on a weekend night, when the women will be older, I'll dress up. If I'm going to run day game in the hipster area of the city, I'll wear a plaid shirt. To maximize your style, choose outfits that make you feel great *and* attract the kind of girl you prefer.

How To Speak And Act

We've covered everything that deals with your inward biological functioning and outward appearance. Next is identifying the best behaviors you can display to women. Note how I used the word "identifying" instead of "changing." There is a situation where any man is ultra-confident, such as when speaking to a group of friends. There is a situation when he can speak in a smooth tone, such as when reading alone to himself. There is a situation where he walks in a masculine way, such as when he leaves the gym. For everything that I will advise you to do, chances are that you're already doing them automatically from time to time. What you want to do is consciously harness these optimal behaviors when you're talking to women.

I don't believe that self-improvement advice or books actually change people. All they can do is enable you to amplify some of your existing behaviors, or ones you're capable of doing, while lowering the volume on less desirable behaviors. You're already born with the ability to connect with a girl, have sex with her, and have a relationship with her, just like a bear is born with the ability to climb trees, catch fish, and relax in the shade. A bear raised in the wild is able to do what is necessary to survive, but a bear raised in a zoo has not had an opportunity to do the things that are within his nature. Instead of hunting, he will wait for food to be served to him. Instead of climbing trees, he will lie down and sleep. Men who have problems with women are no different to a bear raised in the zoo.

The modern culture we've grown up in has taken away our confidence, directed our energies into activities such as sitting in an office all day, and made us feel ashamed to be powerful and masculine. My job is not to change you but to allow you to be the man you already are. So when I tell you to approach women or hit the gym, I'm not changing you so much as bringing out something already within you that will make it easier to connect with women.

An important component is how you speak. Years ago, I read a quote that goes something like this: "If a man is attractive, he can read from the phone book and girls will still want to sleep with him." Imagine a famous actor reading a phone book in his slowest, lowest, and most deliberate tone. Would his female fans still want to sleep with him? Of course they would, and they wouldn't care about the content of his speech, only his sexy behavior.

We're not famous actors, so there must be content to our speech, but the point remains that if you hit all the other attraction buttons a girl has, and speak in a way that appeals to her, you don't have to worry *as much* about content. This is why you often see attractive girls with men whom you'd consider boring. She's not with him for his intriguing banter and jokes, but because of his other qualities that you may not have picked up on.

If I told you the best way to speak to a woman, and you don't currently speak that way, do you really think you could change your manner of speaking? For example, if your voice is high pitched, but I tell you that girls like low-pitched voices, do you think it would be worthwhile going through dozens of hours of training to make your voice a bit deeper? Probably not. We're born with aspects of how we speak that we can't change without strenuous effort, which might not even work in the end, but there are things we can change quite easily. If I tell you to speak slower and louder, I'm confident you can do so without training, because there have been many times in your life when you have manipulated the volume or speed of your speech.

Imagine you meet a girl who is mildly attracted to you. You speak to her softly without enunciating your words. It is likely that she will become impatient and interrupt you by saying that she has to go instead of asking you to repeat what she didn't understand. On the other hand, if she is mildly attracted to you, and you're speaking clearly and audibly, she is likely to stick around for longer out of curiosity. Therefore, the reason you optimize your speech pattern is so that you can hold the attention of girls who are mildly attracted to you, in the hope that they will become strongly attracted over time.

I have five simple tips for making sure that how you speak is not encouraging girls to walk away. The first is to speak louder. If at any point a girl says that she can't hear you, it means she is missing what you're saying and getting discouraged. With the exception of a noisy nightclub, a girl should never have trouble hearing you. Don't be concerned if bystanders are eavesdropping. Pretend that you're doing a good deed by providing strangers with a few moments of entertainment that will enable them to take a break from their smartphones.

Second, speak clearly. Enunciate your words as if you were taking a verbal pronunciation test. While it would be great to have a seductive speaking style, it's even more important to be understood. If a girl doesn't understand you, she will get frustrated and want to leave.

Third, speak slightly slower than your typical speed. Men who get nervous around women start talking fast as if they want to get the interaction over with, but this is not enjoyable for the girl, particularly if you're making other mistakes like talking too softly. Speaking slowly hides your nervousness and conveys confidence, because confident men are so sure that people want to listen to them that they don't see the need to rush.

Fourth, rid your speech of filler sounds or words such as "um," "you know," "like," and "uh." These sounds and words do not add any content, meaning, or substance to what you're saying. Many men use them for no other reason than habit, and would come across as more intelligent if they dropped them entirely.

The final tip is to model a speaker you enjoy. For me, that person is the actor Liam Neeson. I like the heaviness of his voice and cadence, so every now and then I'll watch his acting and absorb his manner of speaking. Of course, I'm not Liam Neeson, and I could never duplicate his Irish accent, but having a model reminds me to utilize parts of my voice that I think women will find attractive.

If you think your speech is below average, or girls make uncomfortable facial expressions when trying to listen to you, I recommend that you join a public speaking club such as Toastmasters, an international organization that I participated in when preparing for my first lecture tour. The club forces you to make prepared and impromptu speeches before a supportive crowd that gives you feedback on how you can improve your body language and speaking.

What you learn at Toastmasters can easily be transferred to game (and some of the material you use in speeches can be used in your conversations with women). If the thought of giving a short speech to a friendly audience makes you nervous, you may have a hard time approaching women, who you know will judge you more critically. Toastmasters can enable you to get the bugs out while improving your confidence.

The main idea is to speak clearly, slowly, and loudly, in a tone that falls in the deeper part of your vocal range, but understand that what's even more important than speaking well is to merely speak. You can still succeed with women if your speech is below average, as long as you put in the effort, but you cannot succeed at all if you don't make any attempts. Get started with what you have right now, and gradually make improvements as time goes on.

Closely related to how you speak is how you act, which includes your mannerisms, body language, and other movements that contribute to your overall vibe. A woman will perceive these things the instant you open your mouth and start speaking to her. It's not helpful to try to micro-manage every little thing we do, such as where to place our left thumb or how to tilt our head. It's better to focus on how we want to present ourselves overall.

If you want to attract feminine girls who prefer to submit to a strong man, you should present yourself as a strong man. To convey strength with how you walk, stand, and move, imagine that you're a caveman hunter looking to spear a wild animal for dinner. The animal could be dangerous, so you're prepared for a life-or-death struggle where you must kill the animal before it kills you. There are five ways to accomplish this vibe.

First, move slowly. Slow movements convey confidence and calm, whereas fast movements convey hyperactivity and anxiety. Second, have a neutral expression on your face, as if you're not affected by your environment and are concentrating on finding an animal to hunt. Do not wear a fake smile, or have an artificial expression that doesn't convey how you're really feeling. Third, ensure your shoulders are upright. This shows vitality and optimal health, as opposed to an office worker who sits all day and begins developing a hunch. You should stand up straight to maximize your height, your chest should be out, and your belly should be in. Fourth, carefully scan people's faces to size them up. Match the hunter vibe by glancing at men to identify potential threats and at women to identify a potential mate. Lastly, make deliberate eye contact with the girls you find most attractive and note if they reciprocate.

Some game gurus advise that you display high energy around girls, but I haven't found this to be universally effective. If you're naturally high energy, by all means show it when appropriate, particularly in venues that match that energy, but faking high energy will come across as phony. Not all girls want a high-energy man, so by acting it out, you mainly attract girls who may not like the "real" you after you relax and return to your normal state.

You can adopt these five tips without having to fake a state that will make you appear drugged out, unnatural, or just weird. Another benefit of the hunter vibe is that you slip under the radar of a mall security guard or potential cockblocker, who won't interpret your understated energy as coming from a "pick-up artist." You're a calm, collected man who moves through life deliberately and occasionally takes action when seeing something of interest.

You don't have to adopt a persona or amplify your energy to be attractive to women. You simply have to convey your strength in a controlled manner that maximizes the receptiveness of any girl you approach. After you ease into the actual approach, you can adjust your energy to a level that's appropriate for the girl and environment.

Chapter Conclusion

You may think that what I've shared so far isn't actual game, but I have raised your game at least 30% if you have studied the seven beliefs and improved your biological functioning, physical appearance, hygiene, style of dress, tone of voice, and body language. All of these things will create such a favorable first impression upon an approach that they will make the ensuing conversation less critical to your results. Hopefully, a girl's initial attraction to you will be such that she'll ignore any minor problems you have with conversing.

What we're doing is no different to how a chef operates a fancy restaurant. He puts most of his efforts not into how the food tastes, but into the lighting, the style of place settings, the shape of the wine glasses, the size of the plates, the design of the dining-room furniture, the appearance of the garnishes, the color of the sauces that are swirled on the plate, and so on. Before you take even one bite of an expensive meal, your mind has been primed to enjoy it, even though the food itself may be average.

The same is true with game. Before a girl is asked to take a bite of you, you've already impressed her with your presentation. If that presentation is excellent, while the taste is just average, the girl will still write a positive review. In a sexual market where girls can choose whom they want to date, you are the dish. How it tastes (what you think of as game) is only one part of the overall package. This is why it's critically important that you take the chapters on internal game and pre-game seriously if you want to improve your success with women.

Even if you stop reading this book right now, without taking my advice on how to approach women and talk to them, your overall game will still take a huge leap, because you've eliminated incorrect beliefs and physical problems that have been hurting how girls see you. You're also probably starting to realize that game is less about trying to convince or persuade a girl to sleep with you and more about allowing a girl to be with you because she appreciates your overall value.

In my early teachings on game, I thought that I had to transform myself into a master player with perfect routines and moves simply to have a normal sex life. What I learned instead is that all the girls I slept with because of my "game" weren't sleeping with a mannequin or an actor but a man with specific strengths, weaknesses, quirks, stories, experiences, and jokes that, in combination, resonated with them on a deep level. Whatever game I did use was only a thin layer on top of the real me. The normal and flawed man I am is still more than good enough to be with a variety of women, and who you are is more than sufficient to get laid. All we have to do is consciously present the parts of us that girls like most to more seamlessly achieve our goal of intimacy.

At the end of the day, the only way to sleep with a girl is to allow her to decide of her own volition to sleep with you, after she's evaluated the "offer" you made when you asked her out on a date, went for the kiss, or invited her to your home. When you walk up to a new girl, you're essentially saying, "Here I am! I'm fit and cool and will add a great experience to your life!" We're all products now, so there is no need to get bogged down in the negative spiral of rejection, fear, and loneliness. Improve the shininess of your product as much as you can and present it to a potential buyer. If you find this to be a bit crass or soulless, I recommend you jump into a time machine and go back to a more traditional era when this wasn't the case.

Ridding your mind of the belief that you have to use persuasion or trickery allows you to seek out natural connections with girls who are already compatible with you, instead of laboriously trying to create them with girls who are incompatible with you.

Unless you plan on being an actor throughout a relationship, artificially trying to create connections where none exist is not sustainable (assuming it can even be done).

You will help bring a natural connection into being by talking to a girl in an optimal manner, texting her without neediness, and escalating in a way that doesn't make her feel like a slut. These things are easy to learn and execute, and will not require you to change into someone else. The last thing I want you to do is to copy what I do and use it on girls. Instead, I want you to use parts of yourself that already exist, and serve them up to a girl you like to maximize the chances that sex or a relationship will occur.

Chapter 4: Attraction

Until the end of time, men will ask, "What do women want?" Dozens of theories have been thought up and hundreds of books have been written in an attempt to answer this question. The problem with general theories of attraction is that they fail to take into account that each girl has her own individual quirks. Yes, all women have common patterns when it comes to attraction, but when analyzing an individual girl, you may find that she prefers a stocky drug-dealer over the archetypal tall, successful, and handsome businessman who the culture promotes as being more desirable.

If you take general patterns too seriously, and try to be attractive to every girl, you will dampen or eliminate a trait of yours that may be intensely attractive to *one* girl. That leads to the following question: do you want to be slightly attractive to hundreds of girls or immensely attractive to just a few? In reality, things are not so white and black, but I hope you can see that slavishly obeying theories of attraction may force you into a general mold that hurts your uniqueness and creates only tepid attraction.

I'm not going to insist that you make wholesale changes to your personality or character. Instead, I will focus on how attraction works so that you understand it, recognize it, and allow it to bloom when it's actually happening. Remember that you're not trying to convince a girl to be attracted to you, but simply advancing the existing attraction that is a result of your initial presentation and vibe.

Types Of Attraction

There are three types of attraction: pre-minute, post-minute, and reputational. One of the three has to be present for a girl to show some interest in you and allow the seduction to proceed. If two or three are present, it's highly probable that sex will result.

Pre-minute attraction is the attraction a girl has for a man she doesn't know after she has been exposed to him for less than one minute. It's a result of his appearance, height, clothing, body language, vibe, and tone of voice. One minute of exposure to someone provides you with more than enough information to decide whether or not you want to keep interacting with that person. If a girl has no pre-minute attraction for you, she will either reject you outright or let you talk out of politeness or boredom before eventually ending the conversation.

Most men can substantially improve their pre-minute attractiveness by employing the techniques I described in the previous chapter. This is critically important, because if a girl doesn't have pre-minute attraction for you, you won't have an opportunity to engage in deeper interactions.

Although you can optimize your appearance and body language, your genetics will put a ceiling on the pre-minute attraction you can create in girls within a specific environment. Once you hit that ceiling, you cannot increase their initial response any further.

I noticed that my pre-minute attraction rose or fell depending on the venues I went to. Then I noticed that it changed in different cities and countries. The good news is that merely going to another place can increase your pre-minute attraction. My advice is to maximize your pre-minute attraction where you live now, at least for a year, and then experiment to see how you fare in other locations. A way to guarantee weak results is to change your environment before doing any work to improve your game.

The second type of attraction is post-minute attraction. It's based on what you say, the stories you tell, your sense of humor, background, job, hobbies, experiences, and how well all of these things connect with your body language, vibe, and general demeanor. A girl will begin to take note of these things about one minute after you initiate contact with her. With post-minute attraction, we're starting to transcend first impressions and physical appearance. Most of the sex you get will be from girls who give you above-average marks on both pre-minute and post-minute attraction.

If your pre-minute attraction is weak, girls will not give you much of a chance to build your post-minute attraction, except in scenarios involving your social circle. It is also possible to overcome poor pre-minute attraction if you have a hidden talent, such as being able to play the guitar or make funny jokes, which can be perceived by a girl after she has written you off. You may have had the experience of changing how you feel about a girl you dismissed after discovering she has a high-level talent like being able to sing.

The third kind of attraction is reputational. This means that your reputation preceded you and she was interested before you knew she existed. One common way to build reputational attraction is for girls to see you with other women. For example, imagine arriving at a nightclub with one or more attractive girls who show intense interest in you. Another girl may notice, become attracted to you, and move closer, or give you signs that she wants to be approached. Some game gurus advise that you take hot girls to bars and clubs, but if you already know hot girls and hang out with them, you probably don't need to approach more.

Reputational attraction can also happen within a social circle, where a girl you've yet to meet has heard that you're super cool or that you have slept with a hotter girl. She'll be much friendlier when she sees you at future events. Keep in mind that reputational attraction can also work in reverse: gossip about your adventures with unattractive and obese girls can decrease your attractiveness among the girls who had previously considered you for intimacy. This is why you may want to conceal from the world any ugly girl that you're sleeping with. False rumors, such as a vindictive ex-girlfriend telling everyone that you abused her, can also hurt your reputational attraction. Ironically, this type of rumor may actually help you to sleep with women who prefer "bad boys."

The strongest form of reputational attraction is fame. If you have fame on the level of a Hollywood actor or pop musician, thousands of attractive girls will be willing to sleep with you, not so much because you are talented, but because other people show that they like you. A girl's brain rationalizes that you must be a high-value man if you have high social proof, even if you are a high-school dropout who is addicted to drugs and can't get his life together. In the past, a girl's parents selected her husband, because females make disastrous decisions based on short-term thinking and the use of flawed shortcuts, but today, we can use their flaws to our advantage.

You don't have to be an international celebrity for fame to enhance your reputational attraction. Local fame or even minor local status can be just as effective. I am friends with a man who owns a popular restaurant in a medium-sized city. He has a constant stream of female customers who give him sexual attention. I'm sure you've also heard of bartenders at average venues who get a lot of attention from girls. The main idea is to be well known or have high status within a small community.

Currently, I'm "internet famous." Millions of people around the world have come across my name or heard about me through a news article, but the number of female groupies I meet are small because I'm known over a wide area. Compare that to when I was blogging locally as "DC Bachelor" and had intimate encounters with over a dozen groupies. Since going worldwide, I've had maybe five or six. For most men, local fame or status will always trump minor worldwide fame.

Should you focus on developing local fame, or continue with traditional game through cold approaching? For example, should you try to become a bartender at a popular bar simply to get girls? If you're already on the road to developing local fame, and have a genuine interest in activities or gigs that will also make you attractive to girls, you should definitely put your energy into those activities, but if they don't really interest you, try something else.

A drawback of local fame is that it can be fleeting. What gives you status today might not give you status tomorrow. I've encountered many men who had a great niche within their city, but lost their status when trends changed with no game to fall back on. Think of the stereotypical football jock whose local status faded after graduating high school. Another flaw of local fame is that it's non-transferable. If you decide to move to another city, you won't be able to take it with you.

While standard game is more challenging, it's a skill that remains with you permanently and can be applied anywhere. Ideally, you should develop your game in parallel with your local status, so that you have something to fall back on once your local status fades.

High reputational attraction will compensate for low pre-minute attraction, but you'll still need to do well when it comes to post-minute attraction. A famous actor who has negative game, where he does *everything* wrong, will fail to have sex with a fan. Your game doesn't have to be perfect, but there is a limit to how many mistakes you can make even if your pre-minute or reputational attraction scores are strong. No matter what your situation, game is not something you can skip out on if you don't want girls to skip out on you.

Attraction Triggers

Now that I've discussed the three main attraction types, we can move on to the specific attraction triggers. These triggers are baked into the game you will learn in later chapters, so what's important at this stage is that you increase your awareness of them.

The weight that women give to the different attraction triggers depends on where they were raised. The triggers I'm about to describe appeal mainly to Anglophone and European women who have a comfortable standard of living. In the impoverished towns and villages of Central America, Africa, and Asia, girls respond less to excitement or novelty triggers than to a provider trigger that conveys stability.

The first attraction trigger is appearance, which can be subjective and depend on a girl's tastes. To hit this trigger, optimize the look you already have, minimize your flaws, and don't worry about the things you can't control, such as your height or baby face. Feeling good about the look you have is as important as looking good, or you won't have the confidence to talk to women.

The second trigger is a sense of humor. Girls like funny guys because humor is an indirect way of showing intelligence, and intelligence is an indication of success and ambition. There is a strong natural component to humor which makes it hard to teach, but I'll say more about this later when I present the Roosh Program.

Even men who are not particularly funny can reveal a lighter side of their personality that conveys humor. It will definitely help your goal of having sex if you can make women smile and laugh, although you shouldn't force it so that your humor comes across as phony or rehearsed. Don't stress if you score low marks on any individual trigger. There are so many triggers that you will naturally possess a handful to exhibit.

The next trigger is confidence. As I'm sure you're aware, every girl in the world proclaims to want a "confident" man. Confidence is the *attitude* a successful man displays, so when a woman says she wants a confident man, what she's really saying is that she wants a successful man. If a girl already knows that a man is successful, perhaps through his reputation, she will automatically assume that he is confident, but if she doesn't know a man's status, as is the case when he approaches her randomly in a coffee shop, she will analyze his behavior and lines to discern whether or not he is successful.

Imagine you approach a girl with your shoulders straight and look her directly in the eyes. You tease her gently and touch her lightly a few times. Every aspect of your behavior is fed into her subconscious, ready to influence her response when you ask for her phone number, a date, or sexual intercourse. If you ask a girl why she said no to a particular man, she'll say something vague such as "I wasn't feeling it," which means her unconscious instructed her to say no based on a lack of attraction triggers, especially confidence.

If you're a young man who has yet to experience success, you may be wondering, "How can I display confidence if I haven't had success yet?" It's the same catch-22 of needing job experience before you can get a job. Luckily for you, we know how confident men behave, so you can fake being confident until you possess real confidence. This is not a perfect strategy, because a girl's subconscious may be able to spot your fakery, particularly if she's already been with successful men, but fake confidence is less likely to be detected by girls who haven't had much experience. The less confidence you have, the more you should focus on girls who haven't been with many men.

The most reliable way to fake confidence is through cockiness, where you say humorous things that display overconfidence. A sample cocky line would be, "I would start dancing, but I don't want to embarrass everyone here with my advanced moves." Would an insecure man who has never experienced success or received compliments utter such a line? He would instead think, "I don't want to dance, because I'm scared people will laugh at me." If you lack confidence, cocky lines would be the opposite of what you're thinking.

Let's transform common insecure thoughts into cocky lines that can increase attraction.

Insecure thought: "She probably doesn't like my beard."

Cocky line: "Do you like men with beards as beautiful as mine?"

Insecure thought: "I hope she doesn't see my big, ugly hands."

Cocky line: "Do you know what they say about guys with large hands?" Pause for two seconds. "That they are very intelligent."

Insecure thought: "My favorite music band is weird. Maybe I should lie about it."

Cocky line: "You don't like my favorite band? We have to break up! I'm sure you'll meet other guys who have the same weird taste in music as you."

Insecure thought: "She keeps touching my arm. Does she like me now?"

Cocky line: "You're very touchy. I'm not just a piece of meat… I'm a real person."

Insecure thought: "I'm an average man. I'm just like everyone else."

Cocky line: "Ever since I was a young child, my mom repeatedly told me that I was special."

Insecure thought: "She's barely talking to me. She doesn't like me."

Cocky line: "I'm not used to girls who are so quiet. How about I buy you five shots of vodka to open you up?"

Insecure thought: "This conversation is so boring. It's not going anywhere."

Cocky line: "Well, this is officially the most amazing conversation I've ever had in my life."

Even if you are genuinely confident, your mind will play tricks on you by planting insecure thoughts that make you feel as if you're not doing well with a girl. Simply take the thought and transform it to mean the opposite so that it will squash the negativity in your mind. The benefit of using cocky lines is that, after a few months, you start morphing into a more confident man.

The next attraction trigger is money. A lot of men mistakenly think money is the *only* attraction trigger and become trapped in a spiral of negative thoughts: "All girls want millionaires… I will never become a millionaire… I will never get sex… I must only sleep with prostitutes." In fact, money is becoming less of an attraction trigger, because most women work and can meet their own material needs, which means they look for men who can fulfill their need for excitement rather than stability.

If you have worked at a typical office job, you know how incredibly boring it is. Forty hours a week in such an environment must be compensated by the opposite—fun. In the case of women, the solution to a boring job is partying on the weekends and finding a man who entertains her and elicits her emotions. The more her money needs are being met through work, the more she will seek out a man who provides an antidote to combat the boredom she experiences for a large part of her week.

If a girl's material needs are not being met through her job, she is already getting enough "excitement" through life's struggles, and she will therefore seek out a man who more strongly hits the money trigger, but because she's not actually starving, and can probably depend on government welfare, she won't choose a man who is a complete bore.

The danger with showing off how wealthy you are to get women is that it attracts a very specific type of woman who is obsessed with money and constantly worries about whether she can land a man who has enough of it.

If you sense that a girl is seeking excitement because she already makes her own money, presenting yourself as well off will turn her off. She simply won't care unless she's consciously hunting for a husband. If you sense that a girl is somewhat impoverished and would like a successful man, or is looking for a husband, you can talk briefly about your job or business. Whatever the case, don't use money as the only means of attraction. It reduces who you are to a number that can easily be beaten by other men in your city. Hit on other attraction triggers to maximize your overall value.

The next attraction trigger is intelligence. This is often displayed indirectly through your humor, conversation, or job. This form of attraction used to be weighted higher when a man needed intelligence to be financially stable, but now most women make their own money. At the very least, you should display a level of intelligence that a girl feels is equal to or above hers.

When it comes to intelligence, it's far more difficult for a girl to "date down" than it is for a man, but if you strongly excel in another attraction trigger, such as appearance, you may get a pass if you seem to be dumb. When you consider that most people don't even read one book a year, the fact that you are reading my book right now means you are likely in the upper 20% of intelligence and will not strike out with a girl because she thinks you're stupid.

Aloofness or emotional cruelty is the next attraction trigger. There is no easier way for a man to show he has higher value than by treating a girl badly. A girl rationalizes it in this way: "If he doesn't care about me, he must be able to get someone better, so his value is above mine, and I must have him." When you're walking down the street every day, you ignore hundreds of girls who may not notice you, but once you've gotten the attention of a girl, such as by talking to her for some time at a party, treating her poorly will indicate to her that your value is higher than hers. This is an essential concept to understand, and explains why you often see pretty girls with men who are assholes.

The easiest way to use this trigger is to be initially friendly to a girl and then begin showing signs that you're losing interest by teasing her playfully or walking away, preferably in an environment where you know you'll see her again or where she has the ability to contact you. It's harder to pull this off with cold approaching, because if you walk away at the beginning, you'll lose all contact with her, so this technique is more useful in the middle and later stages of a seduction, often after sex.

To activate this trigger early on, I recommend that you absorb the following belief: "When I find a girl who seems interesting, I expect her to impress me." If you do, you will act with bemused skepticism and test her with "qualifications" that aim to see whether she works out or knows how to cook.

For some girls, aloofness is not subtle enough—they need a man who harms them emotionally so they can truly feel that their value is lower. While I do not advocate or teach such a strategy, it's important to be aware that we now live in an era where girls are actively seeking out men who will debase them. You'll get hints of this in the bedroom when a girl demands that you cause her physical pain by engaging in extremely rough sex. Almost all girls prefer a man to be dominant, but there is a fine line between dominance and abuse, and if a girl is gravitating towards the latter, she will lose interest in you if you refuse to be abusive. You'll have to decide for yourself how far you're willing to go.

The next attraction trigger is social status, which is simply the quantity and quality of people who like you. A billionaire has a lot of social status because people like him for his money. A local restaurateur has status because locals like him for his food. A club promoter has status because party goers like him for the access he gives them. A businessman has status because people like him for the leadership and jobs he provides. The more you are liked, the more social status you have. The peak of social status is when you are liked by other people with high social status, such as celebrities or world leaders.

For social status to be effective, a girl has to *witness* others giving you attention. If you're famous on the internet, but she meets you in a bar without knowing you beforehand, it will be hard for you to build attraction based on your status unless fans happen to approach you while you're talking to her. However, if she knows you from the internet and then sees you in a bar, reputational attraction will kick in, and she'll give you clear indicators of interest.

A girl who is social or outgoing will want to date a man who has higher social status than her. If you have zero social status, meaning you are a lone wolf in a big city without any friends, your ideal target is a shy girl who doesn't have social status either, because a girl generally doesn't want to date a man who scores lower on a quality than she does. The reason day game is such a great tool for the lone-wolf type of man is that a girl can't detect his low social status. This is not the case in a bar or nightclub, where she can easily size him up based on who he's hanging out with. This is also why I don't approach a girl in a club if I see her talking to bartenders, the DJ, or the club owner, because it's clear that she is seeking a guy with the highest social status in that venue. As a lowly patron, I cannot compete on social status with those men, so it would be a waste of time to approach her.

Social status is a useful shortcut for women to judge the value of a man. In the distant past, a man who was loved by everyone in his tribe was providing it with such great value that he was in a position to reap the most rewards. In the modern era, a man who dedicates his life to clubbing or maintaining a rolodex of nightlife contacts will be perceived as having higher social status by women than a doctor or businessman, simply because women want to achieve high status in social environments. The main idea is to pick a hunting ground frequented by a lot of attractive women and then become well-liked there. If you approach a girl in a venue or within a community where your status is known, she will be far more receptive than if you're just another random guy.

The final attraction trigger is romantic connection, a feeling of being drawn to a person from sensing an emotional bond, similar to what you see in romantic movies. While these movies give far too much weight to romantic connection and its importance for stable relationships, it's still an important value that women idealize and want to experience.

When you're a young man, you will feel "butterflies" in your stomach when you start meeting pretty girls, mostly because you overestimate what these girls can add to your life. As you get older and gain experience, you move from seeking a romantic connection to more practical considerations, such as whether a girl can serve your needs without causing you harm. However, even when women get older, they will regard romantic connection as more important than morals or values. They don't require a romantic connection for sex or short-term relationships, but when it comes to long-term relationships, they expect to fall head-over-heels in love with a man.

Some men try to manufacture a romantic connection, but this makes them appear needy, because girls can easily sense when men are forcing something that should be experienced naturally. It also presupposes that we know all the nuts and bolts of interpersonal connection, which we certainly don't, so what you think of as a connection may be partially valid from your point of view, but not the girl's. Through game we can simulate basic attraction and rapport, but what romantic connection is, and how it comes into being, is something for girls to feel rather than for men to analyze. If a girl sees you as high value, and there is a natural fit between your personalities, she will likely perceive a romantic connection, but if you try to manufacture this connection, it will be perceived as fake and disturb what would have developed organically.

The best you can do is allow a girl to decide that a romantic connection is present after you display your most attractive traits. For her to experience this deeper feeling, there has to be the seed of a genuine bond present, so the proper game maneuver is not to try to manipulate the connection. It's a matter of sheer luck, because in a lifetime of dating you may meet only three or four girls with whom you share a strong romantic connection.

If you attempt to analyze why a woman is attracted to a particular man, you'll find that it stems from a mixture of appearance, humor, confidence, money, intelligence, aloofness, social status, and romantic connection. If beards are suddenly trendy, girls will like men with beards because of the social status they convey, not necessarily because these men have hair on their faces. If a girl likes a man who created a tech start-up, she's attracted to the man's intelligence and his potential to make money, not necessarily because she likes technology or business. As social trends change, women will become attracted to different things, but they all boil down to a combination of the eight main triggers described above.

It should now make sense to you why girls are attracted to "successful" men (intelligence, money), or "trendy" men who look cool (appearance, social status), or abusive men who treat them like crap (confidence, aloofness). This shows that you don't need to hit all the triggers to have a relationship with a girl—hit one or two triggers strongly, or hit several triggers slightly.

When I cold approach during the day, I hit the triggers of appearance, confidence, and humor. I don't hit the money or social status triggers, and I begin to hit aloofness only when a girl starts to commit to me. When I cold approach at a nightclub with a group of cool friends, I add social status to the mix. The nature of attraction triggers explains why men who are completely different from each other can attract women in their own way, and why copying me or another man will hurt more than help, since the potency of one man's mix of triggers will be different from yours.

Attraction Destroyers

More important than increasing attraction is not destroying any natural attraction present. Even if your attraction triggers are weak, it's still possible for you to do well with women if you do not display any attraction destroyers. If you are new to game and are struggling with girls, it's likely you are showing more destroyers than triggers.

The first attraction destroyer is neediness. Nothing turns a girl off quicker than a needy man. This is where you contact her often, reply to calls or text messages much faster than she does, compliment her more than she compliments you, buy her gifts in the hope that she'll like you, or display any other behavior where you show that you care about her deeply when she doesn't reciprocate in the same way.

Small gestures that may seem innocent, such as telling a girl you like her or that you're "looking for a girlfriend," also detonate a deadly nuclear bomb when it comes to her attraction. Girls tolerated needy men in the past only because they didn't have dating choice, but now that they can date anyone, needy men are the first to get rejected. Even basic compliments have become dangerous, and are best given infrequently only after a girl has complimented you sincerely.

Men who are needy incorrectly idealize girls as being able to enhance their life significantly, mostly because they lack experience. These men also don't think highly of themselves and believe that being with a pretty girl will make them feel better about who they are. Since neediness is a deeply ingrained trait that can take years to get rid of, the best option for a needy man is to not act on that neediness, with the understanding that doing so will lead to rejection. By pretending not to be needy, even though needy thoughts still flow through his mind, he will eventually gain the experience that kills neediness at its root. If you have this problem, adopt the following belief: "I will not act on the needy and anxious thoughts that enter my mind, and will allow girls to be far needier than me."

Desperation is the next attraction destroyer. No girl has ever said that she is attracted to a man because she pities him. Surprisingly, some men try to use pity to get girls to sleep with them by disclosing that they are virgins or extremely lonely. That doesn't work! Other examples of showing desperation to a girl are complaining that you are treated badly by other people, are unlucky with love, or haven't had sex in a long time. You should also not portray yourself as worthless, sad, depressed, or loveless. Share your true feelings with your male friends if you need support or advice, but never with a woman, even if you've had sex with her.

The next attraction destroyer is meekness, where you present yourself as scared, spineless, or unable to make decisions. This shouldn't be confused with shyness, where you are introverted around new people, although shyness and meekness often go hand in hand. A meek man is hesitant to stand up for himself and reveal his opinions, interests, or desires. He has trouble making decisions and would rather have other people make them for him. One of his biggest fears is offending or challenging someone and having to face a confrontation where he has to defend or explain himself. Meekness can be a useful quality when you're before an authority figure such as a judge or priest, but not when you're around women.

A common physical trait that coincides with meekness is

speaking softly and slumping your shoulders. While bad posture is far from ideal, speaking softly signifies a number of negative traits that will consistently make you unattractive. Speak in a strong voice from your stomach or chest to harness the deepest and loudest parts of your vocal range. Experiment by visualizing air originating and flowing from different parts of your torso as you talk.

A behavioral trait associated with meekness is the fear to make a move. It's not easy to try to kiss a girl, especially when you're starting out with game and are more sensitive to rejection, but risk-taking is essential if you want intimacy. There are risks you must take in game like with anything else in life, such as starting a business or taking a long trip through different countries. If you want to reap the rewards that come from these endeavors, you must overcome your fear of failure and take the risk. If you don't then move aside, because there are many other men who are ready to try.

The dating game is incredibly competitive, just like a professional sport, and you'll have to put up or shut up. If you expect a girl to take risks or make moves on you, I have bad news: she won't. Nature has decreed that men must take risks to prove their strength in order to access a woman's vagina. Despite the inroads that feminism has made in our society with giving women a contrived level of confidence, they still expect you to make the first move, along with all the subsequent moves that escalate into sex.

I can't think of anything that makes me feel more masculine than when I take a risk and succeed. Even when I fail, the failure hurts much less than I envisioned, and it teaches me how to increase my chances of succeeding in the future. Remember the belief that every failure puts you one step closer to success. If you do not embrace this concept, you'll miss out on intimacy with girls who like you but gave up because you didn't make a move. Girls can be attracted to you all day and night, but if you're not cashing in on their attraction by making moves, you will get less than the man who barely builds attraction but acts in a fearless manner.

Meekness tends to coincide with anxiety, an emotional state that causes a man to exaggerate small problems or worries. Anxiety can be hidden, but if you're in a long-term relationship, a girl will begin to sense it and interpret it as weakness. Anxiety is a problem for men who had an excessively comfortable and safe upbringing. If you never had to solve serious problems on your own when you were young, you will be more anxious when you encounter the challenges of adulthood. Men who want to reduce their anxiety should look into Stoicism or Eastern philosophies like Buddhism, Zen, and Taoism, which can bring a sense of perspective and balance to how you view life.

You should aim to temper your attraction destroyers and strengthen your attraction triggers. This can be done only by taking action: optimize your look, do approaches, go on dates, and push interactions into the bedroom. Only after taking action can you reflect on what you did right or wrong. You will not improve without taking action, so don't think that you can memorize everything and then do great on your first try. Knowledge is only entertainment until you put it to use.

The Fluidity Of Attraction

A girl will have a preference for certain attraction triggers and a disgust for certain attraction destroyers based of her unique genetics, background, and experiences. The type of man she's ultimately attracted to is out of your control. We reviewed a list of attraction triggers and destroyers that are common to most girls, but there is no way of knowing which ones will be most important to a particular girl. This is why it's silly to become attached to a girl before you enter a relationship with her, because odds are you won't be offering her the mix of traits she desires.

It's more useful to maximize your triggers and then find a venue or niche where you are likely to find girls who are attracted to the mix you offer. For example, if you have a strong appearance trigger because you are good looking, your preferred venue may be a cheesy nightclub where looks are weighted heavily. If you are an artist, it would make sense to penetrate a social circle of artists or volunteer to teach art classes. If you are fair-skinned, perhaps you should go to Latin America or Southeast Asia, where girls may see you as a white god. Ideally, the method you use to hunt for girls should enable you to showcase your strengths.

You may be wondering whether there is a more efficient way of knowing what a specific girl's attraction triggers are. Why don't we simply ask them? I actually tried asking girls what they wanted so that I could deliver the right type of game. As you can guess, it didn't work, and my success rate decreased. The first reason it failed is that most women don't consciously know what they want. Almost all women will say they want a confident, nice guy who treats them well, but they often sleep with men who are not that nice. Essentially, you have to give women what they don't know they want.

Second, a girl will never admit that she wants a cocky man with high social status, because it would reveal that she is vain and shallow. She has convinced herself that she wants a "good" man, but this is precisely the type of guy she will instantly friend-zone unless she's in a panic to get married. Assume that you know more about what a girl wants than she does and proceed accordingly.

Also, it would be incredibly difficult for you to change your game on the fly even if a girl gave you credible information about her triggers, such as details about an ex-boyfriend who broke her heart. It's tough enough to approach a girl, show our value, and converse with her, but now we have to adapt our game in response to feedback that may or may not reveal what she really wants? Forget it!

While it's possible to make minor changes to your game in the middle of a seduction, such as not telling a type of joke that a girl doesn't find amusing, it's difficult to adjust your entire strategy. If you try, you'll get too into your head, focus on your behavior instead of evaluating hers, and come across as less authentic. The better strategy is to stick to your game plan and see it through to the end, whether or not it results in rejection. If you make a mistake in a seduction, or realize that you could have done something differently, make changes with the next girl you game.

The work of improving your attraction ability should be done *in between* interactions, where you come up with ways to overcome your stumbling blocks. That's why a man who asks for advice about a particular girl almost never succeeds, because he's too focused on insignificant actions instead of being the most attractive man possible.

The Three Types Of Game

Now that we have a firm understanding of attraction and how it works, we can move onto the three types of game that reliably cater to women's most common attraction patterns. There are infinite variations within each type of game, so think of them as foundational starting points.

The first type of game is clown game. If you're reading about game in books or on websites, this is the type of game you're learning. You're taught how to be an entertaining, exciting, confident, cocky, aloof, sexy, and outgoing "alpha male." The man who goes to a nightclub to dance with girls is using clown game to entertain a girl, the good-looking man in a nice suit is using clown game to get a girl excited about his appearance, and the man who is abusive is using clown game to add drama to a girl's life. They are all using mainly external factors that can be copied, changed, and manipulated. You can learn how to dance to be entertaining, how to improve your appearance to look more attractive, and how to treat a girl badly to give her the drama she craves. Even when you think you're not using clown game by being yourself, you're still using it because how attractive you are to a girl will depend on factors related to your look, personality, or status instead of your family background or ability to take care of her.

Clown game is required in economically developed countries where women have excess choice on who to date, and where they can meet their need for security and material comfort without having to get married. In other words, if a girl intends to pursue a career, or already has one, she will require clown game.

A woman was loyal and feminine in the past because she needed a man's resources in order to survive. *She* was the one who had to put on the clown mask in order to get material resources from a man, even if she hated him. Now that women no longer need men for resources, they can take off the clown mask and give it to men, who have to act and perform to be attractive. This has allowed women to steadily regress to their true nature, which can often be foul and nasty.

The environmental constraints that encouraged a woman to be a lady were removed a long time ago, allowing her now to tickle her desire for fun, excitement, validation, and attention, things her female ancestors also wanted to experience but couldn't, because they needed the approval of a man if they wanted to continue receiving his resources and protection.

These days, a girl can have sex with 1,000 men without harming her ability to survive. She can quit her promiscuous lifestyle at any time and easily find a man who will wife her up, as long as she maintains her appearance, whereas in the past she would've been regarded as a vile prostitute. Back in an age when there were no air-conditioned offices that make it easy for women to work in, she'd have no job, no government welfare, and no man would be willing to marry her, because she had been ridden like the town bicycle. Today, she can be the *world* bicycle and be greatly rewarded for it, which is why you must be the clown if you want to sexually access her or even normal girls who don't ride the cock carousel as aggressively.

When I was learning game, I assumed that clown game was the only type of game to which girls would respond, but then I started traveling. My clown game stumbled in poorer countries where girls required material comfort instead of feeling "empowered" by having fast and easy sex. This led me to recognizing the second type of game, provider game.

Provider game is where a man displays that he's a good catch through his resources, stability, chivalry, spirituality, and character. It involves telling a girl that you have a stable job that pays a solid middle-class income suitable for creating a happy family. You talk about how you put your family above your own needs and would not hesitate to sacrifice your well-being for their sake. You're a classic gentleman who honors family, tribe, and God, without showcasing your appearance, running cocky game, or telling jokes.

When women depended on men for basic needs, and a woman's father had to approve of her future husband, the provider male was usually rewarded with a wife without having to date or worry about creating a positive first impression as is the case today. He courted one girl, often a virgin, met her parents, received their blessing, and asked for her hand in marriage before sampling her sexually. He was expected to provide for his wife in good times and bad. Being good-looking, attractive, or confident played only a small role in whether or not she selected him, particularly because her parents had to approve of the man she married. As long as a man had the means to provide for a family and was seen as a good man, he could get a wife.

It could be argued that this arrangement was a form of servitude for a man, because he was beholden to provide for a woman who did not bring in additional resources, but it was the most direct and logical path for a man to fulfill his biological role in creating life. With a dedicated mother at home, his children had the greatest odds not only of survival, but also of being raised in a way that protected them from toxic external influences. The implicit pact was straightforward for both sexes: the men brought home the bacon and the women enjoyed that bacon to maintain the family home and raise healthy children.

Unless you're dealing with an impoverished or ultra-religious girl, you won't find many women under the age of 30 who are looking for a provider, and if you find one who is, it won't be through cold-approach game at a nightclub or supermarket, because a girl who is looking for a provider is reluctant to consider men outside of her immediate social or religious circle. Therefore if your default game is based on displaying your provider status and stability, you will experience a spectacular inability to get laid. You will be toyed with and discarded by women who are looking for a man with tight clown game instead. Going up to a girl and telling her about your stable job or profession would've worked in the past, but unless your job conveys exciting status, such as a DJ or club bartender, a girl won't care, and she will actually find you less attractive because of it.

Provider game strikes a logical and economical deal with a moderately young girl and her family. It is *not* getting married to a reformed slut well past her prime after she had her fun. The reformed slut will want a man who has provider qualities, but that alone will not be able to satisfy her because she is addicted to behaving impulsively, as her sexual history clearly shows. The worst thing you can do is to use provider game on a slut. Thanks to modern divorce laws, a man has far more to lose than a woman when a marriage fails, so a provider-type arrangement should include unspoiled goods for the man, which is what a virgin or a girl with a tiny notch count delivers.

The ship has sailed on being a provider as poor countries become more developed and religion plays a smaller role in people's lives. Even countries where traditions remain strong, such as India, are starting to see decreased rates of arranged marriages, but you may still encounter environments where showing slight provider traits could serve you in the third type of game, hybrid game.

Hybrid game is mid-way between clown and provider game, but it almost always leans more towards clown game, because any environment where you can cold approach a woman who may consider you for sex will require exciting triggers to establish attraction. With hybrid game, you drop in aspects of stability, such as your job, cozy apartment, and your healthy relationship with your family to show that you are a "good" man, but you do this in *small doses* after building a foundation of attraction through your appearance, vibe, and personality. Since provider game is rarely applicable, and won't return until the aftermath of a nuclear holocaust, you are effectively left with two options: clown game and hybrid game. Which one should you use and when?

If a girl is born in an English-speaking country, and you meet her anywhere *except* a small conservative town, use full clown game to maximize your results, where you do not convey that you are a stable or honorable man. In small towns where religion is still important, use hybrid game. Foreign girls who have been in the West for a year or two may respond to hybrid game, but they will come to expect clown game upon achieving material comfort. If you travel to South America, Eastern Europe, or Southeast Asia, use hybrid game as your starting point and then make adjustments to take account of the local culture and the type of men you notice doing well with women. In Western European countries such as Denmark, Germany, France, and Spain, lean heavily towards clown game in big cities.

Another indication of which game to use is based on how virginal a girl is. If she's had three or fewer sexual partners, hybrid game will be more effective. Her naivety and social awkwardness will be the most relevant clues that she has a low notch count. On the other hand, use clown game if she's experienced, which will be obvious if she is comfortable talking to men she doesn't know.

The more Westernized, rich, and experienced she is, the more clown game will be required. The more foreign, poor, and virginal she is, the more hybrid game will be required. In your city, you will have favorite venues for meeting girls, and the girls who frequent these venues are likely to be similar, so you won't have to worry about switching your game for every approach. When I'm in the United States, I use clown game every single time unless I meet a foreign girl who speaks bad English. The odds of finding a "good" girl in my home environment are so incredibly low that making exceptions for any American girl will lead to failure.

When I'm abroad, I use hybrid game on sober girls and clown game on inebriated girls, although every year I amplify my clown game slightly as foreign countries become more economically successful. The more wealth you see around you, the more you'll need clown game, because the last thing a girl needs in a rich environment is a provider.

You may be wondering if you can gauge a girl's financial situation to decide which type of game to use. The problem with this idea is that it takes many hours of getting to know a girl to find out her real financial status, and by that stage it will be too late to make adjustments to your game. Also, poor girls can make themselves appear "rich" with a few fashion tricks that don't cost them much money. Your best bet is to establish a default game based on where you are and resist making adjustments unless you have strong evidence to the contrary.

Girls who require hybrid game still want to feel attraction, but they also ask themselves whether you are the right choice based on practicality and long-term potential. A girl who requires clown game alone does not think of these things, and even if she does and you rate poorly, she will still sleep with you as long as she's strongly attracted to you.

With hybrid game, the optimal strategy is to move the interaction forward in an entertaining and fun manner while casually or indirectly displaying aspects that show you're a stable man. In essence, hybrid game means you can be yourself instead of exaggerating your hobbies to appear more interesting. You also don't have to downplay the fact that you may have a "boring" career. With girls who require clown game, you often have to conceal your stable attributes so they will think of you as edgy, aloof, or exciting.

As a country advances economically, girls will transition from requiring provider game to hybrid game, and finally, to clown game. When I first arrived in Poland in 2011, I had to run a hybrid game that wasn't too clownish. Fast forward seven years and it's clear that I need to run full-blown clown game to attract girls of the same quality. I didn't change much myself, but the girls sure did, and that was a result of Poland's rapidly increasing economic success and the widespread adoption of smartphones.

After reading about clown and hybrid game, you may be wishing for the days when provider game dominated, especially if you're a stable man with a reasonable income. You probably don't want to play the clown or put in a lot of work for what may be only a fleeting sexual encounter. Instead, you want to meet one good girl with whom you can start a family. I often feel the same way, but the bad news is that we were born in the wrong era. Unless you can embed yourself in a hyper-religious community, entertaining nostalgic fantasies will merely make you more frustrated, because you will not find the virtuous woman who exists only in your mind. It's best to accept reality and work with what the universe offers you.

Chapter Conclusion

I hope this chapter allows you to understand *why* you have to say the lines and perform the moves that we'll get into shortly. Once you make the connection between the theory of how attraction works and why you should speak to a girl in a certain way, game will feel more natural to you.

How did I come to understand attraction triggers, attraction destroyers, and the three types of game? Through *action*. In the beginning, I was like a parrot repeating lines I read on the internet, but it was through parroting those lines in thousands of attempts that I detected patterns and developed theories. A theory may help in the application of game, but it's no substitute for game itself. I cannot stress enough that the only way you will improve your game is by taking action. You can read 100 books on game and attraction theory, but without action, your sex life will be no better.

You're now ready for me to teach you the *Roosh Program*, which is a protocol of big action steps that will start getting you results.

Chapter 5: The Roosh Program

In 2012, I wrote an article called "The Roosh Program." It was intended for men who wanted to learn game but didn't know how to get started. It has withstood the test of time, providing thousands of men with an effective, action-oriented method to improve their results. I've since made refinements based on the feedback I've received to better accomplish the goals of improving your self-confidence, attaining competent game, enjoying sexual success, and not getting overly jaded about women and their true nature. While I wouldn't go as far as describing the program as fun, I'm certain that you will find value in every step and understand how it will bring you closer to your sexual goals.

Each of the steps I'm about to describe is essential. If you're not doing all the steps, you're not doing the program. If you're not ready to implement the program in its entirety, you may fall short of your intimacy goals.

Step 1: Improve Your Body And Appearance

The chapter on pre-game was dedicated to achieving the first step of the program. If you haven't started that improvement, now is a good time.

Girls can select the men they want to have sex with, and they've clearly shown that they would rather have an attractive man than not. You can have the best verbal game in the world, but if you're knocking one or two points off your overall score because you haven't fixed problems such as poor dress sense or obesity, you will severely harm your chances with women.

I understand that focusing on appearance can be perceived as superficial, but women are now more superficial than ever, and if you want to bed the most attractive of them, you have to improve your look. Make the changes that you're comfortable doing then stop when you feel they're making you too feminine or gay, because girls will sense if you don't feel good about your presentation.

Step 2: Study One Game Resource At A Time

A game resource, whether a book or a workshop, connects your mind with a man who has spent hundreds or thousands of hours thinking about the goal you want to achieve. I'm not an expert at game because I was born an expert, but because I've spent more time running game and analyzing it than 99.9% of men.

As much as I take pride in the fact that the information I'm giving you is effective and accurate, no one man has all the answers. Extract all that you can from my work and then implement the teachings for a period of time. When your results hit a ceiling that my work can't help you rise above, whether in a few months or a few years, find another teacher or resource that can help you.

One thing I don't advise is studying multiple resources at the same time. This will just lead to confusion. Ride the wave of this book as far as you can, and when you feel you're no longer moving forward, try another resource. Just don't try to ride two waves at once.

Step 3: Start A Muscle-Building Workout Routine

Lifting weights improves your appearance, increases your testosterone levels, and improves your self-esteem and confidence. These are *precisely* the attributes you need to be successful with game. If there is one keystone habit that will improve your results with girls, apart from actually interacting with them, it's lifting weights. It's so critical that I simply can't envision an effective game program that excludes it.

If you're an absolute newbie and have never been to the gym before, I recommend *Convict Conditioning*, a book that focuses on callisthenic exercises where the resistance is your own body weight. The program focuses on six exercises that target your abs, back, chest, legs, spine, and shoulders. Each exercise is divided into ten stages. You start at stage one, complete what is required, and then advance to stage two. Each stage gradually increases the resistance until you make it to the last step and perform feats at the level of a male gymnast.

With this program, you don't need to go to the gym at all, and the only equipment required is a pull-up bar, or access to one in a neighborhood park. The downside is that it doesn't build a lot of bulk, but it will give you an athletic body that girls will notice when you take off your shirt. If you're not crazy about joining a gym, and don't particularly want to build big muscles and eat carefully planned meals, I highly recommend this program.

The second book I recommend is *Starting Strength*, which requires you go to a gym, or at least set up a home gym. It advocates doing compound exercises that work multiple muscle groups at once, such as the squat, deadlift, and bench press. The program is simple in that you do only a few exercises per session, but it will take time to nail down the correct forms, especially for the squat and deadlift, where your unique anatomy could make it difficult to perform the standard form.

For each exercise, you'll perform three sets (groups) of five repetitions each, all at the same weight. Once you can complete all three sets, you increase the weight slightly for the next workout and repeat the process. With *Starting Strength,* you'll see faster gains and more muscle bulk, assuming you eat the required amount of protein, but the chance of injury is high if your form is not ideal. My short torso, combined with my long arms and legs, have made it difficult for me to properly squat and deadlift, so I've sustained minor short-term injuries that forced me to stop doing those exercises. If your body is better designed for compound exercises, and you don't get injured, you can see large gains that are more noticeable compared with callisthenic exercises.

A variation of *Starting Strength* is *Stronglifts*, a program that you can find online. It's essentially the same as *Starting Strength*, but instead of doing three sets of five repetitions, you do five sets of five repetitions.

These three programs, and virtually any other fitness regimen, use the same principle for building muscle mass: increase the weight or resistance over time. The best analogy is that of an ancient Greek Olympian who decides to start carrying a newborn calf across a field every day. As the calf grows, the Olympian has to carry a heavier load, but the daily increase is so small that it does not pose a challenge for his muscles. Eventually, he's carrying a bull across the field without difficulty. The only way your fitness regimen will fail is if you're not steadily increasing the weight.

Don't worry about which regimen out of the hundreds that are available is the "best." Instead, stick with one for a year or two, get the most out of it, and then seek out another when you feel you have plateaued. It's exactly the same strategy we apply to game instruction.

When I started lifting weights, I did not increase the weight except for the bench press, so my strength increased only somewhat. Then I found *Starting Strength* and saw rapid gains within a year until I sustained injuries that prevented me from moving forward. I then did *Convict Conditioning* for a while, which gave me gymnast strength but not much in the way of bulk. Since then, I've settled on my own customized program of going to a gym six to eight times a month and doing a mix of compound and callisthenic exercises that keep me fit, maintain my testosterone levels, and give me a bit of bulk.

Our sedentary lifestyles cause us to sit at home, sit at work, sit in cars, and then sit at home again. We are performing a fraction of the physical movement our ancestors did. This decreases our muscle mass, testosterone, and overall fitness. If you don't have a job that involves manual labor, you absolutely require a regimen that simulates this manual labor just to ensure proper functioning. Once we add the fact that girls will be more attracted to you for looking healthy, fit, and muscular, and that you'll be more confident to talk to them, you can clearly see that the benefits of lifting weights far outweigh the cost in terms of time and energy.

The only danger of lifting is getting your ego involved and trying to be as big as the next guy, where you exceed your original goals and start injecting yourself with various chemicals and substances. Both game and lifting can be dangerous when you're no longer performing it for your benefit but for the benefit of your ego, which can never be fully sated. There will always be another man who is bigger or who gets prettier girls than you, so keep your goals internally focused on what you want instead of trying to beat others. As long as you like what you see when you look in the mirror, there will be girls out there who think the same.

Step 4: Do 100 Approaches

If you want to get good at game, you need to practice game. The most efficient and effective way to practice game is to approach girls you don't know and take the interaction as far as you can. You are free to run game on girls you already know, but it's likely that these girls have already created an unattractive impression of you that is unlikely to change. Refine your game using cold approaches before attempting to use it within your social and work circles.

Some game purists judge men on *how* they get laid. If you used your looks to get laid, that's "not game." If you used a smartphone app to get laid, that's "not game." I'm not such a purist, and I believe that you should use whatever means are available to reach the sexual comfort you desire, but beware of using shortcuts that merely postpone the work you'll have to do anyway. For example, say there is a special girl in your social circle you really like. You use my advice and manage to get into a relationship with her. The relationship is blissful for one year before it ends. Then what? Your ability to meet girls is no better than before you started, and your situation may, in fact, be worse if you don't like any of the other girls in your social circle.

Let's imagine another man who embarks on his first 100 approaches. He makes it up to 80 when he meets a girl he likes and gets into a relationship with her for one year. At the end of that year, he still retains the experience from those 80 approaches that led him to getting a girlfriend in the first place, completely independent of his social circle. Now that he is single, he simply has to start approaching again, which will be easier for him than it was before.

By doing cold approaches, you develop a reproducible skill that you can use anytime you want. You become less dependent on temporary situations and luck to meet girls.

While I won't discourage you from internet game, the 100 approaches have to be done face-to-face. The biggest problem with the internet is that girls have complete price discovery. What this means is that online girls know their *exact value* on the market and the hottest man they can attract, making it hard to create a situation where you can date up, or even date girls on your level.

Because the internet has long been flooded with horny men ready to sleep with anything, online girls are now under the impression that they can get a better man than they could in real life. Any internet game you use will automatically result in getting lower-quality girls. On the street, it's possible to meet a pretty girl who doesn't quite know how pretty she is, and therefore decides to date you even though your value could be higher, but on the internet a slightly pretty girl receives such an insane amount of attention that she won't settle for less.

Another reason I advise against internet dating is that it reduces your entire value to physical appearance. Your aesthetic is important, but as I have pointed out, it's only one of many factors that girls use when weighing their attraction for you. The problem with online dating is that looks are often the *only* factor that girls use. If you don't have above-average looks, you'll become frustrated by how much work it will take to date a moderately cute girl, whereas a top 1% Chad can use lines that would get you blocked yet still have girls lining up for dates. It's better to meet girls face-to-face where you can display your complete value.

The third problem with meeting girls on the internet is that the golden goose stops laying eggs as soon as you figure out how to make it lay eggs. Algorithms are changed often, so the minute you master a site, something happens and your results go down. I've lost count of how many times I've heard men tell me "OK Cupid is not as good as it used to be" or "Tinder sucks now." You'll achieve the best results with online dating if you crack a new site quickly and extract as many sexual rewards as you can before it stops delivering.

On the other hand, cold approach game is like riding a bike. Once you know how to ride one bike, you can ride many different kinds of bikes, even on different terrains. Because I know how to cold approach, I can go to any city in the world and meet a new girl within a couple of hours, day or night. The outcome is completely dependent on me and the work I'm willing to put in, not algorithms and other factors beyond my control. I can't emphasize enough that cold approaching is one of the most beneficial skills you can master, ensuring that, besides the occasional dry patch, you will not suffer from a lack of sex.

Learning how to cold approach will also boost your general social skills with friends, family, and coworkers. It will turn you into a conscious social being and not a robot who only knows how to copy and paste lines as if operating a computer logic tree. Tackling your first 100 cold approaches will give you a vast amount of knowledge, confidence, and skill, putting you on a solid path to enjoying female company on your own terms, regardless of your location or station in life.

If you're a total beginner and haven't done more than a handful of cold approaches, I'm going to lower your expectations and tell you straight up that your first 100 approaches will probably not result in a lay. Instead, I mostly expect that you will have short conversations with girls who will politely leave before the two-minute mark. You may have a handful of longer conversations that will lead to you exchanging phone numbers, but the girls may not respond when you contact them. The main goal of your first 100 is to face your anxiety head-on, practice building attraction by showing your best traits, and identify the signs a girl puts out when she is interested in getting to know you.

To get started, I advise you do at least five approaches every week. Less than five and you risk putting so much space between approaches that you will feel rusty or nervous at the beginning of the next session. Five approaches can easily be done in two hours on a Saturday afternoon in the middle of any city, so you will not be able to use lack of time as an excuse for skipping out on the program.

You are free to do more than five approaches a week, but it is not mandatory. One advantage of doing a smaller number of approaches is that it encourages your mind to "make them count" by only approaching girls who seem to be more open, such as ones who give you eye contact or move slowly. If you plan to do 50 approaches a week, for example, you'll approach bad targets, such as girls walking fast or wearing headphones, with no noticeable improvement in your results. When starting out, keep your weekly approaches to between five and twenty.

To prevent becoming confused about which game strategy to use during your first 100 approaches, I recommend that you focus on either day *or* night venues, because each type of venue requires a slightly different strategy. If you're a night owl, enjoy drinking alcohol, and have many friends who like to party at night, night game will be a better fit for you. If you are more of a loner who doesn't have many friends to go out with, and you're not a big fan of alcohol, day game will be better. A sign that you don't have the personality for night game is if you're not already doing it when you picked up this book. When I first encountered the game community in 2001, I had a large group of friends who enjoyed going to nightclubs, so it was a logical decision for me to get started there.

You are free to change course after your first 100 approaches. If you started with day approaches and want to try night game for your second set of 100, go right ahead. It's likely you'll find that night game is more expensive, takes more of your energy, and is more competitive, but the girls you meet are more eager for fast sex. Day game is less fun, takes more time to yield sex, and can be harder to warm up for, but it gives you one-on-one access to more girls without interruption. Nightclubs and bars are in decline both in the United States and abroad, so unless you particularly like the night scene, you should plan to experiment with day game at some point.

I'm not going to lie to you and say that doing your first set of 100 will be a piece of cake. If you've had a relatively easy and comfortable life, this will be the most challenging thing you embark on from the standpoint of social risk, and no one will be there to hold your hand and keep you motivated. Whenever you are filled with doubt, you have to ask yourself whether or not you want to get this aspect of your life handled. Only through work can you achieve the sex and relationships you desire.

When I first started game, I knew less than 5% of what I'm teaching you now. I was nervous during those initial approaches, but I was so motivated to be successful that I was able to quiet the saboteur within me who wanted to protect my ego from risk and rejection. It's okay to chicken out on an approach every now and then, but ultimately you should be able to do what it takes to accomplish your goals, especially when the knowledge I'm giving you will only result in a worst-case scenario of a girl exiting a conversation with you. If you still can't gather up the balls to approach, when so many thousands of men are doing it every day, I can only conclude that you are not horny enough to be with a woman, and you're reading a book like this so you can feel knowledgeable about game without learning how to be competent at it.

I've been careful to market my game books without insinuating that I have a magic formula. Yes, there are many tricks I share that you will find helpful, but they are part of a grand mission where we transform our time, energy, knowledge, and courage into sex and love. Most men, however, are not capable of this mission. I don't blame them, because putting in effort and taking social risk is hard, but you should regard any excuse you invent for not doing 100 approaches as just an effort by your mind to sabotage you. If you live in a small town, travel to a bigger one on the weekends. If you're tired after work, experiment with ways to improve your energy. Even having a physical disability is no excuse for inaction, because I know men who are deaf yet still approach women. Convince yourself that you want it badly enough so that you will find a way to make it happen.

Your goal when approaching shouldn't be a complete lack of anxiety or nervousness. That is unnatural and will make you come across as a robot or actor. It's actually helpful to have some anxiety or trip over a few words so that girls don't get the impression that you do this all the time. There is nothing in the chapter on attraction that states a girl desires perfection or flawlessness in a man, and being too smooth and practiced may cause girls to think you're not being genuine. Allow your anxiety to bring authenticity to the forefront, but don't let it prevent you from approaching at all.

We need a basic strategy for completing our first 100 in a way that facilitates our learning, maximizes our results, and keeps us motivated to finish. I would have failed you as a teacher if I taught a program that you won't have the will to complete or that burns you out, so I have devised guidelines to keep your progress steady and sustainable. For day approaches, I recommend you do one approach a day, at least five days a week. Find a time during the day that is convenient and walk around a crowded part of your city until you find a girl to approach. Unless you live in a small town, you should be able to complete this approach in no more than one hour. Many men can do at least three approaches per hour in a medium-sized city.

For it to count as an approach, the girl must hear you. If she pretends she didn't, but you're sure she did, it still counts as an approach. It also counts if she says something like "I'm sorry but I'm late for work" before running off. This type of response may seem insignificant, but oftentimes it will encourage you to do more than the minimum. If you want to do more than one approach a day, especially when you're feeling sociable, by all means do so, but it's not required. The guideline I'm giving you is strong enough to be effective, but not so onerous that you won't be able to commit to it.

Earlier, I stated that lifting weights is a keystone habit that will improve other areas of your life. One approach a day is the keystone habit of game. When you wake up knowing you have to do one approach, which may take up to an hour, you start making changes to your lifestyle and schedule that will help you to advance your game.

First, because you know that you'll be presenting yourself to a girl later that day, you take care how you dress and groom yourself. Second, you are more conscious of your mood. You start looking for opportunities to be more social in preparation for the approach, such as being extra friendly to a store clerk or coffee shop barista. Third, you start seeking venues where attractive girls gather.

When you do your one approach of the day, it's fine if you're not in a sociable state. You'll learn that doing the work, no matter what state you're in, is far more crucial. It's fine if all you can think is, "Alright, just do this one approach and get it over with." If you happen to get in the mood after doing your one approach, you can then decide whether you want to do another.

Be careful about using the same indoor venue every time you approach. It's okay to do your approaches in malls, supermarkets, coffee shops, bookstores, and so on, but don't use a particular venue more than three times a week. If the venue is small, it's better to approach there only once a week.

For example, if you know of a large mall where there are always lots of girls, use it only three times a week, and don't do more than two or three approaches per session. This will ensure that you will not be targeted by jealous staff members or security guards. I know this guideline will be tough to maintain if you live in a small city that has only one indoor mall, but you'll have to be conservative when it comes to the number of approaches you do so you don't burn out venues. This means that some of your day approaches will have to take place outdoors, even in the middle of winter.

I'm not teaching you a style of game that is dangerous or

illegal, but the world has become so sensitive to displays of masculinity that if employees or feminist bystanders suspect you are trying to pick up a girl, they may jump to the conclusion that she's being harassed. Their response will be to treat the girl like she's a little child and you like a potential rapist. Because you will be using some indirect game and not saturating any one venue, I'm certain that spectators will not give you a hard time. On the other hand, if you walk up to a girl aggressively and immediately get physical, it's inevitable that someone will confront you in an attempt to "save" her.

Approaching at night involves a change in strategy, where you adopt a batch method of doing multiple approaches in one session. If you go out once or twice a week at night and stay at a venue for at least two hours, and our weekly goal is a minimum of five approaches, you'll have to approach about three girls per visit, which is roughly one girl an hour. That doesn't sound like a lot, but sometimes it can be difficult to find approachable girls in a night venue, meaning that you will spend most of your time waiting by the bar until an opportunity presents itself. Also consider that many night approaches will involve a girl who doesn't want to talk to you after your opening line, which further exacerbates the waiting game.

At the peak of my night game, I used a ten-approach rule. When I went out for the night, I did not return home until I had done ten approaches or had met a girl who liked me. This forced me to be properly rested before I went out to start early so that I had enough time to do all ten. As the club scene around the world declined, particularly in the United States, I began finding it impossible to find ten attractive girls in a venue who were not part of a huge group or with a boyfriend. I started to hop from bar to bar, doing one or two approaches in each one. Then I started walking on the streets and approaching with a simple opener: "Excuse me, do you know a good bar around here?" Funnily enough, I found that I preferred picking up girls on the street than in a club. There was no noise, no cockblockers, and it was free of charge. Whatever approach goal you set for yourself, your mind will find a way to accomplish it in a way that suits your nature most.

The night scene has deteriorated so rapidly that I think a ten-approach rule may encourage you to do garbage approaches instead of focusing on the real goal: finding a genuine connection. Therefore, I advise you to start with a goal of five and increase it only if your environment is rich with attractive women. Every time you go out at night, you're not allowed to return home until you've done five approaches. It's not an excuse if all the bars and clubs suck, because you still have the option of walking around and doing street approaches.

A minimum approach rule motivates you to talk to enough girls to establish a solid connection, so never put the rule above connection itself. On most nights I went out, I did not hit ten, because I connected with a girl before that and spent the rest of the evening with her. Guidelines and rules are not ends in themselves but a *means* to the end you desire. The problem with many men is that they get caught up in number goals and forget why they got into game in the first place.

If an evening out in your city doesn't allow you to approach at least five girls you find attractive, particularly on weekends, I can tell you with certainty that night game will be a tough grind. An alternative strategy is to go out every night for a short amount of time to do only one approach. This is easiest if you live within walking distance of a nightlife zone. The problem with this method, however, is that you develop a mentality of "I'm not staying here for long." That prevents you from pushing hard with your interactions, which is important in night game to reduce flaking. Planning to do at least five approaches during a night out is more likely to lead to success.

Your first set of 100 approaches, whether during the day or at night, will establish a baseline of what will be your lowest results. Things can only get better after that. On the other hand, it's possible that your normal personality is highly conducive to getting laid, and all you needed to succeed was to increase the number of interactions you had with girls without having to significantly improve your game.

I find that counting my approaches is discouraging, because I see firsthand how challenging game is and how much work it takes to get a single lay. I know that there is only a small chance I'll sleep with a random girl I pick out of a crowd. I also understand that this is a numbers game, a statistical strategy that has little bearing on my worth as a man. There have been great men of history who couldn't get laid in a whorehouse while serial killers and other criminals have a never-ending supply of eager women. Your ability to get laid within a certain year and environment is more an accident of space and time than a reliable indicator of your overall value, because if you had been born 500 years ago, your interactions with women would have been completely different.

An alternative to counting is using time-based goals to estimate when you've completed 100 approaches. For example, if you average about ten approaches a week, the end of your set of 100 will be ten weeks from the date on which you start. You don't have to be exact.

If you don't approach, and don't have a social circle full of girls, I can guarantee that you won't succeed. Out of all the steps in the program, approaching is the most important, because it's the only one that puts you into direct contact with women.

Step 5: Watch One Episode Of *Seinfeld* Every Day

Popular in the late 1990s, *Seinfeld* was an American sitcom starring Jewish comedian Jerry Seinfeld. It was set in New York City and centered on the lives of four main characters as they sought happiness with work, friendship, and dating. The show's unique style of humor may not be for everyone, but it's excellent at teaching you two things through example: (1) how to be generally humorous in a way that girls like, and (2) how to have long, meandering conversations about nothing without being boring (in other words, how to "ramble"). If you think that your social skills are low and could be improved, watching *Seinfeld* is better than reading books that teach conversational skills, because you can effortlessly mimic the show's characters.

Rambling is the art of chatting for prolonged periods of time.

This skill is essential in cold-approach situations. When girls claim they like a man who is the "strong, silent type," they are stating that they want to experience reputational attraction from a man who is pre-screened, but because you'll be approaching girls who don't know you, you'll have to build attraction using language, and until a girl decides she is definitely attracted to you, you'll have to talk more than she does.

In a cold-approach scenario, the interaction won't last even five minutes unless you can maintain it by dominating and steering the conversation through your ramble. It's the main vehicle that adds to your post-minute attraction, and it has to be particularly solid if a girl's pre-minute attraction for you isn't strong. In other words, you have to *keep talking* during the early stages of an interaction, even if she's not giving you much verbal feedback.

If you're not a chatty person, and odds are you aren't, I advise you to start new interactions with a chattiness level that is on the high end of your range and then slowly revert to your normal level over the course of several dates. Ideally, you want to maintain high chattiness until you get the girl into bed. After that, you can be more of your natural self, knowing that if a girl isn't sufficiently attracted to you after sex to accept less ramble, the connection is weak. If you don't want to change your chattiness level at all, and your conversations with girls are punctuated by long silences, you'll have to depend on meeting girls who are highly chatty and have strong pre-minute attraction for you.

Regularly watching a show such as *Seinfeld* will teach you how to ramble through hundreds of realistic situations while giving you a structure for telling simple jokes that enable girls to enjoy their time with you. The humor in *Seinfeld* plays well just about anywhere: I've employed it successfully in over twenty countries within North America, South America, and Eastern Europe. I've also lost count of how many times I've used lines from the show word for word.

There are comedy shows that are funnier and more interesting, but there isn't one as applicable to game as *Seinfeld*. At only twenty-two minutes per episode, it is an entertaining and passive way to learn conversational game, and it has the additional benefit of warming you up for social interactions if you watch an episode before you go out to approach, like I often did at night.

You can buy used DVDs of each season for only a few bucks online, and I have seen pirated copies on torrent sites. The first season has only five episodes and is the least funny. The second season gets better, but the show really hits its stride in the third season. You can start with season two and work your way up. I advise you not to binge watch, so that your mind will have time to absorb the conversational ideas of each show.

Step 6: Limit Masturbation To Once Per Week

When I was a teenager, the only porn I had access to were images downloaded from my dial-up internet connection and an old copy of *Hustler* magazine that a friend stole from his father. Compare that to the situation today, where videos containing every sex act imaginable and featuring girls of all shapes and sizes can be instantly watched for free. Because porn is so easy to access, I can't really blame men for choosing to rub one out instead of stepping outside and doing an approach, but this behavior makes them even more dependent on porn while they lose the ability to be intimate with a real girl. In the late stages of a porn addiction, the brains of some men become so rewired that they can't get an erection during sex unless they imagine their favorite video clips.

When it comes to game, the problem with porn is that it wastes your horniness, which is the fuel that feeds the game fire. The hornier you are, the more motivated you will be to talk to girls. Horniness may be a bigger determinant of your success than knowledge, because having the irrational, illogical, and unquenchable need to thrust inside a girl will strongly push you into interacting with one. Many men forgo the amazing power of horniness by dissipating it at home through masturbation, or they desensitize themselves to the allure of flesh-and-blood girls by watching videos of naked girls getting banged by giant cocks.

Your horniness must be elevated to the point where it will help you to reach your game goals. For most men this means masturbating no more than once a week or once every two weeks (forgoing masturbation altogether may result in a sexual emergency that causes you to pursue fat girls). Not only will you be more motivated to approach girls when you're horny, but you will persist in any interaction because you desire to have sex immediately. When you know you can relieve your horniness by going home and pulling up your favorite porn clip, you won't care much about the outcome of your approaches. You'll do your approach quota of the day simply to say you've done it.

Some men advocate not masturbating at all, but I worry about the long-term effects this has on the prostate gland and testicles, so I recommend you masturbate at a bare-bones level that will ensure your horniness on days you want to approach. For example, if you batch approach on Friday and Saturday nights, your masturbation day can be Sunday so that, by the time Friday rolls around, your balls are about to explode. (If you're not horny even after limiting your masturbation, check your testosterone levels and make appropriate changes to your diet and lifestyle.) You should also masturbate if you're experiencing an emergency of blue balls in the event a girl turned you on during a date but didn't let you sleep with her.

You may have encountered advice that tells men it's better to get rid of horniness through masturbation because girls can "smell desperation." There's a big difference between desperation and horniness. Desperation is often present in a man who has low self-esteem and thinks that he doesn't deserve better, causing him to display neediness instead of sexual desire. Horniness is a man on a mission who places himself in a hyper-masculine state by controlling how much he masturbates. The desperate man comes from a place of loneliness while the horny man comes from a place of animalistic vigor. Game is hard enough that if you aren't horny, it's unlikely that you will have the motivation to put in the work needed to succeed.

Even when you do masturbate, I strongly advise against using porn. Quitting porn will make you extremely sensitive to subtle flashes of female skin or the sight of a tight skirt, propelling you to approach and persist in your interactions. If you quit porn, you may start getting spontaneous erections in the presence of clothed women. Your erection becomes a sort of homing beacon that tells you which women are most worth pursuing, an ability that porn robs you of.

I can't stress how incredibly harmful porn is to a man's game and sex life. If you use porn as an aid to masturbate only once a week, the harm will be small, but don't discount the cumulative effects of using porn for a decade or more. I started to limit porn when I noticed that it pushed me to approach girls who looked easy, ensuring a stream of short relationships that went nowhere. Porn is hard to resist, because it makes masturbation easy and pleasurable, but it reduces a man's overall horniness, sabotages his game efforts, and makes him attracted to the trashiest girls.

Depending on your current masturbation habits, this step will either be the easiest or the hardest part of the program. As long as you limit masturbation so that you can maximize your horniness, I'm confident that you will fall into a routine that best suits your game. Start with masturbating only one day a week and see how that works for you. If it's lowering your standards to an embarrassing level, or causing you to ejaculate too quickly when you do have sex, try increasing it to twice a week, but I wouldn't recommend masturbating more often than that unless you're experiencing pain in your testicles.

Step 7: Write Down Notes And Observations In A Dedicated Player Notebook

Imagine you start a relationship with a new girl, date her for a while, and then she dumps you. You get over her and are ready to dive back into game so you can meet another girl. There's just one problem: you can't recall the exact game you used to get her in the first place. You proceed to have several difficult weeks before finally shaking off the rust.

Now imagine if you had a customized game manual that contained your best lines, moves, and techniques, written in your own hand. You'd be up and running in two weeks or less. This manual is simply a notebook that you keep when you're actively gaming. You occasionally write down what worked for you, what didn't work, your favorite lines, good places to approach, and so on.

If you used a specific move that allowed you to achieve sexual success, why would your mind forget it? Because it prefers to vividly remember the things that caused you pain, not success. Your memory is great at helping you avoid committing the same mistake twice, but it was not designed to help you seduce women like we currently have to, and it often forgets the fine details. For this reason, we need a notebook that will help us remember details that might have been inconsequential in the days of traditional dating and marriage, but which today can mean the difference between sex and no sex.

It's likely that you'll forget big chunks of your game if you take a break of two months or more. When you get back in, you'll remember the macro concepts but forget micro moves and lines. Once your game reaches the upper intermediate or advanced level, it won't be a big deal if you don't remember everything, because you've already internalized the main beliefs, but your success rate will suffer if you're still in the beginner or early intermediate stages.

After you do a handful of approaches or go on a couple of dates, open up your notebook and update it with brief notes about what you did right or wrong. Use bulleted lists and short sentences so that it will be easy for you to later review your observations and conclusions. Highlight important ideas with stars and circles. Write down tasks and experiments you could try in the future. If you keep this up for six months, you'll have effectively created a customized game plan that works exclusively for you. Your notebook will be extremely helpful whenever you return from a break, greatly reducing your anxiety when it's time to run game again.

Another benefit of your player notebook is that you will be able to see your progress over time, providing a source of confidence and satisfaction. When I look back at my first game notebook, I can't help but feel immense pride. I was a complete newbie, unaware of even the basics, but I was putting in an honest effort every week and could pinpoint exactly when I came to the major realizations that I'm passing on to you now.

When you reach an advanced level, where you are running game unconsciously, you won't need your notebook anymore, or even this book. All the information I'm giving you will provide a foundation that enables you to get started, but you should be sufficiently motivated to create a game plan that works best for you. After about two years of game work, you'll be able to start taking off the training wheels.

Step 8: Read One New Book Every Month

I have highlighted how important it is to be able to ramble in cold-approach scenarios, where you are expected to talk more than the girl. Watching *Seinfeld* will help with this by giving you a basic structure for rambling. Reading one book a month will further aid your conversations by giving you information and knowledge that you can share directly with girls. This will liven up your conversations and make you appear both intelligent and interesting.

The first few minutes of any approach will be similar, particularly if you're using the same lines. You'll automatically remember certain sentences, jokes, or answers to common questions. As the conversation gets longer, however, you'll encounter new territory. This may create anxiety if you're not a natural rambler, but if you read one new book a month, the knowledge you accumulate will enable you to talk about a number of interesting topics. The books create a warehouse of ideas and topics that are readily available for you to use in a conversation.

It doesn't matter what books you read as long as they aren't about overly technical subjects like computer programming or engineering. If you read books about things that interest you, the ideas will be simmering in your mind, and you'll want to share them with someone else. As I write this book, I've been reading a lot on Taoism, so my current girl gets to hear me talk about Tao when we're together. A couple of months ago, I was reading about globalism, so she got to hear me explain who is behind central banking. These topics keep our conversations interesting, and explaining what I've read to someone else enables me to commit the knowledge to memory.

With the vast amount of online content available in the form of articles, memes, apps, and video clips, reading books has declined in popularity, but I'm a firm believer in the value of books, because the author has put a huge amount of work into organizing information or narratives in a seamless way. Online content is like candy that tastes good but which is deficient in nutrition, lacking the benefits provided by the more balanced meal of a book. If you get into the habit of reading books along with watching *Seinfeld*, you will be able to spit casual humor and display depth and intelligence instead of simply interviewing girls by asking boring questions.

Step 9: Take A Break After A Set Of 100 Approaches

Once you have completed a set of 100 approaches, I advise you to take at least two weeks off from approaching to relax and reflect. What were your most obvious weaknesses that you need to work on in the next set of 100? Which strategy would make the most sense in the future based on your natural strengths? What type of feedback have you received from girls? What stage of the seduction are you having trouble getting past? Spend a couple of free evenings with your game notebook to review notes, add new realizations, and reimagine some of your memorable approaches or dates to analyze what you did right or wrong. It's also helpful to pause after sleeping with a new girl, even if you didn't complete a set of 100 approaches. Stop completely if you enter a relationship.

Towards the end of your break, draw up a list of the things you want to try during your next set of 100. This may include new opening lines, conversational pieces, moves, or venues. If you're completely stuck and have no idea why you're hitting a wall at a particular stage of the seduction, ask a man you trust for advice. Then update your auto-suggestion list to help you overcome hurdles and undertake new actions.

Your first set of 100 should produce a huge jump in how comfortable you are with doing approaches, but don't be disappointed if it didn't yield much in the form of dates or intimacy. The most important result you want from doing the first set is to feel more comfortable during approaches 91 to 100 than your first ten.

An unwanted side-effect of doing your first set is feeling burned out and starting to dislike girls. If your sexual drive is strong, you can be tempted to do twenty or more approaches a week, but you may pay the price in the form of fatigue or frustration. In order to enjoy game, and be motivated to stay in it for years, your path to success should be slow and steady. There is no rush! Don't be like me, who turned game into a lifestyle by jam-packing so many approaches into a short amount of time that it started to feel like a job.

As you get older and gain experience, you will have to take longer breaks from girls so that you won't get tired of them. I take frequent breaks until I eagerly crave the company of women and can't wait to interact with them again. If you find that you're not in the mood to talk to women, or you've become disappointed with their behavior or attitude, take a long break or seek out a different kind of woman by trying new venues.

Once you're done with your break, start a new set of 100 approaches. Feel free to switch from night to day game or vice versa. Maintain your workout routine, *Seinfeld* viewing, book reading, limitation on masturbation, and your player notebook. Each additional set of 100 that you do will be easier and yield more success.

Time Management

How much time does it take to do the program? Working out three times a week takes two to six hours. Reading a new book every month takes up to two hours a week. A *Seinfeld* episode a day will take almost two hours a week. Approaching five girls will take at least three hours a week. You're looking at a *minimum* commitment of ten hours every week.

You may already be doing some of these activities, such as working out or reading, but even if you are, you will need to dedicate more time than before. The good news is that, once you've reached your game goals, your time investment falls dramatically, especially if you get a girlfriend. Instead of spending hours a week approaching new girls, you will spend it with your girlfriend doing more relaxing activities that are important to you. There is light at the end of the game tunnel.

Let's say your life is so incredibly busy that you can't do at least five approaches a week, and you don't know when your workload will ease. If there really is no way you could better organize your time, I'd recommend an *absolute minimum* of one approach a week while including as many of the other elements of the program as possible. If you do one approach a week, it will take you two years to do a set of 100. This is not ideal, but it's better than nothing, and it will keep you engaged in game at a bare-bones level until you're ready to commit more time to it. It is better to do a sub-optimal version of the program than nothing at all.

If, on the other hand, you have enough free time to accelerate your learning, be careful not to dedicate your life to the game, because it will put you on a hedonistic treadmill where you focus on quantity instead of quality. If game becomes the most important thing in your life for a prolonged period, there is a high risk that you'll burn out.

Chapter Conclusion

If your reason for getting into game is to sleep with a lot of girls without making a commitment, the program will help you get there as you cycle through multiple sets of 100 approaches. If your goal is to get a girlfriend, the approach part of the program will end once you get one. Either way, always put your needs above the program. If you meet a girl you like, take a break from the program for as long as you are with her (just be careful about letting yourself go physically by stopping your workouts). If you've just slept with a new girl, you don't have to go out the next day and do an approach simply to hit an arbitrary approach quota.

The point of the program is to increase your satisfaction with life through intimacy with women. When you are successful and sleep with someone new, savor it by allowing the joy to flow through you before rushing out to do more approaches. You should also not feel ashamed or weak if you're getting fatigued and need to lower your commitment to game while you focus on other areas of your life. The girls will still be there when you're ready to return.

Since the program is meant to maximize your value and improve your success rate in the most efficient manner possible, it's rather mechanical, especially when it comes to counting your approaches and taking notes. This is the cost of fast learning, but I am confident that after a few sets of 100, you will reach a level where you can apply game in a less methodical way.

One day, you won't have to count your approaches and you won't have to set weekly goals. You will go out and talk to girls when you're in the mood to talk to them, and the only "guidelines" you'll have to follow are those of your instincts and sexual desire. The most important game concepts will have become etched into your brain, and you can move into a natural game that consists largely of you being yourself while "game angels" sit on your shoulders, reminding you of helpful do's and don'ts each time you interact with a woman.

Chapter 6: Approaching

Suppose that you stopped reading this book once you reached the end of the previous chapter, before continuing to the specifics of approaching and dating. What would the result be? You already know the right beliefs, how to optimize your appearance, and how attraction works. You also have a self-correcting game program. If I told you to go approach right now based on what I've shared so far, you would eventually get there, because the most important components for success are in place.

I'm telling you this because sharing the specifics of game will both help and hurt you. It will help because you will have powerful lines that have definitely worked for me and many other men, but it will hurt because you will be tempted to copy the lines like a robot, causing you to come across as less natural and spontaneous.

I've been teaching game for many years, and I know that many men want a plug-and-play system where they simply need to know exactly what to say to get laid. They want an easy solution where they don't have to go through the steps of discovering game on their own. Use what I'm about to teach as a starting point, but make your own modifications that more accurately reflect who you are.

Think of this book as a recipe for a Chinese stir-fry dish, where you have a lot of leeway on which vegetables to throw into the pan, instead of a cake recipe where the ingredients have to be precisely measured. You can add or subtract a lot of components and game will still work. Prepare the dish according to the recipe for the first few times to understand how the chef intended it to taste, and then get to work making your own modifications.

Accepting Rejection

I have good news and bad news. The bad news is that a large majority of girls (96% to 99.9%) do not want to have sex with you any time you offer it, and nothing you do will change their mind. Even if you become a millionaire and develop huge muscles, they will still not want to be with you. You're simply not their type. Do not lament the fact that most of the world's female population refuses to receive your lovemaking.

The good news is that even if 99.9% of girls in the world don't want to have sex with you, that still leaves *seven million* girls who do. If you plan on living for forty more years from today, you would have to sleep with 500 girls every single day to bang them all. No matter how low your confidence may be when you start out in game, there are an incredible number of girls out there who will give you a chance. They may not be supermodels, and they may not be your first choice, but they are fully capable of providing you with intimacy.

While game is meant to improve your value to the point where you are more attractive to desirable girls, a significant part of it is to play the numbers game and let luck fall on your lap. Many men get good results not necessarily because their game is stellar, but simply because they are talking to more girls than before, making it more likely they will encounter one in that group of seven million. After reading this book, you will do more approaches and then thank me for teaching you a "game system," but a big chunk of that system consists of getting you out the door and interacting with more women.

It's helpful to understand why we have to do so many approaches just to meet one girl. Apart from the fact that most girls will not be attracted to you, many of them are already being serviced by a man they like. If a girl's goal is to get the highest-value man possible, and she's already dating a man who is higher value than you, there is no reason for her to consider you, not even for a minute.

Another reason a girl may reject you is that you approach her when she's not ready to entertain an offer from a man she doesn't know. Perhaps she's in a rush, her mind is preoccupied with something else, she just had a fight with her mom, she's on her period, she just got an internet dating match from a hot guy, she has mental health problems, or her herpes is flaring up. It is quite possible that a girl who rejected you today would have responded positively if you had approached her a few days previously when her mood was different. It's for these reasons that you must be detached when running game and not dwell on rejection.

A man may have to do eighty approaches to get eight numbers that lead to three dates that results in one lay. At each stage of the escalation, girls who are not interested will drop out. Sometimes I go on a hot streak where I have to do only a handful of approaches since my last lay to sleep with a girl. At other times, I go on a cold streak and have to do more than fifty. Even though I'm the same person who is living in the same city and going to the same places, the law of statistical averages means that I won't achieve identical results. Every time you have a hot streak, there must also be a cold streak to maintain balance in the universe.

Fact is you have to build *quantity* of approaches to achieve quality. Your results are correlated with the effort you put in, up to the point you mindlessly approach anything in sight with a desperate or thirsty vibe.

The reality of the numbers game should prevent you from becoming attached to every girl you meet, even if you sense some emotional compatibility. Since the odds that any one prospect will make it through your entire game funnel are less than 10%, you should control your fantasies about the girls you meet, no matter how hot they are, to avoid setting yourself up for disappointment. Even after you have sex with a girl, you should manage your feelings carefully, because it's not uncommon for a girl to have sex with you a couple of times, get bored, and then disappear off the face of the earth. Not until she starts sharing her feelings and profusely complimenting you should you begin investing in the relationship on an emotional level.

It might be hard for you to accept that so many girls won't

like you, but it's actually liberating because it creates such a low expectation of what your results should be that you are less likely to become discouraged when going through a rough spot. There is no rule, mandate, or law that says the majority of girls you talk to should be attracted to you. This fact saves you from disappointment and stops you from getting too attached to a prospect who is canceling dates (flaking) or wasting your time with petty bullshit. As long as you make your best effort and escalate with girls who like you, success will be around the corner.

The truth about rejection is that we reject girls *more* than they reject us. Our rejection comes before we've spoken a word to them, when we evaluate how attractive they are. Whether you're in a club or doing day game, you carefully judge if a girl is pretty based on her facial features, hair, body size, and clothing. If you decide she's not hot enough for you, there is no approach, meaning you rejected her. She may not realize this, but it happened nonetheless.

When I'm out approaching, I reject more than 90% of girls off the bat without desiring to know them at all. The main difference between men and women is that women can go through life with their egos intact since they don't know they're being rejected. On the other hand, our egos must constantly face the reality that not every girl likes us, because we put ourselves on the chopping block each time we convert our sexual interest into an approach. Our attempts to get laid are immediately checked by reality, while a girl can live in the clouds without being aware of all the instances where she is getting rejected by men who don't think she's good enough for sex.

Thankfully, most girls reject us in the gentlest manner. They usually say, "Sorry, I have to go" or "Sorry, I have a boyfriend." You may experience harsher rejections, often in a night setting, when a girl laughs at you, barks at you to "Go away," or turns her back to you. We can also imagine the worst-case scenario.

Pretend you walk up to a pretty girl in a bar and deliver an opening line. She looks at you, laughs, says "Fuck off!" and throws her drink in your face. Everyone stops to stare at you.

You put your head down and walk back to your group, humiliated. You feel like absolute hell as you dry yourself off. *This* is the absolute worst possible scenario that you'll face in public, and most likely you won't even come close to experiencing it. Even if it happens, you'll start getting over it within an hour, and probably laugh about it the next day, because as a man you were born with the ability to overcome difficulties in a way that women were not.

Whenever you're anxious about approaching a girl, visualize the worst case and how you have the masculine ability to survive it. While some men find it helpful to think positively and visualize success, that doesn't work for me and many others. I imagine the worst case, accept it, realize I'm not made of glass, and then harness my desire and masculinity to accomplish the goal I want. If you're the type of man who is more motivated by visualizing a positive outcome than a negative one, by all means do so. Choose the strategy that is more likely to push you towards taking action.

Understand that you are not like one of those tiny dogs that shakes uncontrollably unless it's held tight. You are not a woman who cries because she dropped her phone in the toilet. You come from a line of men who have successfully reproduced and been through war and near starvation. On a scale of one to 100, getting painfully rejected by a girl is at most a seven compared with the difficulties your male ancestors had to face. Chalk up those rejections as one of the "no's" that is statistically needed to get a "yes."

Even if the worst-case scenario does not make you anxious, you will still have "approach resistance," which is your mind's way of telling you that you're about to embark on a difficult task. It will whisper sabotage in your ear: "Wouldn't you much rather masturbate to porn instead? Wouldn't you rather watch a movie instead of going out?" Resistance is common in any activity that requires a burst of will, such as going to the gym or writing a book like this, and it has nothing to do with the fear of a negative outcome.

To get rid of your approach anxiety, be pessimistic. Imagine all kinds of rejection and failure until you get numb to it, then do a handful of approaches to prove to yourself that your worst-case visualizations are delusions. To get rid of resistance, force yourself to do it, because resistance is just a matter of will, not fear. It may be helpful to give yourself some type of reward once you've done your daily approach quota. For example, I cannot eat a piece of cake today unless I do my approaches, or I cannot use the internet tonight unless I do three approaches in the bar. If rewards don't work, your problem may be that you don't desire intimacy enough. Is your testosterone level healthy? Are you refraining from masturbation? Do you have any unresolved health issues? Resistance is normal but shouldn't be insurmountable. If it is, think of what you can do to increase your desire to be with women. This could mean taking a complete break from game until you strongly crave the feminine.

Anxiety will decrease over time as you begin having successful interactions that show you there was nothing to be nervous about in the first place. Resistance will wax and wane, depending on your desire and what other parts of your life are consuming willpower, but it won't go away completely. If you have a busy life where you're working out at the gym every day, spending hours on your business, and learning new languages, you may not have much willpower leftover for cold approaches, particularly as you get older and your sex drive decreases. The winning formula for effortless approaches is to have a strong desire for sex, accept worst-case rejection scenarios, and have plenty of gas in the tank from not using it on other difficult tasks.

Even though I have been writing books for over a decade, I still face resistance every time I sit down to work. After writing a paragraph or two, I stare into space and dream of the many easier things I would rather be doing than trying to translate the thoughts in my head into words on paper, but I force myself to write it, knowing full well that at one point it will be over and I can relax. Similarly, you will reach the point where you will enter a relationship with a girl and be able to relax for a period of time as well.

The Approach

Most of game is based on the cold approach, where you initiate conversation with a girl you don't know. This is a relatively new behavior that our male ancestors did not have to do in order to meet girls. In the past, men would meet girls from their tribe, extended family, church, or circle of friends and be more than satisfied if they married the first girl they had sex with. Today, men have much more choice about who to select and go out with, but girls have even more choice than men, because they don't have to put in any special effort or run game to get suitors lining up around the block. It may take you a few months to approach 100 girls, but a pretty girl can get more than 100 responses in a single day on a dating app.

It's because of the massive choice girls have that we have to maximize our value and sample a large number of girls through cold approaching. As social circles get smaller and society becomes more atomized, most men simply won't be able to experience sexual relationships at all without approaching.

Cold approaching is a form of sales where you contact a pool of potential leads with the goal of converting them into buying customers. A commercial salesman will first get you to fill out an online form where you indicate what interests you. Then he will contact you with information that contains a sales pitch. One example of this in game is when you approach girls after they show some interest, such as making eye contact. You then try to convert that interest into a sale in the form of sex. The reality is that to close one deal, you have to contact more than one lead. You will never, ever have a close rate of 100%, not just with cold approaching but also when you're using reputational attraction like fame.

The amount of effort you'll have to expend to make a sale depends on the quality of the product you're selling (your overall game and value) and how receptive the prospect is (her attraction to you and her desire to get laid). If you want a high conversion rate with piss poor game, you'll have to focus on girls who are less attractive, because they will more likely be attracted to you.

If you want a high conversion rate with hot girls, your value has to be sky high, or at least higher than that of the girls you're pursuing. After some time in the game, you'll be able to strike a balance between your value and the prospects you desire.

We can begin to see why men fail at game. Why does a salesman have cold streaks when he can't seem to sell anything? Because his prospects don't want what he's selling or the price is too high. Almost all sustained game problems result from a man wanting girls whose value is higher than his own. In other words, he is getting rejected by girls who know they can do better. In a completely free and open sexual marketplace, not every man can get the girl he wants, no matter how much he desires her. A man who is having this problem has to lower his standards significantly while improving his value over time.

Regardless of your standards or value, there is one consistent quality that correlates with success: persistence. As long as you keep your eye on the goal you want to achieve, you can convert your will into results. A persistent man who doesn't let rejection phase him will do far better than the man with tight game who isn't persistent. If a man does one approach, gets rejected strongly simply because the girl has a bad attitude, and curses her before giving up and going home, he will see far less results than a man with lower value who does five or ten approaches on the same night.

The type of man who consistently sleeps with pretty girls is not always the man with the highest value, but the man who leverages his value *with* willpower, time, and energy. I'm not recommending that you dedicate your life to girls, because doing so will set you up for an existential crisis down the line, but I am saying that having low value can be compensated for in the short term if you put in effort. In sales, it's better to pick up the phone and make calls with a poor script than not to make any calls at all, because the day will come when a prospect so desires the product that it barely takes any work to close the sale.

After singing the praises of cold approaching, I have to tell you that I seldomly do it these days. The reason is that my motivation is too low to endure the high failure rate that results when I approach random women who have not given me a sign that they are interested. When I was young, horny, and full of energy, the failure rate didn't faze me, but now that I'm middle aged, I cannot do many approaches a week. I need a way to filter the girls I am able to approach so that I have a significant chance of succeeding before burning out. I do this by warm approaching, where I act based on a positive signal that a girl sends to me or her environment.

Before I describe warm approaching, it's important to explain the two factors that cause a girl to sleep with a man: attraction and availability. We already discussed attraction, where a woman has high interest in you because of something she values, such as your looks, vibe, or reputation. However, a girl will not decide to sleep with you based on attraction alone—she also needs to be ready and open to meeting a man. This means her penis pipeline must either have a free slot or be completely empty. If a girl has high attraction to you, but her availability is low, you will experience flakey behavior where she gives you her number or makes out with you before disappearing. She doesn't see you as important because other men in her penis pipeline are already meeting her needs.

I have frequently passed up on girls who gave me strong eye contact in night venues because they weren't attractive enough. Did they give up and go home alone? No, because I'd always see them getting hot and heavy with someone else before the night was over. Their interest in me was high, but their availability was also high. I quickly learned that when a woman is showing high availability, she will consider any reasonable prospect. She has sex not because she wants to sleep with a specific man but simply because she wants to have sex.

How does a girl show that she's available? She moves slowly, makes frequent eye contact with the people in her environment, and generally has a deer-in-the-headlights appearance where she seems lost, confused, or worried. She looks like a tourist who just arrived from a faraway land. The next guy with decent game who approaches her has an extremely high chance of getting her into bed. In fact, many men focus on foreign girls who are "fresh off the boat," because they are highly available from not knowing many people.

Let's take the attraction a girl has for you and divide it into three levels: low, medium, and high. Low attraction means a girl is not attracted to you. Medium attraction means she thinks you're an okay catch. High attraction means she really likes you. Let's also divide availability into low, medium, and high. Low availability means a girl is in love with another guy, or her penis pipeline is completely full. Medium availability means she is getting serviced by one or two men but wouldn't mind an upgrade. High availability means she is not getting laid at all and is actively looking for a man to add to her penis pipeline. In order for you to lay any girl, one scale has to register at least a medium and the other has to register a high.

For example, if a girl has medium attraction for you and high availability, or high attraction and medium availability, it's likely that you will sleep with her. High attraction and high availability will probably lead to a long-term relationship. Any other combination will result in failure. Most of the flakes that men experience, especially after a girl showed initial interest, are the result of a girl having medium attraction and medium availability. Being rejected outright is the result of a low score on at least one of the scales.

Most of the girls I have slept with had medium attraction for me during a time of high availability. I know this because they didn't fall in love with me or become particularly upset when I moved on. I was a good catch at the right time and right place, and because I know how to escalate an interaction to the bedroom, they came along for the ride. If you're not a stereotypical good-looking Chad with six-pack abs and a square jaw, the main way you'll be getting laid is through maximizing your look and game to be a good catch for a girl who really wants to get laid. If you are a Chad, your pool of girls will be larger, because you will be able to hit on girls whose availability is medium.

The main way a girl shows both attraction and availability is through eye contact. No matter where a girl is from, she is capable of giving men prolonged stares, day or night. If she is highly attracted to a man, she will lock eyes with his and hope he reciprocates. If she is highly available, she will give a number of men short glances as if she's window shopping. I've been to dozens of countries and found no exception to this rule, although a small percentage of women are shy and stingy with their eye contact. They may use a proximity indicator instead where they stand close to a man or draw attention to themselves by humming, sighing loudly, clearing their throat, or fixing their hair. The vast majority of women, however, use their eyes to signal attraction and availability.

If you approach a girl who didn't give you eye contact, or otherwise signal that she's available, you are betting on her having high interest in you even though she failed to notice you, but let me ask you, if Ryan Gosling, Brad Pitt, or the man of her dreams walked into a room, would she notice him and make eye contact? Of course she would, because a woman can *feel* when a man she finds attractive is near. A girl can also feel when a man is looking at her. If the man staring at her is a Hollywood star with extremely high value, she would definitely lock eyes with him. This tells you that if your eye contact is not reciprocated, you are going into the approach knowing that she almost certainly doesn't have high attraction for you. In this case, you had better hope that she is highly available.

You may be thinking, "But I don't get eye contact from women." You definitely do, but it's from women you are not highly attracted to. Ugly women are invisible to you, in the same way that average men are invisible to hot women. If your overall rating is a six out of ten, I guarantee that girls in the three to four range are checking you out, but you probably have blinders on for that type of girl.

To prove I'm right, I want you to do an exercise. Go out in a public space or shopping mall where there are a lot of people and walk around for at least an hour making eye contact with every woman between the ages of 18 and 45, regardless of their beauty. When a girl reciprocates eye contact, hold it until she looks away first.

Count the girls who lock eyes with you for at least half a

second. They have medium or high attraction for you. The girls who hold eye contact for at least two seconds have *very high* attraction for you. Also note the girls who give you eye contact for less than half a second. These girls have medium or high availability and wanted to check out the man who was checking them out.

When I'm in the mood to run day game, I approach a girl who either gives me a stare or is walking very slowly while looking lost—preferably a girl who is doing both. At night, I stand in the middle of the bar and approach girls who give me a stare or a proximity indicator by standing near me. These are warm approaches, where I talk only to girls who are displaying signs of either high attraction or high availability. I have a *twenty times* greater chance of sleeping with a girl from a warm approach than from a cold approach, where I did not attempt to read the signs beforehand.

A girl's attraction and availability can vary depending on the time of day. She can be feeling sociable during the day and accept your approach, but annoyed at night and reject it, or vice versa. There is no perfect way to predict when a girl will be open to you.

One major problem is that girls are usually staring at their drug of choice—their phones. This is particularly true in large cities. There are times when you may feel that you've entered a land of zombies and not one girl is looking at you or any other guy. The reason a girl doesn't look at men is because her penis pipeline is full. Who do you think she's texting on her phone? Not her mom, that's for sure.

If a girl has a full penis pipeline, the last thing she will do is make eye contact with men in public, because she knows they may approach her. She hasn't any space to entertain a new man in her life, so she deliberately withholds eye contact. When one of her star players gets a cock injury and can no longer service her, she will start making eye contact with men again, because as I've mentioned, girls are not scared of shopping for men with their eyes when they're in need of a new cock. You will save yourself a lot of grief by not approaching a girl who is doing her best to ignore all the men in her environment.

An indicator of your attractiveness is based on the type of girls who give you sustained eye contact. In the Eastern European city where I currently live, I get eye contact mostly from women in the six to seven range. Therefore, my attractiveness to these women is a seven or eight (one point is added because girls like dating up). If I approach a five that is available, it will be quite easy to get her into bed since my value is definitely higher than hers. On the other hand, what would happen if I approached a nine? Rejection, unless I strongly hit one of her attraction buttons or she has heard positive things about me from other people.

If you get sustained eye contact only from girls who are no higher than a four, your rating in that city is about a five. This rating will change if you improve your look, find niche venues, or move to a new city, but the eyes don't lie. The type of girl who makes eye contact with you tells you where you stand and what type of girl you should focus on if you don't want to experience sustained rejection and possible game failure.

If a man doesn't get eye contact from girls above a four, it would be a waste of time for him to approach anything above a five. Since we're living in an age where it's easy for girls to date up, most girls do not have to sleep with men who have lower value. If your appearance rating is low and you want a hot girl, you'll have to draw on the reputational elements of local status or fame.

Another danger of doing *only* cold approaches is that you internalize a needy vibe. If you're jumping at the prospect of a pretty girl, and even run after her as many men do in day game scenarios, you are telling your subconscious that you're thirsty or desperate. You may not actually be desperate, but spam approaching dozens of girls a week who showed no signs that they're interested in you leans towards neediness, and that vibe will be obvious to the girls you talk to, whether or not you are aware of it. This is why I advised you earlier to approach less than twenty girls a week, because this will make it hard for you to internalize and exhibit a needy vibe.

The more girls I approach, the worse my success rate. If I cold approach ten hot girls a day, I may get the phone number of only one girl who will eventually flake on me. However, if I warm approach only two girls a day, I may also get one number, but now I have a high chance of getting sex. Approaching more girls will lead to more results only if you're doing warm approaches or are approaching in venues where you're one of the most attractive guys. Otherwise, your success rate may actually decrease.

Because of my advanced age, I mainly stick to warm approaching, but I will cold approach if I'm feeling energetic and sociable, or if I see my "dream girl" and don't care whether or not she gave me signals. It's perfectly okay to cold approach a girl who showed no indicators of interest, but going hog wild and approaching everything in sight is not a viable long-term strategy.

Early in your game journey, you'll have to "waste" time with cold approaches to gain experience on how to escalate encounters with girls who are interested in you, because even if a girl has high attraction or availability, you still need competent game to move things to the bedroom. The fact that men still need optimal game to sleep with women who are interested in them says a lot about the degraded state of society, but I don't expect this to improve in our lifetimes.

If you're in the beginner or intermediate stage, I recommend you do a mix of cold and warm approaches. When you become experienced, or can go for longer periods without sex, do mostly warm approaches so that you don't burn yourself out. Whatever the case, you're going to have to face your fears, put in the effort, and get rejected.

Indirect vs Direct Approaching

Before I get into the mechanics of an approach, you have to know the two main styles of approaches and what they entail. Indirect approaching is when you begin an interaction with a girl without immediately referencing the real reason you approached her (you are attracted to her and want to have sex with her). An indirect approach can be asking a girl for directions or inquiring where she got a certain article of clothing because you want to buy it as a gift for a female relative. At some point, the conversation will move from the innocent opening topic towards the fact that you are interested in taking her out on a date.

Direct approaching is when you tell a girl something about her appearance or vibe that you like (or don't like). Your opener is about her, not something external. Since it will be more obvious to the girl that you like her, it takes less of an effort to move the conversation into asking her out on a date. The downside is that you first have to amp your mood to overcome the extra internal resistance that is present when attempting a bolder approach.

There have been endless debates about which style of game is better, and I can write several pages analyzing the pros and cons of each method, but the bottom line is that both indirect and direct game work and can be useful in your game arsenal. I personally lean towards indirect game, because there is far less resistance for me to ask a girl for help than going up to her and complimenting her. Another advantage is that you are less likely to get into trouble with security guards or police for "sexual harassment." A man who exclusively does direct game within a small geographical area is also far more likely to be blacklisted and marked than a man who does indirect game only.

The biggest downside of direct game is that it takes significantly more will to execute. It also forces a girl to decide quickly whether or not she likes you. If you don't blow her away with strong pre-minute attraction based mostly on your appearance, she will not want to participate in the conversation.

Indirect game, on the other hand, allows you to bring in more post-minute features of your value so she isn't forced to decide immediately whether or not she wants to continue talking to you. Your pre-minute attraction still has to be strong, but not as strong as with a direct approach. In situations where you know that your pre-minute attraction is high, such as a girl giving you eye contact or a smile, direct game may be more efficient in eliminating the few minutes of introductory ramble that you would have to do in an indirect approach.

In situations where there is no sign that a girl is interested in you, indirect game is better, because you won't be forcing her to make a snap judgment about you—she can "feel you out" for a bit instead. Indirect also has the advantage of allowing you to judge the girl for a minute or two and evaluate other attributes apart from her beauty, such as her manner and attitude.

If you're a beginner, I recommend you start with indirect game, whether during the day or at night, and experiment with direct approaches when you're feeling sociable or in a good mood. For night game, I generally increase my proportion of direct approaches, because I'm taking advantage of a looser mood thanks to alcohol and the fact that I receive more eye contact. For day game, I use indirect about 80% of the time.

Day Game

Day game is where you approach a girl anywhere besides a bar, nightclub, or similar establishment. The places I've approached girls during the day include coffee shops, streets, supermarkets, bookstores, malls, parks, concerts, wine festivals, and libraries. Anywhere a girl can be found, it's possible to approach her in a way that can lead to a conversation, and if you're able to have a conversation with a girl, you can get her phone number, and if you're able to get her number, you can take her out on a date and have sex with her.

During the day, I imagine that girls are like scared cats. If you begin too strong by getting into their personal space or touching them, they'll immediately withdraw. Girls today may be hyper-socialized to interact with men, but while they're sober, their primal nature still dictates suspicion towards a man they don't know. Just as if you were approaching a skittish cat, be as non-threatening as possible when you deliver your opening line so that she will feel at ease. This is especially important if you have a hyper-masculine appearance with huge muscles or an imposing beard.

In my book *Day Bang*, I went into minute detail about how to stop a girl, but I now believe that information was overkill. If you want to talk to someone, how do you do it? You put yourself in front of that person, start speaking, and they give you their attention. This means you have to get close enough to the person and speak loud enough so that there is no doubt you are talking to them.

In a quiet setting, such as a café, the space between you and the girl can be bigger and she will still know that you're talking to her. In a noisy and busy setting such as a street, however, you'll have to get closer to her and speak louder so that she knows you're addressing her. If you tried to stop a girl on the street and she didn't notice you, try to move closer on your next approach. If you tried to talk to a girl in a supermarket and she didn't hear you, try speaking louder. On the other hand, if you spoke to a girl and she immediately moved backwards, crossed her arms, or appeared scared, you were either too close or too loud. During your initial day approaches, tinker with your volume and proximity with the aim of getting a girl to stop what she's doing and listen to you with a warm and curious expression on her face.

I prefer to keep my openers simple and as universal to a number of different venues as possible. Approaching is hard enough without having to complicate matters with an involved opener that requires precise delivery to pull off. Instead of teaching you dozens of openers, I will teach you the pattern to use so that, even if you find yourself in a venue that has yet to be invented, you'll know what to do without needing further instruction from me. The point of the opener is not to make her attracted to you, but to initiate a conversation that you can maintain. If you can think of an opener that will allow a conversation to develop without a girl getting scared, use it.

Indirect

If you're doing an indirect opener, the approach begins when you casually position yourself face-to-face with a girl. In situations where you have to chase after her, or suddenly pop up in front of her, a direct approach would be more suitable, which will be explained later.

Indirect approaches are easy to do when she's already near you. Examples include a girl standing next to you at a bus stop, sitting on a park bench next to a path you're walking on, sitting at a coffee shop table next to yours, and perhaps most commonly, a girl walking towards you on the sidewalk. You simply have to move towards her until you're within her line of sight and begin talking when you're near enough for her to hear you. If she's walking towards you, simply step into her path, make eye contact, and deliver your opener.

To give her a clear sign that you are indeed talking to her, always start with "Excuse me." This will eliminate any doubt in her mind that you're talking to her, and it suggests that you are a safe man who is not about to do something dangerous.

Of the dozens of indirect openers I've tried, there is a common pattern to the ones that work best: they involve asking a girl for help. The most reliable way to get the attention of a pretty girl is to make her feel virtuous by helping someone in need. This allows her to accomplish her good deed for the day, tapping into her womanly need to be helpful and nurturing, while unbeknownst to her, she gives you precious minutes of her attention that you can translate into sexual attraction. It also allows you to screen out girls who do not want to meet a new man, because if she's not willing to help a stranger in need, regardless of his real intentions, she is not interested in adding someone new to her life.

The biggest benefit of this "elderly opener" style is that it's incredibly easy to do (you've already asked for help dozens of times in your life). The main downside is that you have to talk about something for a couple of minutes even though it may not interest you, but I'm sure you'll agree that the potential benefits far outweigh the cost. It's one of the most powerful techniques that you will learn from this book.

When you open by asking for help, you will look more authentic if you appear slightly confused. Taking advantage of a girl's innate desire to help someone in need starts with your facial expression and body language, which should match those of a man who needs information. Let's look at examples of openers you could do on the street.

"Excuse me, do you know where I can find a coffee shop around here that has the best coffee (or tea)?" Coffee shops are common, so you're not asking her for the nearest one. Instead, you're asking for the "best" coffee shop, which will require her to stop and think. Now you might be wondering, "What do I say after I open?" Imagine you are a man who really wants to find the best coffee. What kind of coffee are you specifically looking for? What types of places have you already been to and what did you think of them? What is the ideal cup of coffee you'd like to have at this moment? What kind of activity did you just do that may require a burst of energy or a moment of relaxation? If you put yourself in the shoes of someone who really wants to find the best cup of coffee, several questions and comments will naturally come to your mind that you can relay to the girl to deepen the conversation. This is why it's best to ask for help on something that interests you, so you can talk about it effortlessly for a fairly long time.

If you're outside of the United States, or in a country where English is not commonly spoken, you can try an optional variation. Before your opener, ask, "Excuse me, do you speak English?" If she says "Yes" or "So, so," you can proceed with your normal opener. What I've found is that this line is really the same as asking, "Excuse me, do you have some attraction for me?" You give her an easy way to bow out of the conversation if she doesn't find you attractive or want to meet a foreign man. You'll notice that many girls will say "Yes" even though their English is terrible. This means they are attracted to you and don't want their poor English to prevent a possible connection.

The worst thing you can do is to memorize word for word what you're going to say after the opener. That wouldn't be a conversation but a script, which will come across as forced, robotic, and unnatural. Ideally, you should memorize only your opener and then wing it based on some keywords in your mind.

In the meantime, I will be generous with examples so that you know the level of chattiness you will have to replicate.

Here are some things I've said when asking for the best coffee:

"I know there is a coffee shop over there, but the coffee isn't good. I tried it recently and their roast is too dark."

"You look like someone who is a coffee drinker. Are you?"

"It's hard to find good coffee in this city/neighborhood."

"I usually drink coffee only two times a week, so each time is a special occasion. I can't just go into any coffee shop."

"I read on the internet that a new coffee shop opened, but I can't seem to find it. Have you heard of ________?"

"Are you an expert on coffee? I have a high standard. I'm a bit of a snob."

"The last coffee shop I went to was called Costa Coffee. It sucked pretty bad. I was traumatized, almost."

"I'm thinking of buying a home coffee-maker called Aeropress, because it's so hard to find a good brew around here."

I mix in statements and questions based on my initial query. Reminder: do not memorize these statements! Why would a girl want to sleep with a man who is reading lines to her like a parrot? Use my examples to understand how I tackle a topic from different angles to allow a girl to give me rich responses that I can work with. If a girl's availability or attraction for me is high, and she feels engaged with my coffee chat, she will begin considering me for intimacy.

Keep in mind that after approaching, you have to continue talking *about the initial topic*. Some guys, when their mind goes blank, start to ask personal questions, but this is unnatural. You don't ask someone to help you with something mundane and then suddenly ask them personal questions. Stay with your opening topic until the conversation naturally flows into another topic, which it will if she likes you.

Here is a complete example of a coffee approach I would do. Before approaching the girl, I put myself in the state of mind of a man who is genuinely looking for a great cup of coffee. Ideas come to me about the things I'd be concerned about, but I don't try to memorize full sentences apart from my opening line.

> Me: "Excuse me, do you know where I can find a good coffee shop around here?"
>
> Her: "Yeah, there's a Starbucks right there."
>
> Me: "I don't like Starbucks. Their coffee is burnt and only tastes good when you add a lot of sugar. Do you know something more local?"
>
> Her: "I don't normally drink coffee so I'm not sure."
>
> Me: "I'm a bit of a coffee snob so I have high standards. I'm looking for something more hipster or Italian inspired."
>
> Her: "Have you heard of Moose Coffee?"
>
> Me: "I haven't. What is it like?"
>
> Her: "Well, it's kind of hipster, but I haven't had their coffee."
>
> Me: "I see. Do you have a favorite place that is close to here?"
>
> Her: "I just go to Starbucks."

At this point, let's imagine that I go blank and don't have anything more to say about coffee. I will hit her with the first piece of bait, which is meant to gauge her interest and make the conversation more personal.

> Me: "*Where I come from*, there are a lot of good coffee shops. So I'm used to quality."

The "Where I come from" (WICF) bait allows a girl to ask about you. If she bites on it, you can move the conversation into more personal matters, but even if a girl is attracted to you, she may not bite the first time, so you have to channel what you learned from watching *Seinfeld* to keep chatting. Then after a minute or two, you can drop the bait once more by using a new observation that follows "Where I come from." Sometimes, it takes three or four drops until a girl will ask you where you're from. Only then can you move the conversation into a personal chat where you get to know each other in a fun way that does *not* involve interrogating her with a barrage of questions.

Let's say you ask a girl inside a café whether the book she's reading is any good. Here is what four WICF drops might look like: "Where I come from, people don't usually read books like that." "Where I come from, there is an indie bookstore where all the hipsters hang out." "Where I come from, most girls read *Harry Potter* and *Twilight* instead of books like yours." "Where I come from, the libraries are old and no one goes to them." Simply connect an observation from your hometown with the topic you're discussing. The drops don't have to be refined or perfect.

Use WICF as bait even if you're approaching a girl in the city that you're originally from. If the girl asks where you're from, your answer can be along the lines of "I'm from here, but was raised in so-and-so neighborhood." If she doesn't bite, you will have to keep rambling. Use her responses to share further experiences and thoughts, or keep talking about coffee or whatever topic you used in your opener. As long as she's still standing there, facing you, not turning in another direction as if she wants to walk away, or not acting as if she's in a hurry, you should keep talking about whatever comes to mind until you feel it's time to drop the WICF bait again, which acts as an exit ramp to move the conversation into the personal.

I advise against making things personal before she makes the *tiny* investment of asking you where you're from, or you'll draw in bored girls who want you to entertain them without having to make a scrap of effort in return. I find that a girl will bite on the first or second WICF attempt if she has high attraction for me. If it takes three or more attempts before she bites, the best you can hope for is that she has medium attraction and high availability.

The beginning of the approach consists of asking for help, rambling about the topic for a while, and dropping the WICF bait as many times as necessary until she asks about you. You may think there should be more to it than this, but up to the point where you drop bait, whether or not a girl is attracted to you will be determined by how she feels in your presence, her availability, and how she interpreted your appearance, body language, and vibe. This means you don't have to *try* to attract her. Most of the attraction work was done before you walked up to her, and now you just have to *be,* with the sole requirement that you need to be chatty until she invests in you. The more lines and routines I give you, the more you'll prolong conversations with girls who won't follow through with dates.

Here's another example. Currently, I am mildly obsessed with pugs, a goofy breed of dog with a wrinkly face. I can ask a girl where to find a pet shop and talk about pugs for some time, because I know so much about them.

Me: "Excuse me, do you know where I can find a pet shop around here?"

Her: "Yeah, there's one in the mall."

Me: "It doesn't have the kind of animal that I'm looking for. Do you know of another one?"

Her: "I don't. What are you looking for?"

Me: "A pug."

Her: "What's that?"

Me: "It's an ugly dog with a smushy face." I show her a picture on my phone.

Her: "I don't know where you can get a pug."

Me: "It's not a very popular dog because it has so many

wrinkles and can't breathe properly. It also snores."

Her: "I've never seen it before."

Me: "It has special needs, so you have to take care of it almost like a baby. Do you have a dog?"

Her: "No, I don't. I have six cats."

Me: "Only six? Well, I think a pug will give me more joy than a cat. If you wanted to buy a rare dog around here, where would you go?"

Her: "I would go on the internet and find a breeder. Here is a website you should check out..."

Me: "Okay, I will check. Where I come from, pugs are very popular, but I don't see them around here."

If the girl doesn't bite on my WICF bait, I would keep talking about pets in general for another two or three minutes. My second WICF bait attempt could be, "Where I come from, people treat their dogs more like children. It's a little weird." Maybe I could ask her about cats, talk about another animal I like, or if I get stuck, change the topic completely by using one of my favorite segues: "By the way, you don't look like you're from here." If she likes me, she'll ask why I think that. If she doesn't, it will show in her body language: she will step or turn away. If that happens, I can wrap up the conversation by saying, "Well, thanks for the help." I have never gotten anywhere with a girl whose body language became more closed as the conversation went on.

If you don't like coffee or pugs, don't ask about them, but if you like tea or hamsters, ask about those instead. As long as you can talk about something, it's worth using it as an opener. For example, let's say that I need to hang a picture frame in my house. I don't have nails, so I make a mental note to buy some from a hardware store in the next few days. I then walk down the street and see a girl I like. I wasn't expecting to run into a pretty girl, so the only thing on my mind is the picture frame and nails.

> Me: "Excuse me, do you know where I can find nails around here?"
>
> Her: "Nails?"
>
> Me: "Yeah, like nails you hammer into the wall. I have a picture that I want to hang, but I'm having trouble finding nails."
>
> Her: "There's a hardware store three blocks down." If I accept her answer, the conversation will be over, so I need to refuse it. In your approaches, adopt a slightly snobbish attitude where her answers are never good enough. This has the effect of prolonging the interaction.
>
> Me: "Oh, I was there before. They don't have the type of nails I want."
>
> Her: "I'm sure they have hundreds of different nails."
>
> Me: "Yeah, but I need extra-thin nails because of the delicate photo frame I have."
>
> Her: "I don't know another hardware store."
>
> Me: "Have you ever had to buy nails before?"
>
> Her: "Yeah, at the store I just mentioned!"
>
> Me: "Where I come from, there is a special hardware store that sells just the nails I need, but I can't find it here, so I'm not sure what to do."

If she didn't bite on my WICF bait the first time, I could try again in a minute, or hit her with a "You don't look like you're from here" segue.

The "game" in this approach is not my conversation about nails—it's that I did the approach in the context of the Roosh Program after I optimized my value. If a girl is open to meeting a new man, has some attraction for me, and likes how I move and talk (even about nails), then I'm in.

I hope my examples take a big load off your mind about how it's okay to be normal. You don't have to worry about making her attracted to you by being someone you're not.

In my earlier game work, I pushed men into wearing a mask when approaching, but the problem is that, even if it gets you more girls in the short term, you will burn out from the amount of effort it takes to be someone else. My revised game method is sustainable, allows you to be yourself (for the most part), requires only a few memorized lines, and depends more on natural attraction instead of fake attraction that has to be maintained with masks and constant game consciousness. If you want to bang a new girl every week, you'll need to put on a heavy mask, but if you are content with a handful of mini-relationships or one long-term relationship every year, you can keep things as easy as I have described.

With the first style of indirect openers, you're asking for directions or help. You'll often use these when you are outdoors or in a mall. The second style is more often done indoors, where you ask a girl if there is another store similar to the one you are in.

Say I'm in a bookstore and I see a girl I like. Here's my opener: "Excuse me, do you know where there is another bookstore?" I will then say that this bookstore doesn't have what I'm looking for. Sometimes, I'll grab a book off the shelf before approaching to use as a prop during my conversations.

After a couple minutes of ramble, your WICF bait could be: "Where I come from, the bookstores are much different because of so and so." If you're in a clothing store, you can ask where to find a different one, because you want a certain style of shirt. If you're in a coffee shop that's about to close, you can ask where to find one that stays open late. If you're in a park, you can ask where to find one with more trees or water features. Wherever you are, ramble about what specifically you're looking for and then drop WICF bait. Here's an example where I'm in a supermarket:

Me: "Excuse me, do you know where I can find another supermarket around here?"

Her: "I think there's one down the street."

Me: "Because I'm trying to find cashew butter, but this supermarket doesn't have it."

Her: "I don't know where you could find that."

Me: "I read an article that says cashew butter has one million times more antioxidants than peanut butter, so I'm ready to try it out, but I can't find it anywhere."

Her: "Maybe you can order it from the internet."

Me: "Order food from the internet? I've never done that before."

Her: "Yeah, I do it all the time."

Me: "What do you order on the internet?"

Her: "I order wine, usually. I like a special type of vintage."

Me: "Interesting. I just buy the cheap wine that's on sale."

Her: "I take my wine very seriously."

In this example, the girl gave me some juicy material when she brought up wine, allowing the conversation to move off cashew butter. Because of this, I could delay dropping my WICF bait a bit longer and enjoy the conversation by probing her interest. When the conversation reaches a natural pause, I'll drop the bait and connect it with our current topic. For example:

"Where I come from, people aren't big wine drinkers. I don't know much about it." Try to be as truthful as you can in your conversations so that you don't need to spend energy trying to remember which white lies you told.

The last style of indirect opener is asking a girl whether or not something of hers (or something near her) is "good" or not. You can apply it to her laptop, smartphone, article of clothing, beverage, meal, book, magazine, or anything else she happens to be using. You can also use it on objects near her, such as a food product in her shopping cart or on the shelf in front of you. Adopt the vibe of a man who is deeply curious about the item in question and wants to know if it's worth buying or sampling. Even if you already know all about the item, pretend you don't, and ask some questions about it. This style of opener is the easiest way to generate a conversation because girls have a lot to say about the things they own. Here's an example:

Me: "Excuse me, is that a good phone?"

Her: "My phone? Umm… yeah, it's good."

Me: "I'm thinking of buying a new phone because my screen is too small. What model is yours?"

Her: "It's the iPhone 1000X, enhanced selfie edition."

Me: "And you like it? It doesn't have many problems?"

Her: "Well, it's not a perfect phone. It's not very good at multitasking."

Me: "I need to multitask because I like to have fifty apps open at once. How is the camera?"

Her: "It's very fast. See, look." She loads the camera app on her phone and takes a picture.

Me: "I have problems with my camera. Look at the types of photos it takes." I show her a few photos that subliminally reveal my value. "I read an article that people take 100 pictures a day with their phones now."

Her: "I take way more than that! I love taking pictures!"

Me: "What do you take pictures of?"

Her: "Mostly selfies, often in my bathroom. It takes a while to get the angles right."

Me: "Where I come from, people love taking selfies in the gym."

I could have asked about her phone's internet speed and its battery life, or made comments about how fast technology is advancing. In both of the above examples, I used an "I read an article that..." segue that allows me to stretch a fact to receive richer responses. As you may have noticed, I don't take approaches seriously, and amuse myself by saying some weird things that are on my mind just to see how a girl will respond. If she gets curious about me as a result, even better.

WICF bait doesn't have to fit perfectly—its main functions are to gauge her attraction and segue off the initial topic. You don't have to use it in cases where the conversation is going so well that she's asking personal questions without being prompted. There'll be many situations where you forget to use it because the chat is enjoyable and the girl is giving you lively responses. WICF bait is there to help you if you need it, but it's not mandatory.

In all of the above examples, I could have stayed with the initial topic longer before dropping WICF bait, so don't become too attached to what I've presented, and definitely don't memorize any of the dialogues. Only remember the opener, your first piece of bait, and any useful segues such as "I read an article that…" or "You don't look like you're from here."

I hope you're currently thinking that my method is easy. The problem with some game gurus is that their methods have turned getting laid or meeting women into a secondary goal behind elevating their status through feats of game that impress other men. Picking up a girl in a supermarket through an indirect opener, getting her number, and having sex with her after two dates is less impressive than running up to a girl on the street, spouting a set of memorized lines, performing elaborate physical moves that spin her around, and ending with a forced kiss on the lips, all while being filmed by a hidden camera. The purpose of that spectacle is not to meet women, but to feed the guru's image of himself as a modern Don Juan and increase the sales of his products.

My style of game may be boring to watch, assuming you even notice it as game in the first place, but it's effective and simple. It's not only important that the method I teach actually works, but also that you can use it with minimal willpower and energy. If a style of game will work only when you're in your mid-twenties and bursting with energy and horniness, it won't be sustainable.

It's also important not to confuse attraction with the temporary intrigue that results from being entertained. You often see intrigue on people's faces when they witness a magic trick. Their eyes open wide in awe and amazement, but this is not attraction. If the magician stops doing tricks, the "attraction" ends. As soon as a pick-up artist runs out of energy or memorized routines, the "attraction" will also end unless a girl is genuinely attracted to him.

I could put on a good show right now by approaching a girl and bombarding her with entertaining conversation, and in your eyes it would look like she's attracted to me, but she may not even return my text a day later. Once I'm no longer entertaining her, she has time to think that she does not feel that attracted to me. On the other hand, if there is genuine attraction, she will return my text, not because she wants more entertainment, which is easy to find anywhere, but because she wants to be in my presence.

Don't waste your time trying to create attraction. Instead, find a girl who is already naturally attracted to you. Earlier I said that if only 0.01% of girls in the world are attracted to you, there are still seven million girls who would jump in your bed. Simply find those girls. They're in your city, your town, and your neighborhood. They will pass through your favorite cafés, bars, and shops. Maximize your value as much as possible, especially around the attraction triggers discussed earlier, and walk up to girls with an opener. Once you find one of the seven million, she will make it easy for you, to the point where you won't even need half of the techniques I'm teaching you.

If you want to sleep with girls who don't have natural attraction for you, but want to feel good about yourself or impress your friends, things will be very difficult. You will have to put on a mask, pump yourself full of energy, and entertain girls in the hope that they will change their mind about you. You will have a hard time converting phone numbers into dates because you'll be pursuing girls who mainly see you as a momentary distraction or an entertaining performer, and you may not even like the girls you do end up sleeping with.

Compare this with a man who runs game because he wants to be intimate with a girl so that he can relieve his horniness or connect with someone new, not because he wants to alleviate his insecurities. His game is more natural and flowing. He is less tense, because he knows it's just a matter of time before he gets lucky. His energy is like a candle, slow and steady, instead of a raging fire that burns out quickly. He doesn't feel superior when he sees a handsome man with an ugly girl, and he doesn't feel inferior when he sees an ugly man with a hot girl. He exists in his own bubble where he cares only if *his* relationships satisfy him, not the rest of the world.

You'll be pleased at how easily you can forget many rules and guidelines I'm giving you and still succeed with women. Consider that you've likely had thousands of conversations in your life. You already have the foundational experience to approach women. Look into the eyes of a girl you like and walk up to her. Words will pop into your mind. Say them. If she likes you, she'll respond to your statements by revealing who she is. Say something else. Enjoy the conversation and gradually escalate the intimacy with her.

Meeting girls is hard only when you're goal-oriented, when you're thinking of a phone number or sex. You then feel the pressure of trying to say the "right" things to reach your goal. Don't try to attract her through conversation—simply have a conversation. Harness the chattier side of your personality, particularly early in the interaction, and say what you want. Use my segues and bait only if you need to. If she doesn't like what you have to say, wish her a good day. If she likes it, her statements will become richer and she will begin asking you questions.

Going into any approach, you should have fewer than thirty words memorized. A clear mind ensures you can make a clear connection. Ask any man about the last girl he slept with and he will probably say it was "easy." When there's a natural connection, it's always easy. When there is no natural connection, it's hard, and you are likely to fail in the end. The most challenging part is doing the approaches, but once you make them, simply be chatty and find out whether she is one of the seven million girls on the planet who is already predisposed to liking you. If she is, that seed of natural attraction will grow into something bigger. Successful game is less about creating something from nothing and more about *noticing* when something is already there and then taking advantage of it.

One challenge is that you'll come across pretty girls when you're least prepared to run game. Although you may block out a certain time every day for approaching, you'll regularly encounter opportunities outside of it. It would be unrealistic to tell you to "always be on" and take advantage of every single girl you see, because this would create too much tension within you, leading to anxiety. The best you can do is to have two or three default openers ready to use in the most common situations you find yourself in.

My two go-to openers are asking where I can find a big supermarket or a great coffee shop. If those aren't suitable, I'll do a "Is that any good?" opener. And that's it. You don't need to customize an opener for each girl. If you try to do that, you'll lose out on opportunities from not being able to act fast enough.

By having default openers, the only thing that can prevent you from approaching at any time is your mood, not a mental block.

Another problem you may encounter, especially when using indirect openers, is how to go from talking about things such as coffee, books, and supermarkets to a more personal chat that will allow you to get her number, because there has to be a moment where you transition from rambling about something you may not care much about. In most cases, when a girl is attracted to you, she will start showing signs that she wants to get to know you, usually after you drop WICF bait or use a segue. She may also start asking you questions out of the blue that allow you to consciously forget about moving the conversation to deeper matters.

Indirect rambling is merely designed to make a girl feel comfortable and safe, paving the way for a more personal chat during a time when it's unlikely she's been drinking. You don't need to have a rigid plan for how you are going to steer the chat in a personal direction, because then you are missing the conversation, and she will pick up on your unnatural vibe. You must enjoy talking to her about any topic that comes up, which is why it's helpful to use openers about things you're interested in.

If you hate animals, and you open a girl by asking her where you can find a pet shop, how pleasant will the initial part of the conversation be for you? I like pets, and I can talk about them at length to anyone, so if you put a pretty girl in front of me and tell me the topic is pets, I will enjoy that conversation. I'll wait patiently for her to give me rich answers that I can comment on instead of rushing through the topic. If I run out of things to say, and feel that it's time to transition the conversation to something else, I will use a segue or drop bait.

My typical strategy in a day approach is to keep dropping WICF bait, spaced out every few minutes, until she asks where I'm from. If she doesn't ask after four drops, I know she's neither attracted nor available, particularly if her body language shows that she's drifting away from me. Unless a girl is drugged, she will want to know a man's name and where he comes from before sleeping with him. If a girl doesn't care about where you're from or where you live, she won't sleep with you—it's as simple as that. If she doesn't bite on your WICF after four attempts, she's not interested, and is only talking to you because she's bored or wants attention. Whatever the reason, move on.

You may be wondering if it will sound weird to keep saying "Where I come from" followed by some kind of statement. I don't know if it is from the girl's perspective, but I do know that the interaction can't move forward unless she makes a tiny investment. Looking back at some of my approaches, it seems almost comical how I keep dropping it: "Where I come from, the coffee is usually burnt… Where I come from, people usually drink espresso coffee… Where I come from, there is only one coffee shop in the entire city… Where I come from, I used to live next to a coffee shop." After the fourth drop, if she doesn't bite, I'm out, though deep down I know that her attraction for me is low if she doesn't bite after the second drop.

If she bites on your WICF bait, or asks a question related to your life or who you are, you've gone from being a man she had no idea existed to one she wants to get to know. At the very least, she's curious about you and will now dedicate more of her attention to you. Your mind should register that you're doing well, but don't let that fact take you out of the conversation. Look into her eyes, pay attention to what she's saying, and let your instinct guide your responses. If your instinct is wrong, and the girl gets angry at you or runs away, there will be time later to think about what happened and find ways to correct your mistakes, but don't second-guess yourself while you're having the conversation. Once you're strapped into the roller coaster, hang on tight and enjoy the ride. You can analyze the various twists and turns after the ride is over.

When a girl bites on your bait or asks a personal question, she's engaged in the conversation and wants to know more about you. You can now retrieve some information about her, such as by using the "You don't look like you're from here" segue to find out where she's from, or by asking her direct personal questions, but you should not switch to interview mode where you hit her with a barrage of questions. Continue to ramble and be chatty.

A good rule of thumb is to ask her one or two personal questions for every one she asks you. As long as you remember to be chattier than normal, and to fill in the gaps if there is a prolonged silence, you're executing optimal game. Give long-winded answers and explanations that allow her to respond richly. If you get stuck, ask a question or make a comment about the environment you're sharing with her, even if it's something as simple as the weather or a fluffy dog walking by. Think of ramble as the main course of your conversation and questions as the dessert.

Since you are a human being and not a robot, you will certainly go blank and have nothing to say. When this happens, simply look into her eyes and smile softly. If she likes you, she will ask you a question to keep the conversation going. If she doesn't like you, she will politely leave. Use moments when you're stuck as an opportunity for deep eye contact, holding it until either she speaks or you come up with something to say.

I purposefully use the silence technique when a girl is enthusiastically talking to me with positive body language but hasn't bitten on my WICF bait after two attempts. This is a confusing situation that makes me wonder if she's interested in me but too shy to ask a question. The ultimate test is to fall silent and force her to show her cards. If she genuinely likes you, she *will* ask a question at that point. Even the shyest of girls will ask questions of a man she's attracted to instead of letting him walk out of her life forever. If she just wanted to be entertained, and you end the entertainment by falling silent, she will excuse herself.

If the conversation ends because you couldn't think of anything else to say, brainstorm things you could have said after the fact. What additional statements or questions could you have thrown in to maintain the conversation? If you repeat this exercise after approaches where you ran out of things to say, your mind will soon start feeding you ideas *during* the conversation. There is no "failure" or "rejection" if you see every interaction as a learning experience that can increase your overall conversational ability and game.

Even when a chat is more personal, it may be hard for a girl to know what your intentions are. Are you simply a chatty guy who's like this with everyone he meets, or are you really interested in her? At some point, it will be helpful to show that you are interested by giving her a compliment, often called a "statement of intent," so that she knows you aren't merely being friendly. This will also prevent her from being taken by surprise when you ask her out on a date. Pay a genuine compliment about anything but a girl's looks. Here are two examples:

"By the way, you're really nice. A lot of people around here seem so serious or angry, so it's cool to meet such a warm person."

"By the way, you have a great positive energy. A lot of people around here come across as anti-social, so it's a surprise to meet someone who is so outgoing and helpful."

This tactic doubles as a way to test her interest, because if a girl doesn't like you, she'll panic when she discovers that you like her and find a quick way to eject from the conversation by saying that she "has to go" or "has a boyfriend." When a girl likes you, and you pay her a mild compliment, she will be excited that you may like her too. You can also compliment her humor, vibe, or grace.

Paying a compliment helps her to understand why you moved from the indirect topic to wanting to date her. She will think, "Okay, I think he likes me now. He's probably going to ask for my number." That's fine, because if she stays in the conversation after that thought enters her head, success is right around the corner.

You can also experiment with dropping customized bait to provoke different reactions. Copy the WICF format to bring up something that you think will make her curious enough to ask a question. For example, if I approach a girl about a pet store not long after traveling to Russia, I could say, "When I was in Eastern Europe, I saw pugs everywhere and decided I had to have one. They're so ugly that they're beautiful." She may ask where in Eastern Europe, or inquire about my love of pugs. If I just came from the gym after a hard workout and opened a girl about finding a café, I may say, "I just came from a place that made me insanely tired, so I need coffee." As long as your bait is missing a key piece of information, you make it easier for her to bite if she wants to learn more, which counts as her asking a personal question.

If you're not a Chad, a girl won't be impressed with the things you're doing apart from traveling, playing in a band, being a DJ, owning a nightclub, being a professional athlete, or appearing in a Hollywood movie. Dropping bait that involves your job or hobbies will likely just make her bored. It's better to rely on maximizing your appearance and allowing your masculine personality to interest her via your ramble, vibe, and humor. Technically, you can be a "loser" with no hobbies, but as long as you are attractive and are fun to chat with, you'll still do well with girls. Paradoxically, not trying to impress her with your accomplishments will impress her, because you're not like all the other guys who use their career in a futile attempt to build attraction.

The sad fact is that most girls won't care if you're a successful doctor or businessman, and you may be better off omitting that information in the beginning stages of a pickup. The exception is if you're in a traditional country where a man's income is valued, but in that case, a girl will ask about your job early on in the conversation, so you won't have to manually insert it as bait. If a traditional girl has attraction for you, WICF bait is all you need to bring it to light.

You've probably noticed that I haven't said too much about body language. The reason is that you simply don't need to read her body language. Trying to do so makes things more complicated. What helps is if you can read the *changes* in a girl's body language as the interaction proceeds, particularly if the change is for the worse. If a girl was facing you directly early in the conversation, but then took a step back, started breaking eye contact more frequently, or turned her body away from you, she is losing interest. Unfortunately, I find that it is virtually impossible to regain a girl's interest once it's lost. You can verify her disinterest by using the silence technique and watch as she quickly exits.

The flip side is if her body language becomes more positive as the interaction goes on: she moves closer to you, gives you more eye contact, and is not distracted by loud noises or her phone. Even if you're unable to notice a change in a girl's body language, this won't harm your results because verbal confirmations are built into my teachings. The WICF bait, the segues, and the silence technique are all ways to judge interest, ensuring that we will never walk away from a girl who actually likes us.

The material I've covered so far is sufficient for you to have basic conversations of two to ten minutes in length. (I'll tackle tips for having long conversations later.) Once a girl asks you a personal question, enjoy getting to know her while she gets to know you. Infuse the conversation with your personality and humor, all without conducting a one-sided interview.

Direct

The main advantage of direct day game is that you can skip one to five minutes of ramble and start with a more personal chat that is easier if you're not much of a natural rambler. The disadvantage is that your pre-minute attraction has to be higher for a girl to continue a conversation with a man who makes it clear from the beginning that he has romantic intentions.

I've often encountered statements that a direct approach creates attraction because the man comes across as bolder and more confident, but this applied more in the past when girls weren't getting approached as often as they are now. Also keep in mind that a girl's player radar is more sensitive today, causing her to be skeptical of a man who approaches directly without appearing nervous. Therefore, direct game is most useful for men who are high on the attractiveness scale.

A man will get at least a phone number if he goes indirect on a girl he could have gone direct on, but he may not get a number if he goes direct on a girl that he could have gone indirect on. This is why I recommend that you lean towards indirect game, because it's easy to implement, versatile, safe to use in anti-male environments, and you won't lose girls who have high attraction for you.

There are two situations I may use direct. The first is where a girl gave me lots of eye contact or a smile. In this case, I could simply ask, "Do I know you from somewhere?" I would inquire if she's been to a certain café or bar recently, throw out "You don't look like you're from here," and a conversation is sure to develop. She'll probably ask me personal questions without me having to drop bait, and generally do a lot of work to maintain the conversation.

The more common situation I use direct is where I can't arrange an "accidental" collision during the day. If there is no casual way to get in front of a girl or beside her, and you have to speed walk to catch up to her, you should go direct, because it would be weird for you to follow her just to ask about a coffee shop, for example. Indirect openers are structured so that it seems you asked her a question because she happened to be near you, not because she's attractive, and that if an old lady had been there instead, you would have asked grandma the same question.

Direct makes it obvious that you are talking to her because you're into her specifically. Despite this, I structure my direct openers to give me plausible deniability that my interest in her is moderate instead of heavy. Why show that she has completely won me over? There's *zero* benefit in announcing your solidified attraction if a girl hasn't first announced hers. Your bold compliment will not be rewarded with sex. It's better to be somewhat vague and mysterious for as long as you can, at least until she invests in the interaction and shows some interest. Otherwise, running up to a girl and profusely complimenting her can be interpreted as needy behavior.

My strategy when going direct is to make a statement that is specific enough to warrant singling her out from the crowd, but not so flowery that she immediately puts me in the "He loves me" box. I therefore show concern or curiosity instead of sexual interest.

Let's say you're strolling down the street and notice a pretty girl walking towards you. You were unable to get beside her to do an indirect opener. You can now do a direct opener by speed walking after her. As you begin to pass her, put your hand up and say "Excuse me" until she notices you. You may have to say it a few times, especially if she's wearing headphones. Another option is to make a U-turn directly in front of her, forcing her to stop.

Here's the default direct line I use when stopping her: "Excuse me, I was walking in that direction, on my way to so-and-so when I saw you, and I noticed that you have a very sad walk." The opener begins with explaining what you were doing and what made you stop and talk to her. It finishes by observing that she has a sad walk. You're a safe man who was just going about his day until his eye was caught by a girl who seemed to be sad.

She will probably be surprised and reply, "Umm… okay." Follow up with: "It looks like you had a hard day at school or work. I just wanted to make sure that everything is okay." At this point, she should crack a smile and insist that everything is fine. The more she smiles, the more she's enjoying your approach. If she has a frown or looks scared, the approach will probably be ending soon.

Even if a girl smiles, does it mean that she will throw her arms around you and ask you to have sex? No. You still have to ramble so that a conversation develops, because she will not take the lead and do all the work for you. In a direct opener, the ramble will be more about her than something external like with an indirect opener.

Once she answers that she is okay, go on to describe what about her walk seemed sad, without insulting her in any way. We're trying to pique her curiosity, not make her feel bad. Here's how you could continue: "I know it's impossible for you to see how you're walking, since you don't have a mirror, but I felt a sadness in it." She will insist that everything is fine, and now you can make a general statement: "I noticed that in this country/city/neighborhood people seem a bit happy, so you stuck out as different. Maybe you're not from here?" Or you could ask: "Maybe you're new here?"

You can eventually drop WICF bait into the mix to connect her sad walk with the general environment you're both a part of:

"Where I come from, people have happy walks, even if they're sad on the inside. They give the appearance that everything is great."

Let's do an example that brings it all together. I'm in the shopping mall and get a short look from a cute girl on the other side of the concourse, suggesting that she is available. I follow her a bit and notice that she's heading for the exit. I do a speed walk and catch up to her outside the mall.

Me: "Excuse me, I was browsing through the mall when I saw you, and you have a very sad walk." My face is one of concern.

Her: "Uhhh okay."

Me: "Maybe you're very sad that you couldn't find a certain item. Or you had a tough day at work or school. I just wanted to make sure everything is okay."

Her: "Oh, everything is fine, but thank you."

Me: "Usually, people are happy when they shop, because they can spend money, but I didn't see that in you. Did you find what you needed?"

Her: "No, I was just browsing. I didn't want to buy anything."

Me: "I see. I came to buy some socks, but I have not been successful. In this mall, there are not a lot of good shops to buy men's clothing. Maybe you didn't see me beforehand, but my walk was sad too."

Her: "Haha."

Me: "Where I come from, malls mostly have men's stores."

Her: No response.

Me: "Do you know another mall around here?"

I started with a direct approach, but she gave weak responses that didn't help me out. Since she didn't turn away from me, I kept going, throwing in an indirect question to see whether it would change the situation. I find that going slightly indirect after a direct approach is a good way to calm a girl who is a bit freaked out that a man chose her out of a crowd for a conversation.

If a girl has a happy walk, approaching her with the "sad walk" opener wouldn't be congruent, so tell her what you think about her happy walk. Set up a contrast by saying how she stands out from the crowd.

> Me: "Excuse me, I just ordered a cup of coffee when I saw you walking that way, and you have a very happy walk."
>
> Her: "Oh, thank you."
>
> Me: "I was not having the best of days, so when I saw your walk, I wondered what kind of day you were having to be so happy."
>
> Her: "I had a great day at school, and my sister just got married!"
>
> Me: "Oh wow, so I was right. I would also be happy in that case. I noticed that a lot of people here have sad walks, so you definitely stand out. Have you noticed how people walk sadly?"
>
> Her: "Yeah, people here are kind of sad. I think it's just the culture."
>
> Me: "It could be, because where I come from people have very happy walks."
>
> Her: "Where are you from?"

You could tell this interaction would go well when she started inserting details about her life. For the sake of brevity, I dropped

WICF bait a bit early, but you don't have to use it until you're ready to test her interest or want to change the topic. You only need to understand the general pattern of these examples.

When you approach with the "sad walk" opener, you'll be surprised how often a girl says, "Actually, I have been having a bad day." Unless a girl is smiling and skipping like a happy child, she will often interpret her day as "bad." Your opener shows that you understand her on a deeper level and are genuinely concerned instead of simply using a "pick-up line," though technically it is a pick-up line. Even if she is enjoying your approach, you still have to ramble while not interviewing her. Once a girl bites on your WICF bait or asks you a personal question, the interaction is almost identical whether you go direct or indirect.

What I like about the "sad walk" opener is that it's direct enough to show a girl that you singled her out from the crowd, but indirect enough to not put her on a pedestal. Of course she will suspect that you like her, as many girls do even when you approach them indirectly, but she won't have verbal confirmation, and as the conversation continues, you can indicate that you are impressed or surprised by her great personality or energy instead of her looks.

I haven't been able to find any direct opener as good as sad or happy walk. The potential alternatives either put her on a pedestal ("You look cute/nice") or make you seem like a dandy ("Your style is great"). It's worth experimenting with a range of different openers to see what type of reactions you get.

In my experience, the flake rates from indirect game and direct game are the same (what does make a difference is whether the approach was warm or cold). Your approach style won't significantly affect your pre-minute and post-minute attraction values, and any emotional rush a girl gets from a bold direct approach will diminish by the time you contact her.

Pick the approach style you feel like doing that is appropriate for the situation. If you feel like approaching indirect, ensure you can arrange an "accidental" collision with a girl you see in public. If you feel like approaching direct, try to avoid complimenting her appearance, especially when you are trying to date up. Instead of asking whether direct or indirect approaching is better, ask which method you're more likely to use consistently with the least amount of approach anxiety or resistance. For most men, the answer leans towards indirect, but direct can be a fun way to spice up your day if you're feeling energetic and sociable.

Instant Date

An instant date is where you ask a girl to join you at a nearby location for coffee, tea, a drink, ice cream, or simply to sit on a park bench. If you have the time, an instant date can substantially deepen your connection with a girl.

Before I go into how to do an instant date, it's important to state that there is only one way to know for certain whether or not a girl likes you: she allows you to get physical with her in the form of touching, kissing, or sex. Just because a girl goes on a date with you, instant or otherwise, that doesn't mean she likes you. You may find this hard to believe, because you would not go on a date with someone you don't like just to kill time, but girls do this all the time.

I've lost count of how many dates I've been on with girls who refused to allow me to get physical. They liked the attention, entertainment, and free beverages I provided, but nothing else. Therefore, if a girl agrees to go on an instant date, either it's a huge sign of interest or it means nothing at all, and you won't know until you try to escalate physically.

Accept that you'll have to waste your time on girls who show interest but don't want to sleep with you. If you don't want to have your time wasted by women at all, I suggest you become celibate because 90% of game time will be lost in the wind on girls who are not serious about you. You have no choice but to endure these losses to get to the wins.

What's odd is that sometimes you will sleep with girls who gave you their number after only a two-minute conversation while girls you went on two-hour instant dates with won't even reply to your first text. Don't discount short interactions, but also don't get excited when you get a number from a girl who seemed to be very into you, because you won't know what she really feels until you start getting physical. That said, instant dates *tend* to increase the likelihood you'll see a girl again because they select for girls who are serious about meeting a new guy.

Trying for an instant date enables me to find out if a girl is capable of going on a real date with me, which takes far more time and investment. If a girl seems free, but doesn't want to spend "fifteen minutes" to have tea with me in the moment, why would she schedule four hours in the future, not to mention the time it takes to put on make-up and transport herself to the venue? If a girl says no to your instant date, the chances that she will go on a real date with you are almost zero.

Once you're talking to a girl for at least five minutes, and she has shown interest by biting on your WICF bait or asking a personal question, try for an instant date if you're in the mood. The first step is to ask about her plans: "What are you doing right now? Do you have plans for the rest of the day?" If she says something like, "Oh my God, look at the time, I have to go," or she mentions something specific she has to do, abort the instant date, wrap things up, and get her number. Otherwise, proceed by asking for the instant date: "Do you have fifteen minutes? I know a place where we can get tea/coffee/ice cream." Point in the direction of the nearest café or ice cream shop so that she knows it's not far. You can add, "Because you seem fun to talk to." Girls will often say "Okay," and then you begin walking to your first "date."

If a girl says no to your instant date, give it one more shot by saying, "Are you sure? I don't have much time either, but it would be nice to get out of the hot/cold/noise to sit down for a couple of minutes." A good habit is to get at least two "no's" to any instant date or change-of-venue suggestion before giving up. If she still refuses, but doesn't want you to think she's not interested, she will provide a reason for saying no.

You just invited a girl who has been talking to you for at least five minutes to sit down with you for another fifteen minutes. If she sees you as an attractive man, has a free spot in her penis pipeline, and doesn't have other plans, she will definitely say yes. If she says no, end the conversation and walk away without getting her number. Realize that a girl will make *huge* sacrifices for a man she is attracted to. Fifteen minutes is far from a huge sacrifice.

If a girl says yes to the instant date, it isn't a guarantee she'll have sex with you, but you are making sound forward progress. Walk with her to the venue you suggested and continue chatting with her. Be aware that, if you're a complete newbie, a possible danger is that you will use up all your first date conversation topics during the instant date and be more anxious during a future date. This is true for me when I'm talking to girls in a foreign language. I use all my best conversation on the instant date and have little left over for the first date. At the same time, instant dates are a good warm-up for real dates, and should help increase your confidence for them.

Once you're on the instant date, you can pursue two different strategies. The first is to show additional value in a thirty-minute period that leaves her wanting more. You're like a movie with an ambiguous ending that hints at an exciting sequel. The main attraction here is curiosity, where you touch on something interesting about your job, your travels, or anything else that you believe makes you an attractive man, and say, "It's a long story. I can tell you next time," as if a future date is a foregone conclusion.

If you tell your entire life story during the instant date, you will deflate the balloon and give her little to look forward to. Don't let a girl feel bored after she discovers the best things about you from a single meeting. Unfortunately, the brains of modern women have been so primed to seek entertainment above all else that men have to package their lives as if they were a soap opera, doling out key information in increments.

Unless you're absolutely sure you can go all the way and sleep with her that same day, I recommend you exit the instant date at the peak moment she is showing interest or asking for more information about your life. Look at the time and say, "I have to run, but I really enjoyed our chat. How about we meet another time and continue it?" Get her number, give her a playful high-five goodbye, and leave with the knowledge that, at the moment you left, she was definitely interested.

Exiting early sets up the possibility of her worrying about whether you rejected her. This is perfect, because you're forcing a girl to think about her flaws and value instead of analyzing yours. It does seem a bit "evil" that making girls anxious tends to increase their attraction for you, but this is the reality of human nature, and girls do it to us all the time.

If you want to go beyond thirty minutes, and her schedule is free, you should try to sleep with her that day because the iron is red hot. If you don't strike, you may lose the opportunity forever. I dislike that girls will sleep with me when they're in the mood yet not even contact me a few days later when they're not, but there's no sense in fighting female psychology. When I do instant dates and don't bow out at its peak, I prepare to go all the way, no matter how many hours it may take.

The best same-day bang strategy is to make several venue changes over an extended period (at least two hours), until the final venue is your or her home. Although this may seem hard if you approach her in the early afternoon when she still has things to do, it becomes easier if your approaches are in the late afternoon or early evening after she has finished work or school.

Enjoy your tea, coffee, or ice cream in the first venue for about an hour before bouncing to a second venue nearby, which should serve alcohol and have more intimate seating. Stay at this venue for an hour or two and then bounce to a third venue that feels even more intimate. This is where you should try to kiss her. The fourth venue will be your or her home. For same-day lays, I recommend three separate venues, because it will distort time and make her feel as if she's known you longer than just a few hours. Even if this strategy doesn't give you a bang, you should get at least a heavy make-out session.

My general guideline is to spend at least an hour in each venue, though you can stay longer if it feels natural to do so. You can also go to more or fewer venues depending on local conditions, but don't rush to get a girl home. She should see moving to a home as a way to deepen the connection by listening to music, having more drinks, or cooking a meal. A side effect of that will be having sex, which is more likely to happen if she has had at least two drinks. If she senses you are pushing too hard for the bang, she may activate her anti-slut defense mechanism.

So far, I haven't said much about touching. This is because it plays only a minor role in day game. I used to think that touching *created* attraction, but I no longer believe this to be the case. Instead, touching mainly primes a girl for deeper physical contact, particularly kissing, because if you want to kiss a girl, you will first have to spend an hour or two making her feel comfortable with your touches. When you're doing normal day game without instant dates, you don't need to worry about touching. Due to the culture's sensitivity over "street harassment" and other boogeymen that feminists are whining about, I would not touch a girl unless she bites on my bait or asks a personal question.

One touch you can use in a same-day bang progression is the arm-in-arm move. On the way from the second venue to the third, or on the way to a home, put out the elbow of your arm that is at her side and say, "I don't want you to fall down." She should take that as a cue to hook her arm through yours. This is not as intimate as hand-holding, but it's a great way to escalate to longer touches that make her feel comfortable with you. If a girl accepts this move, she will soon be ready for a kiss.

The trajectories of your instant dates can vary widely, but one common scenario for me is to do the arm-in-arm move when walking to the third venue, pause before entering the venue, and get close to her face to see where I stand with the kiss. At the very least, I should be kissing her towards the end of our stay in the third venue, or soon thereafter. We'll talk more about touching, kissing, and changing the venue to a home in the section on night game.

Getting A Phone Number

The majority of phone numbers you get will go nowhere, no

matter how much interest a girl showed when you met. The reality is that most of the intimacy you experience will result from being in the right place at the right time with the right value that an available girl was looking for at that moment. Almost all girls now choose to have sex with a man based on emotional reasons, and since emotion is like a cloud that constantly moves and changes shape, a girl who likes you today may not want to talk to you tomorrow. Don't get frustrated at a reality that you can't change. Don't get upset at girls who flake or don't respond to you. If you persist on playing the salesmanship game, you will eventually be the recipient of a pleasant intimate encounter.

If a girl asks you at least one personal question, you have enough interest to try getting her number. Ideally, I like to wait until a girl asks me two or three personal questions, but if she's attractive enough, I'll go for it if she asks only one.

The shortest and easiest way to get a number is through a closing move that indicates you have to leave, pays her a minor compliment, and asks for her number. Look at the time and say, "Hey, I actually have to run, but you seem cool. Do you want meet some other time for a drink?" The ball is in her court to say yes or no. I like doing this because it forces her to say yes instead of making it too easy with a line such as "Why don't you give me your number" or "Here, put your number in my phone." Always give a girl an opportunity to declare her interest in you. If she says yes, get her number, exchange names, and be on your way.

She may decline to give you her number and tell you to give her your number instead, or to add her on social networking. Refuse. Insist on getting her number by telling her that you're a man and should contact a girl first, or that you don't use social networking. It's generally a bad sign if a girl resists giving her number.

If you have time, you can try a longer method I first wrote about in *Day Bang* called GALNUC, which gives you useful information for setting the first date while making her feel like she's getting to know you (chances are that you'll naturally hit on at least one part of GALNUC in the main conversation).

Below are the six questions to ask her in the lead-up to getting a number.

G stands for German: "By the way, are you half-German?" I ask about her ethnicity and comment on how she has Germanic features (or those associated with another country). Refer to a country with which you genuinely think she has ancestral links.

A stands for Age: "By the way, how old are you?" I ask her age and make her guess mine. Now that I'm middle-aged, I have stopped asking this question. Skip it if you suspect there's a wide age gap.

L stands for Location: "By the way, where do you live?" I ask this so I can determine a general neighborhood for the first date.

N stands for Name: "By the way, what's your name?" Names are usually exchanged after you get the number so you don't have to ask this question beforehand.

U stands for Usually: "So where do you usually hang out?" The answer to this question will tell you the types of venue she likes, let's her know you're about to ask for the number, and may tell you how promiscuous she is.

C stands for Cool: "I actually have to run, but you seem cool. Do you want to meet some other time for a drink?" If she says yes, take out your phone and get her number.

The key point in GALNUC is to ramble a bit after each question so it doesn't seem like an interview. Currently I do a shorter LUC variant. After it's clear she has interest in me, I say, "By the way, where do you live?" I make a comment related to what I know about her neighborhood before asking where she usually hangs out. Then I tell her she seems cool and ask if she wants to meet again. You can experiment with different ways of doing it. Obviously, only the "C" question is essential.

You'll notice that you don't directly ask for her number—you ask for the date. If you ask a girl for her number, you may get only her number but no date, because you didn't require her to think about making a future time commitment with you. When you ask her for a date, her reaction should be enthusiastic or she won't show up for one. If she starts rattling off excuses to the effect that she isn't sure or is too busy, there is no point in getting her number since she's already trying to weasel out of a date. But if she says "Sure!" or "Okay!" it's safe to say that she's genuinely excited about the prospect of seeing you again.

Something else I do is glean her schedule so that I know what days to shoot for when setting the date. Good days for a first date are Sunday through Thursday evenings when she's more likely to be free. Once she puts her number in my phone, I'll say something like, "Great, I'll text you soon. Maybe Monday or Tuesday night will be good for you?" If she doesn't take a second to think about her schedule and quickly says, "Just text me," I know I'm in trouble, because she's not putting in an effort to make things work, but if she slowly ponders and says something like, "Mondays are usually better," I know she's more likely to come through. You don't need to finalize your plans right then and there, but you should be asking for a date and making her think about going on one instead of simply getting her number.

It's important to understand that what I'm teaching you is an optimized starting point. Never feel that you're doing it wrong if you don't follow exactly what I say. I'm giving you the basic structure and the most important steps, but you can modify them so that they work even better.

Remember one of the beliefs: "It's fun to try new things just to see what happens." There are no mistakes when you run game, only learning experiences. If at any point you forget what to say or do, make up something on the spot. As long as you're aware that it's your responsibility to escalate during the interaction—whether it involves getting her number or going for the kiss—you'll be fine.

Night Game

Night game used to be great, at least from the perspective of a man in his twenties living in Washington, D.C. during the early 2000s, but it has become significantly harder since then. The reasons for this decline are the introduction of table service, the rise of dating apps that don't require girls to meet guys in clubs, the decrease in female attractiveness because of the obesity epidemic, and worsening sex ratios to the point that men far outnumber women in most major cities. You can be in a crowded club but not see a single girl who's worth approaching, and if you do find one, her ego can be so gassed up from all the attention she gets that her attitude is vulgar and nasty.

It doesn't help that the age of "rape culture" and #MeToo means every girl is trying to save her friend from "dangerous" men, leading to nonstop cockblocking. That said, there are still plenty of opportunities at night, especially if you experiment with the venues you go to.

Venues

An optimal venue for night pick-ups should have five features. First, it should primarily be a bar, not a nightclub, though a small dance floor is okay. Nightclubs are now "event" destinations that provide "memorable experiences" instead of a frictionless way to meet members of the opposite sex.

Second, a venue should not be so loud that you have to scream in a girl's ear. The louder a venue, the more you'll have to rely on pre-minute attraction instead of your post-minute value.

Third, most of the girls shouldn't be sitting down. It's harder to approach girls who are seated, so you want at least 25% of the crowd to be standing or milling around.

Fourth, it shouldn't heavily feature bottle service. The second a girl enters a club with bottle service, her attitude increases several degrees and her mission becomes more about scoring free drinks and showing off than meeting a man.

Lastly, the sex ratio should not be worse than two men for every one girl. This ratio is still workable since most men are too scared to approach, but once the ratio is three guys for every girl or worse, the girls start to sense their power and turn up their attitudes.

If you go to one of the mega clubs in your city that is advertised on the radio or through flyers, your night is likely to be frustrating and expensive. The only time a mega club is worthwhile is when it has far more girls than men, but that rarely happens these days. You may have better odds going to a bar with only five girls than to a club with over 100, because the former is more conducive to people getting to know each other through conversation.

The common scenario in a big club is that you do about ten approaches, get five rejections off the bat, and get into a long conversation with one or two girls. In a bar on a slow night, you can probably do only three approaches but get into a long conversation with one. A substantial downside of bars, however, is that there is a lot more waiting between approaches. Sometimes you have to wait up to an hour before an opportunity presents itself, whereas in a club there is more constant action. Bar game will sometimes feel more like meditation, but it's a tradeoff I'll accept on most nights.

During the week, one strategy is to hit a neighborhood bar, get a drink, and see whether you can do an approach or two before heading home. On the weekends, you can try to do five or ten approaches, which may require you to visit two or three venues.

I also recommend that you go out at night with at least one friend. While you can go out solo to a nightclub, something I've done hundreds of times, you put yourself at a disadvantage because girls will give you lower pre-minute attraction scores from having no social proof. Can you still pick up when rolling solo? Of course you can, but solo night game is harder than solo day game. The exception is if you particularly like alcohol or are a night owl. The better my day game became, the less I went out solo at night.

Whether you decide to go alone or with a friend, always be friendly with the bouncers and bartenders, because they will be a source of social proof if girls see you interacting with them. Tip the bartenders well, and gradually exchange names with the entire staff after you've visited the same bar or club a few times. If you're not sociable enough to be friendly with the staff, you may be too introverted for night game and should focus on day game instead. Night game success correlates highly with extroverted men, or at least an introverted man who can become moderately extroverted during the hours he spends in a night venue.

Opening

The ideal night-game openers are playful and direct, where you're talking to a girl about herself but nowhere close to paying her a compliment. In fact, your opener may include a mild insult that lowers a girl's value, with the aim of making her realize that you aren't especially impressed by her. Because it is likely that she will be consuming alcohol, you can be much looser in your speech and also touch more than you would during the day.

It's impossible to prescribe one method for approaching a girl in a bar or club because you are likely to encounter hundreds of logistical variations. You'll be confronted with new situations every night you go out, but this shouldn't stop you from doing the approach since you'll never have perfect knowledge that prepares you for everything. Take what you learn here and combine it with your intellect, fortitude, creativity, and knowledge of local conditions to make the approach happen.

When I first got into game, I would approach groups of four or more girls and entertain all of them. This was a big waste of time. Even if there is a group of only two girls, there will always be one girl who is simply not interested in what you have to say (she'll often be the fat one) and cause the other girl to stop paying attention to you. And then you face the challenge of trying to go from a group conversation to only talking to the girl you like.

I came up with a simple solution to overcome this problem: only approach and talk to the girl you like. Maintain a conversation with her without engaging her friends. This means that if you see a group of girls, go up to the one you like and have a one-on-one conversation with her. Let her friends look on—who cares. If the girl doesn't like you, she will reject you quickly, and you won't have expended much energy unlike when you dance like a clown for an entire group only to be cockblocked in the end.

An indication that an approach won't go well is when a girl puts out prior signs of low availability by talking nonstop to her friends or not checking out anyone else in the venue. It's likely this means she has no interest in meeting a man, but if you like the girl, do the approach anyway, especially if she's the only available prospect around.

A girl will be less receptive if her friends are next to her, because she'll be hyper-sensitive about what they may think of her talking to a random guy. To increase the odds of success, I time my approach to when she's away from her friends, either when she goes to the bathroom (I approach her on her way back), goes to the bar to get a drink, or when she is bored and starts looking around.

At night, it's important to make it clear to a girl that you are talking to her. If you approach a girl from behind or the side, I recommend that you tap her on the shoulder three times so that she turns in your direction (I use three taps because a girl could perceive one or two taps as accidental). Do it if she won't see you doing it and has to turn in your direction. This is often the case in crowded or dark venues.

The goal of the triple tap is to eliminate all doubt that you are trying to talk to her, forcing her either to acknowledge you or reject you outright. If girls regularly fail to notice that you are trying to talk to them, you have to triple tap more often.

For night game, there are two classes of openers, one of which you already know—asking for help or advice. Here's an example where I ask a girl whether she can recommend another bar, club, or restaurant for me to check out after describing what is lacking in the current venue:

> Me: "Excuse me, do you know if there's another bar around here that is good?"
>
> Her: "What are you looking for?"

Me: "I don't like the music here. I want something less upbeat."

Her: "Less upbeat?"

Me: "Yeah, my energy is not as high as everyone here. I'm also not as drunk."

Her: "I don't know of any place else."

Me: "So you don't go out often?"

Her: "Actually, this is my first day in the city."

Me: "Oh, you're not from here."

Her: "No, I'm from Australia."

You will customize the conversation based on the bar you want. Adopt the attitude of a snob and reject her suggestions to prolong the conversation. You can also drop in WICF bait and the segues used in day game if you get stuck. Everything you learned in the section on day game can be used more or less as is at night, except that at night you can be more personal.

If your energy is high, you can have a conversation that goes in the opposite direction.

Me: "Excuse me, do you know if there's another bar around here that is good?"

Her: "There are a few."

Me: "This place is not really my style. I want something that has more energy so I can dance all night long."

Her: "You can try the club down the street."

Me: "Do they have raised platforms that I can dance on? I want everyone to see me dancing."

Her: She laughs.

Me: "This isn't my favorite music, so I won't dance yet. So why are you here?"

What I like about this opener is that it filters out girls who don't want to help a man in need while taking the conversation in a fun direction. If she doesn't even want to suggest where you can go, she's definitely not interested. Another advantage of this opener is that you don't have to be drunk or amped up to ask a girl to recommend a bar or club, and it comes across as natural. The more complicated your opener, the more likely the girl will perceive it as a pick-up line and become guarded as a result.

The next class of opener starts with "You look like." This is where you notice something about her and talk about it. I often stack this opener on top of the previous one, meaning that if I don't get a lively response after asking her for a bar recommendation, I will use "You look like" to jump-start the conversation. The first example involves guessing her ethnicity and then explaining it.

Me: "You look like you're from Colombia."

Her: "What?"

Me: "Colombia, the country. It's the way your cheeks are shaped and also your forehead."

Her: "I'm not from Colombia."

Me: "Strange, because if you go to Colombia, you'll see a lot of girls who look like you. Do you speak Spanish?"

Her: "No."

Me: "Wow, I was way off. Well, I'm sure you get that all the time. Maybe your great-great-great-great-grandfather was from Colombia."

Her: "Actually, I have some Spanish in my family tree."

Me: "I knew it! So technically I'm not wrong since Colombians are descended from Spaniards. Where I come from, there are a lot of Spaniards."

You'll notice that the conversation is more playful than the previous examples. There's no rule against this sort of conversation during the day, but I find they happen more naturally in night settings where alcohol is being consumed.

The next "You look like" opener involves guessing that she is from a different state or province. This is more useful with girls who don't look like they are from another country.

Me: "You look like you're from Texas."

Her: "Excuse me?"

Me: "You look like you're from Texas, based on how your style is."

Her: "I'm not from Texas."

Me: "Am I close?"

Her: "Not even."

Me: "That's strange. I'm never wrong with this kind of thing. Are you sure you don't have ancestors from Texas?"

Her: "Oh, I'm sure."

Me: "Well, this is the first time I've ever been wrong… in my life. So, what state are you from?"

Her: "New Hampshire."

Me: "Wow! I was off. It must be the dim lighting. It messed up my senses."

Her: "Okay."

Me: "So why are you in this bar?"

The above example includes one of my favorite night segues of asking a girl *why* she is in a particular venue, which allows you to take the conversation in different directions. A typical answer will be "To have fun with my friends." You could ask about her friends, how she knows them, and her idea of fun. If she says she's at the venue to dance, ask her what kind of music she likes to dance to. (Remember, always ramble about these topics instead of only asking questions.) Listen carefully to her answers for clues on the best way to seduce her. If she says that she loves to dance, you should eventually dance with her. If she says that she loves to drink, get ready to do shots. You can also share your opinion of what you think about the venue.

If a girl asks why you are in the venue, do not tell her you're looking for love, a relationship, or a wife. Even if a girl is looking for commitment, she will be turned off by a man who says he wants it. This is why girls never explicitly state they are looking for love, even if it's what they deeply desire (they think that saying so makes them appear desperate). Showing that you need something, or that you crave female companionship, will lower your value in a girl's eyes.

The closest you can get to stating what you really want is a humorous answer such as "Love at first sight." Even when you're on dates with girls who seem traditional, you should keep your answer open-ended when they ask what you want. Use vague phrases like "I prefer a natural connection," "It's better not to have a plan," and "I'll listen to my gut instinct to know if a girl is right for me."

There is a "You look like" opener that I love doing in foreign countries.

Me: "You look like you speak very good English."

Her: "I speak a little."

Me: "I can tell when someone speaks my language because of how their face looks."

Her: "Really?"

Me: "Sure, you have an English-speaking face. It's all in the cheeks. Are you an English teacher?"

Her: "I'm not."

Me: "Well, you probably could be. It's nice to meet someone who speaks English, since there aren't many English-speakers around here."

Her: "Where are you from?"

I could also have commented on her accent or asked questions about where she learned to speak English so well. This opener is a bit more complimentary than the others, but I find that foreign girls are insecure about their English, and if I boost their confidence, they will be more relaxed talking to me. Being an exotic man certainly helps, and you'll find that foreign girls will be much quicker to ask where you're from.

If you start with an opener that asks for help, you can stack on the "You look like" opener followed by "Why are you here?" These three conversational pieces will yield several minutes of chat if you remember to ramble and think of follow-up questions that dig deeper. While your approach doesn't have to follow this trajectory, it is nice to know they will provide you with a basic structure that prevents you from getting stuck early on. You can use them in any order. Mix and match the components often so that your game doesn't become rigid.

A girl in a night venue will ask personal questions much faster than during the day. Although this will help the conversation flow, you shouldn't read too much into her questions. If a girl asks you just one personal question during the day, you likely have enough interest to get her number, because she's asking when she's sober and unlikely to be feeling very sociable, but at a night venue she's highly sociable and probably slightly drunk. She will need to invest significantly more in the interaction before you should see her as a solid prospect.

The way you answer personal questions at night must also be different. During the day, it makes sense to give mostly straight answers, but at night your answers should be more optimized to build attraction. If she asks you what you do, give an answer like lumberjack, farmer, pencil maker, or whatever you think is humorous. Most men think they can convince girls of their value by telling them they have an important job, but this deflates attraction. You will exhibit higher value if you don't take the question seriously.

When she asks your age or where you're from, answer with "Guess" and make her work for the answer. If a girl says, "I don't want to play games, just tell me the answer," she's already commanding you to jump through hoops for her. Do not comply. She must bend to your will instead of the other way around. Maintain frame by saying, "If you want to know the answer, you'll have to guess."

All of the approach situations I've described so far involve you walking up to a girl while ignoring her female friends, but what if there is a man in her group and you don't think she's sleeping with him? You have two options: approach her when she becomes separated from the group, or approach the man, connect with him, and let him introduce you to the group. The first option is easier and more likely to lead to success, but the second option may be necessary if you are unable to approach the girl when she's alone, or if you're in a foreign country where a man may be impressed with you because you're a Westerner.

When I was in Siberia, my club strategy was to approach men. Being an American was such high value that they eagerly introduced me to the girls they knew, and even if they weren't with girls, they provided me with instant social proof. On the nights you roll solo, it's useful during an approach to point to a random guy you met twenty minutes earlier and say that he's your "friend," especially in a country such as Russia where social proof is far more important than in the United States.

Approach men by asking for help. Use the same lines you use on girls, such as, "Excuse me, do you know if there is another bar around here that is good?" You will find that men are more receptive than women when it comes to offering help. The funny thing is that men will instantly bite on your WICF bait if you drop it, which tells me that men are naturally more curious and engaging when they meet new people than women.

If you're approaching a man who is with girls, don't try to upstage him, because this will cause him to lose face and then not want to speak to you further. Defer to him and compliment him in some way so that he doesn't mark you as a threat to his social group. If he introduces you to everyone, ask him privately which girl is his so that you don't step on his toes. If you're respectful to a man in this way, you'll often find that he will help you hook up with the girl you like by calling off the cockblockers in the group.

The most luck you'll have in a night situation is when a girl comes to the venue alone, though this doesn't happen frequently. The second most ideal situation is when she's with two other girls, because they can talk amongst themselves after you approach your target. If she's with only one other girl, she may feel bad if her friend is left alone, and will not want to talk with you at length unless the friend finds something or someone to keep her busy.

When dealing with large all-female groups, be prepared to get viciously cockblocked by the obese "mother hen" who wants to ensure that all her friends stay single like her. Whether a girl is with one friend or ten, I always plan my approaches so that I have to talk to my target only. If a girl I approached introduces me to her friend or friends, I'll be sociable and friendly around them, but I won't be a clown for them.

My favorite night venue tactic is picking a prime spot at the bar and waiting for a girl I like to order a drink. I then move closer to her so that after she's paid for her drink, I'm within arm's reach. Assuming the bar is not crowded, I'll look at her and say my opener, but if it is crowded, I will triple tap first. The beauty of this strategy is that I select for girls who are drinking, alone, and giving me a proximity indicator. If her friends let her to go to the bar alone, the chances of me getting cockblocked are low. I try to identify girls who are sufficiently independent to make their own decisions about who they'll sleep with.

When popular venues get crowded, people will continually ask you to move from prime spots at the bar so they can order a drink. This used to make me angry, but I realized that positioning myself a few feet away from the bar gives me a better view of potential targets. Another option is to stand at the very end of the bar to more easily scan the entire scene.

If I'm out of position and a girl I like goes to the bar to get a drink, I move behind her, let her pay for a drink, then triple tap. It's important to wait until she's finished with the bartender or else she will be too distracted to talk to you. While you're waiting, don't let any other guy get in a better position than you, because he may be using the same tactic! If the approach doesn't go well, I move back into position and wait for the next girl.

It's a bad sign when girls aren't coming to the bar to get a drink. That means I'm in a place that either has no girls or the girls are not accessible for a standard bar approach. I will then try to find a spot away from the bar where I can do a triple tap, possibly on girls walking back from the bathroom. If that doesn't lead to any approaches, I can safely conclude that I'm not in a good venue and must find another. If other venues are also bad, I will walk the streets. On many nights, I don't go into any clubs or bars, and simply approach girls who are walking in the nightlife area alone. I then use an indirect opener, usually about finding a good bar or a place where I can eat food that is atypical for that time of night, such as ice cream or pancakes with maple syrup.

There are usually two different waves of activity at night. The first wave is composed of people who are out for dinner, happy hour, or casual drinks. The second wave is composed of people attending clubs and parties. To approach on the street at night, it's best to be outside *after* one of the waves. Every city is different, but in my current city the first wave ends at about 11pm. For one hour after that, girls are making their way home, and that's when I do a few approaches.

The second wave ends at about 3am and can be called "garbage hour." The girls will be sloppy and more inebriated. You will encounter many drunk sluts who want to vomit. In Scandinavia, I had a lot of success walking around at garbage hour when I venue-changed girls directly to my apartment. In Eastern Europe, I've had success after the first wave, when I moved her to one or two other bars before trying for my place.

What I like about night street game is that you meet looser girls without having to deal with night venues. The downside is that it's not much fun, especially if you're doing it alone when the weather is bad. It can also make you feel shady, because you'll start to notice that the other men walking around alone at night seem to be engaged in some sort of criminal activity like pimping or drug dealing. Make your night approaches gentle, slow, and indirect so that the girl doesn't think you're dangerous. I always start with "Excuse me" and maintain a good distance from her.

I'm sure you're beginning to notice that day game and night game share many transposable elements. Generally speaking, you'll present a less cocky and playful version of yourself during the day, but this rule isn't absolute and depends on the situation. The reason is that a girl who shows signs of attraction during the day is genuinely attracted to you, so you don't have to be as cocky and playful to maintain her attention. At night, that attraction may be influenced by alcohol and the more social environment that doesn't really signify actual interest, which means you must continue working to confirm whether or not it's real.

At night, there's also a better chance of getting a same-night lay, which we have to push for since it's the only way to deal with the horrendous flaking that happens when meeting girls after dark. Touching her will help you to reach that goal.

Touching

Touching is significantly more important at night (or on

dates) than it is when doing day approaches. During the night time, you'll want to touch early and often to show that you're not trying to be her friend, you're not intimidated by her, and you're a man who goes after what he wants. You also want to take advantage of her hornier state at night, since drinking and dancing serves as sexual foreplay for most girls.

My favorite place to touch a girl, particularly early on, is her forearm or upper arm. When I'm emphasizing an important point or making a joke, I touch her for a second on one of these areas. It's better to touch when you're talking than when she's talking, because she will not be conscious of what you're doing. The earlier you are in the interaction, the more you should touch her when making an important point. Later, when she starts touching you, you can touch at will. More intimate places to touch are the back of her hand and the side of her thigh.

There are no hard-and-fast rules on how often you should touch a girl, but your touches should increase in frequency and duration as time goes on. In the first hour you talk to a girl, you may touch her only once or twice, but in the last hour, before kissing, you may be touching a dozen times or more. The more extroverted a girl is, the more likely it will feel natural to touch her often.

The main benefit of touching is that it primes a girl for a kiss. The kiss is technically touching, so there's no better way to ramp up to it than by doing smaller touches beforehand. When she gets used to basic touches without rejecting them, she will be less likely to resist the "big" touch (a kiss). This is why you should take note if a girl calls you out after you have touched her. It could mean one of three things.

First, it could mean you touched too much too soon. This is common in the first hour of the interaction when she may not yet feel comfortable with you and your hands are all over the place. If she withdraws from your touching at this stage, dial it back a little and re-build with short touches on the arm.

The second reason is that she's testing to see whether or not you're a man. She may ask, "What are you doing?" Simply reply, "Touching you." If she allows you to keep touching her after such an answer, you passed her test.

The third reason is that she decided she doesn't want to be intimate with you at all. You may not find this out until you've talked to her for hours. If she removes your hand from her body, or orders you not to touch her anymore, and there's no playful vibe to her rejection, she's not interested and you should move on. If a girl doesn't let you touch her, she definitely won't let you kiss her.

A longer touch is putting your hand on her shoulder. If you want to emphasize a particularly long point, rest your hand on her shoulder and leave it there for as long as it takes you to make the point. Then remove your hand. Since the shoulder is not a sexual zone, a girl shouldn't object to your hand resting there, so if she squirms out of the way, you should interpret it as an indication of disinterest and take a step back by doing simpler touches. You can also do a prolonged touch on her upper arm with a loose grip, and you already know about the arm-in-arm move that you use when walking outside with her.

Another common move is putting your hand on her upper back when leading her to another spot in the venue or out the door, as if you're guiding her through. If the venue is crowded, it's worth putting out your hand for her to grab it so you can lead the way. A girl is more likely to grab your hand if you've done a few small touches beforehand. Remember that smaller touches pave the way for bigger touches, which pave the way for a kiss, which paves the way for sex. If you don't touch at all, a girl will feel awkward when you eventually try to kiss her, but if your touches are frequent, the kiss will feel like a foregone conclusion to her because the groundwork has been laid.

Yet another move is to rest your hand on her lower back or her hip, which you can do when standing close to her after she has warmly received your other touches. With this move, the hand remains on her for extended periods, as if you're marking your property. The hand is just a way to make her feel comfortable, to know you're there and will protect her from drunk guys. It also has the effect of moving your crotch closer to hers.

I learned touching by noticing how girls touched me. They

would first tap my arm lightly, usually when making a joke or light-hearted comment. If you are confused about exactly how to touch, look at how girls touch guys they like. The only problem is that girls will not touch you first unless they're drunk, because they are more afraid of rejection than men, so get the ball rolling by touching first. As a man, all escalation moves must be done first by you.

The only way to know how far you can get with touching is to monitor her feedback. If you touch her lightly and she doesn't bat an eye, you are free to touch her again shortly and to keep your hand there for slightly longer. If she squirms or resists, take a step back and resume with short touches on her arm. If she repeatedly rejects your touches, even after talking to you for a long time, and you have tried touching her shoulder, upper arm, or forearm, she is not interested in you.

Isolation

Earlier I discussed how taking a girl to multiple venues makes her feel like she's known you longer than she has. We can simulate this desirable effect *within* a venue by bouncing from one area of the venue to another.

If you're talking to a girl in a night venue, go from the bar to the dance floor to the other bar to the outdoor deck and then back to the dance floor. In addition to distorting time, moving around will separate her from the judgmental eyes of jealous friends and provide opportunities for touching as you guide her through the venue, either with your hand on her back or by holding her hand.

Suggest the first move after talking to her for at least ten minutes. If you're at a venue with a dance floor, ask her if she likes dancing. If she says yes, prime the dance by saying, "When a song I like comes on, we'll go dance." Then when you're ready to dance, and your drinks are almost finished, say, "I like this song, let's go dance." If she seems hesitant, gently grab her hand and lead her. The more crowded the venue, the more that grabbing her hand will seem natural.

It's not important to hold her hand the whole way, but take

note whether she squeezes your hand or holds it loosely. The harder the squeeze, the better you're doing, though she's unlikely to squeeze if for more than a few seconds if not much time has passed since you met her. As the interaction continues, you'll notice that she'll hold your hand longer when you guide her around the venue. Just don't overdo it and try to touch her hand constantly, because this can be perceived as needy instead of a sign of confidence.

Dancing is a great opportunity to touch a girl's back, arms, and thighs, but don't go overboard and act like you've never danced with a girl before by trying to make love to her right there on the dance floor. A confident man touches in a way that matches the developing connection while expecting some reciprocity, but you need to take a step back if you're touching her at every opportunity and she's stepping away from you. You want to show that it's not a big deal to be interacting with her.

While dancing, move in close for a minute and withdraw a step or two, and then move in closer before withdrawing again. If you've been dancing for a while, and she's still reluctant to touch you, give her permission. Grab her hand, put it on your shoulder, and say, "It's okay if you want to touch me." The frequency and duration of her touches should then increase.

After you've been dancing for a while, lead her back to the bar or another part of the venue. It is important that you don't ask her what she wants to do. Simply tell her, "Let's go to so and so." If she says no, relax a bit before trying again later. You will need to strike a balance between leading and showing that you are considerate of her preferences based on the feedback she's giving you.

If you're at a venue that doesn't have a dance floor, try to move her to other parts of the bar to "check out" something you noticed. If the bar is small and there's no room to move around, stay where you are and have a long chat. When the energy of the interaction dies down, suggest going somewhere else.

Changing locations within a venue is also a great way to test her attraction for you. Upon meeting someone new, things are most exciting at the beginning when a man and a woman put their best feet forward to present themselves as the ideal sexual partner. If a girl made a small request of you at this stage, such as asking you to wait a minute while she has a quick dialogue with her girlfriends, your instinct is to comply, because you don't want to destroy what could be something great, so it's definitely a bad sign when she refuses a small request to go to the bar to get a drink with you or to have a quick dance. She's potentially *destroying* this new interaction by not complying. This can only mean that she's not that attracted to you.

If a girl doesn't pass your "compliance test," she definitely won't block out hours of her time to go on a date. You need her compliance with small requests before you can get her to say yes to the bigger ones.

The compliance tests I've mentioned so far—moving to another part of the bar or going for a dance—will usually come at least ten minutes after meeting her. You can start even earlier with a tiny compliance test where you suggest moving just a few feet away: "Hey let's stand right here." Or there might be chairs near you: "Hey let's sit down for a second." The tiny compliance test is not required, but it does tell you where you stand with a girl before ten minutes have passed. If she doesn't comply with a small request, you'll know for sure that she's not ready to move forward.

Whenever I get non-compliance, I continue talking to her for some time before trying my compliance test again. If she refuses a second time, I can safely assume that she is not attracted to me but enjoys my entertainment. I will then withdraw from the conversation if there are other prospects in the venue. I may try a third time if she is shy and I think she needs more time to open up.

A girl giving you her phone number is actually one of the smallest compliance tests there is because it requires practically no effort on her part. If you get a girl's number before she passed a few compliance tests, you'll have no idea if she's serious about going on a date with you or not, but if you get her number after she's complied with a handful of tests, your chances are much higher. For some girls, banging you in the club bathroom or a nearby apartment involves less compliance than meeting you again for a date.

Compliance tests can also be done during the day. If you approach a girl on a crowded street that has a lot of foot traffic, try this test: “Hey let’s stand over there to get away from the crowd.” Or there might be a nearby bench and you want to sit down because your “feet are tired” from walking so much. I avoid doing compliance tests too soon before I have had a chance to establish some post-minute attraction, but it’s important to do them starting at the ten-minute mark. Asking her to sit or move somewhere is the beginning of a process that eventually leads to her showing up for a date, kissing, coming back to your apartment, and sleeping with you. Compliance tests train her to say yes to you while providing you with key information about exactly where you stand.

It may take some time before you devise a repertoire of compliance tests based on your approach style and the type of venues you frequent. As long as you understand that a compliance test should cause a girl to put in increasing amounts of effort over time, you won’t go wrong. It’s also fair game to ask her to perform small favors, such as watching your drink while you go to the bathroom or retrieving an item for you from the bar. I’m an independent man and can take care of myself, but I ask girls for small things to keep their investment in me high and also to let me know where I stand, especially before sex.

Kissing

If you lay the proper touching and compliance groundwork, kissing will have a low chance of rejection. When a girl passes your compliance tests and moves around the venue with you while accepting your touches, not only will she expect you to kiss her, but she will *want* you to do so. Going in for the kiss will only feel scary if you try it out of the blue without having touched or done any compliance tests beforehand. Since we don’t take random stabs in the dark, but gradually escalate using touching and compliance, we should know precisely when she’s ready to be kissed.

The number-one way to know that a girl is ready to be kissed is if she doesn't move her head back when you move yours closer to hers while face-to-face. If a girl moves her head back when I put mine a foot (30 centimeters) away, she's nowhere ready to being kissed. If she moves it back only when I get three inches (8 centimeters) away, she should be ready within thirty minutes. I like to do a "fly-by" where I lock my eyes with hers and get close to see how she responds, often while placing at least one of my hands on her hip or lower back.

Let's say I've been talking to a girl in a club for an hour. We've danced a couple times, moved to another part of the club, touched a bit, and I've bought a round of drinks to keep the fun going. Now we're standing by the bar with my hand on her lower back, which she does not object to (if she did, I'd take a step back and try again later). At this point, there are more breaks in the conversation that I use to my advantage by holding eye contact to increase the feeling of intimacy. I suspect she's ready to be kissed, so during a pause in the conversation, I do a fly-by where I get within six inches (15 centimeters) of her face and smile. She does not move her head back, a good sign. Five minutes later, during another silent moment, I do another fly-by where I lock eye contact and move in close, only three inches from her face. This time she giggles and moves her head back. She knows I'm about to kiss her, but is not quite ready.

I have a few options now. I can hit the dance floor with her and turn her on further with additional touching, move her to a different part of the venue, or stay put and do another fly-by later that is also three inches away. Since many girls don't like to be kissed in front of other people, I will pick the option that offers us the most privacy. Once I've done that, I will repeat the fly-by.

Three inches is pretty close, about the length of your index finger. If a girl allows you to get that close to her, she can be kissed. With your heads frozen three inches apart, you can either bridge the gap and kiss her or withdraw to tease her until a later fly-by when you finally do so. When you successfully kiss her, keep it short to maintain sexual tension. You can start to ramp up the passion to reach peak intensity when you're in a bedroom.

I estimate that 25% of girls don't like to be kissed for the first time in public, so you may have to wait until gaining more privacy. Also, a more traditional girl will want you to move way slower. She will not drink much (if at all) or allow you to get too comfortable with touching her. Whatever the case, go as far as you can until you hit a wall of resistance where she rejects a move *three times*. For example, a girl might not want you to touch her waist or lower back. You try three times over the course of an hour, but she resists each time. That's the wall for the night. Or perhaps a girl won't take your hand when you move her around the venue. You try three times and she declines each time, so that's the wall. It could be because she has a predetermined rule of how far she will go with a guy she's just met.

Whatever early resistance a girl is putting up, try to overcome it three times to confirm that you have indeed hit a wall. You can work within the space enclosed by her wall, get her number and move on to other girls (in a part of the venue where she can't see you), spend time getting to know her, or eject completely. The right option will depend on your attraction for the girl, what your goals are, and the intent behind her resistance. If you like a girl and think a connection will develop, work within her wall and aim to bypass it the next time you see her. If you simply want to bang her once, it may be best to eject.

Understand that giving up on escalating after three tries is only a guideline. You should get three rejections at a particular step of a solid interaction before you can even *think* about giving up. If I'm horny and my goal is a same-night bang, I may keep going until she walks away, though I still space my attempts so that I don't look like a desperate sex hound. On several occasions, I've had more than a dozen rejections on my fly-bys before I could finally kiss the girl. There is no way to know exactly whether or not you should give up, but generally, the longer the interaction, the more no's you can accept.

If I've been talking to a girl for only five minutes, and she doesn't comply with my tiny "Let's stand over here" test, I may eject right then, but if I've been talking to a girl for three hours and she pulls away from my kiss fly-by three times while still touching me intimately, I won't give up. The more you feel invested in an interaction, and the more she doesn't seem bothered by your attempts, the more likely you should stay, but you don't want to appear desperate by constantly trying moves without her reciprocation. If you try to kiss her a dozen times over the course of two hours, she may see you as aggressive yet confident, but if you try a dozen times within twenty minutes, she may see you as a creep. As long as you space out your attempts and allow her to put in effort and reciprocate between those attempts, you're not spitting bad game.

Once you've kissed her, don't act like you're falling in love by touching and kissing every second. Play it cool. Expect her to reciprocate and start initiating touches and kisses. Don't completely abandon having conversation—it's still quite early in the interaction and she wants an interesting, attractive man, not one who only wants to grab and kiss her.

How would a man who has no trouble meeting girls act if he kissed one? He would be pleased, no doubt, but it wouldn't cause him to think he had achieved something great. The look on his face would indicate that he's relaxed, not excited. A guideline of how to act after the kiss is to not appear one degree happier or more excited than the girl. If she perceives that you are far more excited than she is, she may lose interest.

If she has to suddenly leave and you didn't have enough time to use the fly-by technique to kiss her on the lips, you can try to weasel one in. Face her and ask for a goodbye kiss on the cheek. After she gives it, point to your other cheek. If she resists, say, "Where I come from, you have to give a man two cheek kisses." After she gives you the second one, say, "I have to give you two cheek kisses too." Pretend this is an important part of your culture. At this point, the girl will know you are playing a sneaky game, but it's likely that she will find it amusing. Slowly give her one cheek kiss, then a second, then stay close to her face for an extra second before giving a third kiss on her lips. I find that if a girl gives you two cheek kisses and allows you to give her two, there is a good chance she will allow a lip kiss.

Many men want to rush to get to the kiss, thinking it will speed up the process of getting a girl into bed, but the correlation on this is weak. Many girls who let you kiss them fairly soon in the interaction are hard to get into bed, and many girls who resist your kisses will have sex with you easily. Whatever the case, don't skip the important steps of touching and compliance. You may sneak in a kiss by tricking her, but it won't necessarily help you to get the lay. By patiently going through all the steps, you build a foundation of attraction that carries all the way to the bedroom.

Same-Night Bang

It would be great if you met a pretty girl in a bar, had a long conversation with her that ended with a kiss, got her phone number, and then arranged a date for a few days later. Unfortunately, the likelihood of this scenario is shrinking, resulting in huge amounts of frustration for just about every man who meets girls at night. Here is the *worst-case* reality: if you get phone numbers from girls you don't kiss, you'll need ten to eighteen numbers to get one date. If you're getting numbers from girls you kissed, you'll need between five and ten. If you're banging girls on the same night, you'll need between two and six. I guarantee you will go through periods where you see worst-case numbers.

Many men think their game sucks because their rate of converting interactions to dates is low, but they're actually doing better than average. Since the dating environment is deteriorating, and girls are getting more unattractive and masculine, your conversion rate may decline even as your game improves. The only way you'll be able to significantly bump up your conversion rate is to have exceedingly high value in a particular venue or within a social circle.

To mitigate the conversion problem, I strongly recommend you go for the bang on the same night you meet a girl. This will not be practical in most situations, especially if you live far from the venue where you meet girls, but the ideal scenario is to meet a girl, spend a few hours with her, try to kiss her, invite her to your place, and move things into the bedroom. If you liked having sex with her, get her number to plan a date. If you don't go for same-night bangs, you'll end up putting in dozens of hours of work for little gain. Without the prospect of the same-night bang, which I am ready to go for with every girl I meet at night, night game wouldn't be worth it because of the maddeningly high flake rate.

Unless a girl you meet says she "never" goes out at night, and this is the first time she's done so in months because of a special occasion, you have to assume that she's a typical girl who, even after kissing you and giving you her number, has little intention of seeing you again. By the time girls are 20 years old, most of them have had a one-night stand or two under their belt, so if she likes a man, she is *fully capable* of quickly going all the way.

Don't be deceived into thinking that a girl is special or good just because she's playing hard to get. Night venues are where people meet to drink alcohol and find sex partners, so her presence in one means that she is, at a minimum, open to meeting an attractive man and going home with him. Unless she's impossibly shy or socially awkward, assume she is that type of girl.

Only by having sex with a girl on the first night, or coming close to it, will she begin to set you apart from the men she merely gave her number to. If you can't stomach the idea of trying to have sex with a girl you've known for only a few hours, and think the whole thing is immoral, night game in venues that serve alcohol is not for you, and you should stick to day game where you have a chance of meeting girls who never go to bars or clubs.

The same-night bang comes into play after you kiss a girl or come close to it. There's much debate on whether or not you should try to kiss before getting a girl home (this question also arises with regular dates). The main argument for not kissing beforehand is that it doesn't make her think that sex is going to happen, increasing the chance she will come over, but my experience shows that kissing before you get her home saves you from wasting *a lot of time* on girls who don't really want to have sex. If I take a girl to my place before we've kissed, she may just want to hang out, which has happened to me countless times, but if I kiss her beforehand, my chances of sex are much greater.

It's extremely frustrating when you can't have sex with a girl you've taken home after investing a large amount of time, so for a same-night bang scenario, I highly recommend you go for the kiss beforehand. Frustration may turn into anger if you spend all night with a girl only to find that she doesn't want to do anything. If she doesn't want to kiss me at a venue, and it's not because she doesn't like kissing in public, I'd get her number and move on to another girl.

At this stage of the interaction, logistics become important. If you don't live near the venue, you may create resistance in her mind to coming over. The further away your place is, the more a girl *really* has to like you to come over. Ideally, your place should be a five-to-ten-minute walk from the venue, something I ensure when I'm staying in a foreign country. The worst scenario is when you don't have your own place at all, such as when living with parents. In this case, you'll have to invite yourself to her place and get the job done there.

Keep in mind that you always have the option of changing venues, a useful way of getting her away from her friends or talking in a quieter setting, but I find that venue changes are largely unnecessary at night if you were able to move her around the venue where you met. I'd change the venue only if I could not escalate and need a better environment to do so.

Men experience dozens of different logistical problems when it comes to getting laid, so it will be impossible for me to offer individual solutions for them all. This is where you will have to use your own ingenuity to overcome any barrier. When I was 26, I lived in my father's basement and was unable to bring girls back. I also didn't have a car, so I'd take a bus and then the subway to hit the city. I would focus my game efforts entirely on getting to a girl's place. Because this happened often, I would go out with my contact lens case and mini-toothbrush to increase my comfort. When a guy tells me that he can't approach girls because he lives with his parents, I know he doesn't want to get laid badly enough, and is just using it as an excuse to not even try.

Let's look at a scenario where you have a private room fairly near the venue. First, you have to allay her concern that you're strongly expecting sex with the "I don't expect sex" routine. Say the following about fifteen minutes before you try to invite her to your place:

> "By the way, there is something I want to tell you. If I ever invite you to my apartment for a drink, whether today, next week, or next year, I don't expect sex. I don't want you to think that just because we're going to my place, I expect it to happen and you have to do it. But if you do want it, I may be able to help you out."

This routine increases the chance that she will come over if she is unsure whether she wants to have sex with you. Your hope is that, at some point while in your place, she will have the desire to sleep with you and then vigorously act on that desire. This routine may be overkill for party girls who are whispering sexual comments in your ear while at the bar, but I have never found it to hurt, and it has the additional advantage of showing that you're going with the flow and aren't desperate to sleep with her.

At least fifteen minutes after doing the routine, go for the invite.

> Me: "So how about we go somewhere else?"
>
> Her: "Where?"
>
> Me: "We can go to my place and relax. I have some drinks and good music. I live only eight minutes away."

If she says no, ask why to see what her objection is. It could be that she can't leave her friends, or some other reason that doesn't have anything to do with you. Try to resolve the objection, which will usually mean more waiting. If her objection is that she doesn't know you well, refer to your earlier statement about not expecting sex. If she still says no, lay off and try again in 30 to 60 minutes, or move to another venue entirely. Sell the move by saying the new venue is "cool" or "interesting." When you ask her a second time to come to your place, give her a new reason to say yes.

Me: "How's your energy? Are you tired?"

Her: "A little, but I'm okay."

Me: "How about we go to my place and chill a bit? It will be easier to talk there."

If she still says no, you can try again later or immediately come up with a new reason: "I think it would be fun, because I have some new music" or "I bought a really nice bottle of wine from Italy that we can try." If you still get a firm no, you can wait before trying again or consider getting her phone number.

You don't have to do the "I don't expect sex" routine if you plan on going to her place, because the assumption is that she can kick you out any time she wants. This suggests that when you go to a girl's place, she has more room to call the shots, although the advantage is that you can leave whenever you like. When she's at your place, that power is shifted to you, meaning she has to behave if she doesn't want to be "rejected" by being kicked out.

I find it more advantageous if a girl comes to my place, especially if alcohol is involved. Some girls get rude and discourteous when they're intoxicated. Having the ability to insinuate that you'll kick her ass out if she isn't lady-like is a strong way to get her to behave. I can also control more variables in my place, such as the music and lighting, which allows for a more flawless seduction, instead of having to deal with her messy room, shabby furniture, or annoying cats.

If you want to go to her place, use the tactic of wanting to get something to eat or drink elsewhere because you're tired or bored of the current venue. Before the attempt, it's a good idea to find out her living arrangements. If it turns out that she's staying with a friend, you can try to sleep with her on her friend's couch, something I've done multiple times. It's not as comfortable, but I won't let a logistical problem get in the way of having sex. It's also helpful to ask how she got to the venue, so you know what arrangements you need to make to get to her place. It's rare that a girl will have driven, so you may have to use a taxi.

> Me: "Are you tired of here yet? How about we go somewhere else?"
>
> Her: "Like where?"
>
> Me: "I like to go somewhere quieter that is easier to talk. Do you have any drinks at your place? We can relax for a bit before calling it a night."

If you're hungry or don't want to drink anymore, ask if she has any food. If she doesn't mind you coming over, she will give a small inventory of what she has. Your response can be simple: "That sounds good, let's do it." You can then begin leaving by saying goodbye to friends, finishing your drinks, getting your coats, and so on. Don't rush or be pushy, but definitely focus on getting her out the door instead of buying another round or aimlessly hanging around.

If she's leaning towards a no, she will say she has no food or her place is messy. Respond by digging a bit more to find exactly what kind of food or drink she has. If she has at least one acceptable item, such as crackers, you can say, "Crackers are perfect. I don't care that your house is messy, I'm a guy." If she's interested in you, she'll accept your answer and you can wind down activity at the venue to head to her place. If she's still resistant, lay off for 30 to 60 minutes before trying again.

It's possible that her resistance has nothing to do with not having food or her place being messy, but because you have not put in enough groundwork or face time. Switching venues may then be a good move, especially to one where you can dance and be more physical. When a girl puts up any sort of wall, I lay off and take it easy for a while, assuming there will be an opportunity to try again later, but if it's a do-or-die moment where either I close the deal right then or we say goodbye, I'm more aggressive and insist on a number of consecutive rejections before I accept the final no. As long as a girl doesn't walk away from you after a rejection, you're still in the game and shouldn't be discouraged.

I have given you a number of guidelines when it comes to timing, but in the middle of a seduction I go by general feel without staring at the clock. Always focus on the girl and the responses she's giving you instead of the time. If you're counting down the minutes and are too goal-oriented, you'll be inside your own head instead of getting into hers. Understand that if you're genuinely enjoying the time you're spending with a girl, she is probably enjoying it as well, making rejection less likely at each escalation stage. Responding according to the unique interaction you're experiencing should always trump following the guidelines I have shared with you.

Another way to get a girl to your place is to use the "Let's go for a walk" move, which works when you live within fifteen minutes' walking distance of the venue (the closer, the better). The benefit of this move is that you can get a girl to your front door, or close to it, without her thinking about the fact that you want her to enter your place. I use this move to get girls out of a venue when I suspect that suggesting a venue change would fail. Sell it as a short walk.

Here's how I do it: "So why don't we go for a walk? This place kind of sucks, and I could use some fresh air. Tell your friends you'll be back in half an hour." What's great about this move is that thirty minutes can turn into two hours because it's easy for her to message her friends that she got "stuck" somewhere and won't be returning. It's also easier for you, because you are asking her to make only a small commitment (a short walk) to which she's unlikely to object, whereas if you asked her to come to your place, she may perceive it as a large commitment and strongly resist.

If she resists going for a walk, find out why and try to sell her an additional reason, no matter how silly. In my second attempt,

I may add, "The mood on the street is good at this hour, and we can get a little exercise." Once she agrees, and you get her outside, start walking to your place at a slow to medium pace. When she asks where you're going, say, "We're going to a place where the drinks are tasty, the music is great, and the seating is comfortable." When you reach the front of your building, say, "We're here." She will look confused, so add, "I live here. How about we grab a quick drink and then head back to the bar?" If she says no, start to sell the cool things in your apartment, one at a time, after each no. Since this is a do-or-die moment, don't give up until you receive at least *five* clear no's. Below are some examples that give you a general idea of how to persist.

After the first no: "I want to play a song from my favorite band to see if you like them. The band is very important to me."

After the second no: "I also have some pictures I want to show you that are not on my phone. I think you'll like them."

After the third no: "I recently bought a new sofa, but my friend said it's ugly and I should throw it out. I could use an opinion on it from a girl with good taste."

After the fourth no: "My place is great to relax. Just because you're coming upstairs, doesn't mean we'll have sex. We don't have much time anyway since we're going back to the bar soon."

After the fifth no: "Okay, well how about we just have a cup of tea? I could use a warm drink right now."

As long as she's standing there and not turning to walk away, I keep inventing random reasons for her to come inside. After each reason, I move towards the building door and motion for her to come in, but I *never* physically pull or grab her—she has to come on her own volition.

One problem with this move is that her friends may incessantly call or text to find out where she is. Instruct her to tell her friends that she'll be back in twenty minutes. If her friends get too annoying, tell her to put her phone on silent.

For same-night bangs, you'll have to develop a customized solution based on your unique logistics, but the main point is not to have a goal of getting phone numbers, because in most cases, a number won't go anywhere. If you intend on running night game, plan for a kiss followed by a venue change to a home. Night venues are great for fostering fast intimacy while both of you are under the influence of alcohol and lust, but they're poor for arranging future meetings.

Even though my same-night bang technique is aggressive, understand that we're simply allowing a girl to do what she really wants, and we always get her consent since she must agree to each stage of the escalation. We may be heavy-handed with our verbal persuasion, but we never force her physically.

Modern girls are extremely comfortable with having random and commitment-free sex with men they're attracted to, so don't flatter yourself by thinking that you are creating sex out of thin air. If you had sex with a girl after many rounds of verbal persistence, you did not really convince her to have sex as much as nudge her into doing what she wanted to do all along.

I used to think of myself as a magician pulling doves out of hats when there were no doves to begin with. I now see myself as more of a chef who combines various ingredients on hand to produce a tasty dish that needed a touch of my talent to come into being. Use the ingredients of the atmosphere created by a bar, club, café, or street corner, plus your game and her personality, to create sex. When you see yourself as a chef, you will be aware of raising the seduction's cooking temperature, flexible when using the ingredients that are on hand, and appreciative of the final sex result that stems from your knowledge and effort.

It is a grave mistake to only get a number from a girl who is putting out signs that she wants to get sexual, such as accepting most of your escalation moves or touching you a lot. Another reliable indication that a girl is considering a fast sexual encounter is when she asks, "Where do you live?" A girl who wants to know this is trying to set up the logistics for the lay. If you don't try to sleep with a girl on the same night when she's putting out strong signs, she may feel rejected and move on to another guy.

A lot of what determines casual sex is being in the right place at the right time, so I make sure to take advantage of good luck. Even if a girl doesn't ask where you live, stick to the game plan and follow my guideline of trying to change the venue to a private room after you kiss.

On the way to your place or hers, I recommend you keep up a light conversation so that she doesn't start thinking too deeply about whether or not she should have sex with you. Definitely do not tell her how you're going to fuck the shit out of her or anything related to sex, because she may start to feel like a slut and chicken out. Instead, recall the night out by sharing observations about the venue you were just in, or make comments about the neighborhood you're walking through. Keep it simple without allowing prolonged silences. If you're traveling on foot, I highly recommend you do the arm-in-arm move and sustain it for most of the walk.

A common problem is that men want to rush an interaction with girls who are not complying with their tests or giving them affection. They are so focused on the goal of sex that they don't seem to care that the girl is not interested in them or their game. They fall into the trap of doing routine after routine without allowing the girl to show interest or compliance. When you learn any type of game system or model, you may be tempted to forget about the individual girl. She shouldn't be a mere afterthought.

You'll gain little satisfaction from your interactions if you treat girls like a video game that needs to be beaten using a special code or move. You will soon become addicted to the achievement of having sex instead of the overall interaction and lose sight of why you got into game in the first place: to intimately connect with women.

No matter how advanced your game may be and how experienced you are, at the end of the day a girl *has to want to be with you.* She has to like you and she has to imagine having sex with you. If this genuine interest isn't in place, which a girl will know for sure within thirty minutes of any interaction (often far sooner), no move or trick will work, and you've missed the point of what game is about. I'm not telling you this so that you will give up when you encounter resistance, since a girl who likes you deeply will still put up barriers so you won't think she's a slut, but so that you will focus on her and the interaction instead of rigidly relying on memorized routines and rules.

Find a girl you think is attractive, talk to her, enjoy her essence, and run the game required to take the interaction to the sex stage, one enjoyable step at a time. Touch her, smell her, listen to her, let her be girly, and allow the lust you have for her lead to pleasure. When you're talking to a girl you don't like, and you just want to put your dick in her, you'll have to fake it all the way through. You'll be like a female stripper who has to pretend she likes dancing on the lap of a drunk customer. If you want to rack up a lot of notches, I hope you're a good actor, because you'll have no choice but to sleep with many girls you don't care about, but if you want to naturally connect with a handful of girls, you can use nuggets of game knowledge and just about be yourself.

I'll talk about what to do when you get a girl in a home later. Now we have to retrace our steps and talk about the consolation prize of getting a phone number.

Getting A Phone Number

There are two situations when you should get a girl's number. The first is when you run out of time, either because she is leaving the venue or you have to leave to catch another appointment. You can get her number in the same way you would during the day: "You seem cool, how about we meet for a drink some time?" She'll probably give you at least a lukewarm yes, and then you can save her number in your phone.

You can also ask for the date in a more direct way than during the daytime by making a firm plan: "You seem cool, how about we meet tomorrow night at eight for a drink?" If she says no without counter-offering, it's unlikely she will accept a date when you text her later. I find that asking a girl to commit to a specific time is a great way to test whether or not she is going to flake, and sometimes I will finalize our plans right then and there, getting her number only in case there's a cancellation.

The longer you've been talking to her, the worse your chances if she decides to leave with her friends. If you've been talking for two hours and are getting close to the kiss, and she decides to go home or bounce to another bar, how serious is her interest? If she has a deep interest, won't she tell her friends to go without her so that she can keep talking to you? In cases where I've gotten a same-night lay, the girl at some point had to choose me over her friends.

It's even worse when a girl ends the conversation without leaving the venue. If she says she's going to dance or use the bathroom, but doesn't return to you, it means her interest level is low. When it's high, a girl will ask where you'll be or tell you that she'll be right back, and then she'll follow through. And if a girl wants to dance, she'll invite you to dance with her. If a girl doesn't come back, she's rejecting you. Approach another girl.

The second situation I get a phone number is when a girl has shown strong interest but I'm not able to push the interaction further. This usually occurs in foreign countries where one-night stands are not as common and I hit a wall when I go for the kiss. Another possibility is that she really wants to spend more time with me, but she can't get away from friends. As long as she showed strong interest, and was fully dedicated to talking to me, I would get her number.

The wall you hit before settling for her number should be high, such as when you go for the kiss or suggest changing venues. If a girl rejects me when I throw up a minor compliance test like coming to the bar with me, her interest level is low, and I won't bother getting her number even if she seems friendly, but if the rejection comes at the kiss stage or after talking to her for hours, her interest level is higher and I will get her number only once I'm certain that I can't escalate the interaction any further that night.

Tactics

Girls With Boyfriends

It's not uncommon for a girl to tell you that she has a boyfriend when you touch her, give her a compliance test, ask for her number, or show some interest by asking personal questions. Should you continue pursuing or should you eject? This is a tough question to answer, morally and strategically.

I have often reasoned, "If she doesn't bang me, she'll bang someone else," although it's possible that I swept her off her feet in a way that only one in a million men could. At a minimum, by sleeping with her, I am interfering with another man's ability to have a relationship with her, or I'm letting her use me to pervert that relationship. Therefore, I cannot justify my action morally, and I will leave it up to you to decide whether or not it's something you want to do.

Getting the phone numbers of girls who have boyfriends is extremely foolhardy because of the astronomical flake rate. If you are unable to seal the deal on the same day or night you met, your chances of sleeping with her will be quite low, especially since she'll want to justify cheating only under the guise of "It was spontaneous and just happened." But it didn't "just happen" if she had to plan to meet you somewhere at a certain time.

Many of the girls you'll sleep with won't tell you that they have a boyfriend. If you are in bed with a girl who has to take a private call, or seems stressed when replying to text messages, she's probably communicating with a man who would regard her as his girlfriend.

The earlier a girl tells you she has a boyfriend, the greater the likelihood she will be faithful to him. If she tells you that she has a boyfriend a few minutes into the conversation, she is highly unlikely to cheat. If she tells you when you first start touching her, she is somewhat unlikely to cheat. If she tells you when you're about to kiss, when your faces are only a few inches apart, she is likely to cheat. If she tells you after you've kissed and are holding hands, she is highly likely to cheat.

If you still want to pursue a girl after she's told you she has a boyfriend, the best move is to reply with a statement that indicates you don't think it's a big deal. I would say, "I don't want to hear about your problems" or "It's okay, I assume that every girl I meet has an obedient dog." Show that her having a boyfriend will not interfere with your plans because you're having fun and enjoying the night, or simply pretend you didn't hear what she said. You can then proceed with your normal game.

If she gives you more resistance than you typically encounter, you should take it as an indication that she will not put out. If a girl with a boyfriend is going to cheat, she won't make things significantly harder after you've brushed off her boyfriend announcement. On the other hand, she may be even easier than a girl who's single if she is deeply unsatisfied with her relationship, and may have gone out with the explicit goal of getting banged by a man she thinks will provide her with something that her boyfriend cannot.

I've reached a point where I immediately eject when a girl tells me she has a boyfriend before we've become physical. Otherwise, I end up wasting my time. If she tells me when we're close to the kissing stage, I will proceed. There are exceptions, but it's easier to have sex with a girl who is horny because she hasn't been laid in a while than with one who got laid within the past few days.

A girl who may be worth pursuing is one who is *about* to dump her boyfriend. This girl will usually conceal her relationship status and act like she's single, but she will still need a lot of comfort over several dates before she switches over to you. In that case, it's helpful if you share the same social or work circle to ensure repeated contact.

You can try pursuing girls with boyfriends to evaluate whether or not it's right for you. One benefit is that it provides you with information about what makes girls cheat, which can be useful when you have a girlfriend. Beware if you see your girlfriend engaging in the same behavior as girls who are prone to cheating on their boyfriends.

Buying Girls Drinks

Buying a girl drinks is logical when you're on a first date, because she's putting in the effort to get to know you. It's unlikely she'll take you for a ride by consuming the drinks and then immediately leaving. Things are a bit trickier when it comes to buying drinks when you're in a night venue and haven't known a girl for more than half an hour. You're not sure if she's genuine about wanting to meet a new man or simply wants free drinks.

If you decide never to buy girls drinks, you will miss out on opportunities to separate a girl from her friends by accompanying her to the bar, and as you already know, alcohol loosens up a girl, allowing her to act on her innermost desires. My advice is simple: buy drinks for girls only once you're having an *established* conversation and want to escalate further. If you want to buy her a drink because you think it'll help your game, go ahead and do so, but don't buy one at the start of a conversation in an attempt to impress her with your money or give her a reason merely to have a chat with you. In night venues, it's a natural part of the scene to buy drinks for the people you're having fun with, whether it's your male friends or a girl you want to have sex with.

My favorite isolation move is moving a girl from a random part of the venue to the bar. I say, "How about you come to the bar with me so we can get a drink?" For the price of a drink, I can now have a one-on-one interaction with her away from distractions.

One warning sign to look out for is if a girl *asks* you to buy her a drink. This shows that she has low attraction and respect for you, because if she really liked you, she wouldn't jeopardize the interaction by making demands so early on. It's rare that the conversation can be salvaged at that point, but you can call her out on her disrespectful request by saying, "Are you the kind of girl who just wants to drink for free all night?" Hopefully, she will apologize or explain that you misunderstood her request.

It's okay if you don't drink at all in night venues. Simply order soda water with lime, which most girls will assume is a vodka drink or a gin and tonic. Bow out of doing shots with an excuse such as "I'm taking a break from drinking" or "I'm driving tonight." I find that not drinking in night venues doesn't hurt the flow or speed of an interaction, because so many other people in the venue are drinking that the girl will consume anyway. The situation is a little different on dates, where she won't drink if it's clear you're not drinking. The consequence for dating is that the girl will have to feel a real connection with you instead of just being horny in the moment, and you'll need an extra date or two before getting laid.

Cockblocking

It's guaranteed that you'll have problems with cockblockers, who are usually a girl's female friends. They will do everything in their power to prevent a hook-up from happening because they are jealous of their friend or don't like you for some reason. The earlier the cockblock comes, particularly within five minutes, the fewer options you have for salvaging the interaction. In a pick-up's early stages, you have not built enough attraction and the girl has not invested much time in you for her to go against the wishes of her friends, so if she doesn't make a token effort to ignore the cockblock and continue the conversation, the approach is lost and you should walk away.

After a cockblock, your instinct will be to get mad or angry, but this is pointless because it just sours your mood and delays your next approach. You must accept that blocking is a part of game, especially at night. Acceptance will be harder when the cockblock comes after you've been with a girl for an hour or two, but this will repeatedly happen to you.

If we analyze the psychology of the cockblocker, we find that she gets very little attention or respect from men. She's like the jealous, aging mother of a beautiful teenage daughter. Giving her a little attention and respect goes a long way to turning her into a wingman instead of a blocker. This may be hard to do if the blocker is ugly and fat, but these are the sacrifices we must make to the game gods.

The first step towards neutralizing a cockblocker is identifying her. You'll know you have one on your hands if a girl often interrupts the conversation you're having with your prospect to "check" on her, or happens to be obscenely ugly and have a bitchy face. On the other hand, if your prospect's friends are occupied with other men or are having fun by themselves, they are unlikely to block. A good guideline is if you sense a watchful presence. If they are close by and monitoring the interaction, you should assume that a block is coming.

Be respectful to the suspected cockblock leader by politely asking her permission to move your girl to another area in the venue, as if she were her mother. First, get your girl to agree with the move. After she agrees, go to the "mother hen" and say, "Your friend is being nice to me. Do you mind if I take her to the dance floor?" Another way to say it: "Your friend is cool. You mind if I borrow her for a minute to go upstairs?" The friend will almost always say, "It's up to her." Then you reply, "She said yes, so we'll be back soon."

Once in a while, the friend will be a total cunt and treat you like dog shit even though you were respectful to her. You can be sterner to make her hesitant about continuing her anti-social behavior. Say, "Are you her mom? Why are you treating your friend like a child? This doesn't seem like a healthy friendship. We're just having a good time." Then look at your girl and insist that she comes with you "for just a couple of minutes." If she refuses, the block was successful and there's not much more you can do.

Another way to prevent a cockblock is to inoculate your girl against it. If she agreed to at least one isolation move, and the blocker is still lurking around, insinuate that her friend is trying to tear you two apart because she's jealous.

Me: "Who is the girl you're with tonight?"

Her: "She's my good friend."

Me: "She's looking over here a lot."

Her: "Yeah, she's just worried about me."

Me: "It looks like jealousy to me. She's not talking to a cool guy and doesn't look happy that you are. I think she's going to sabotage our interaction soon because she looks very jealous."

Her: "No, she's not like that."

Me: "Okay. It's just common that some girls don't want their friends to meet anyone if they don't meet someone."

If the cockblock comes, but your girl defended against it because she likes you, continue with the inoculation: "If she was talking to a guy she liked right now, would she have done that? I'm glad I'm not a girl. Guys don't do that to each other." The purpose of the inoculation is to reframe her friend as an enemy who is preventing her from experiencing love with the potential man of her dreams. You and the girl are on the same team, and the so-called friend is trying to destroy a new romance.

Cockblock inoculation works only if a girl genuinely likes you and has the confidence to stand up for herself. It will not work if you try it too early in the conversation before she passed any of your compliance tests.

You will encounter at least one nuclear cockblock that destroyed what could have resulted in a long-term relationship, even marriage. Things were going well with your ideal girl and her vicious friend ruined it forever. If you're like me, you will be tempted to fly into a rage and call the blocker all types of names. This is a natural response to being wronged, but realize that you never had the girl in the first place if another individual could separate her from you so easily. Your angry response may feel good, but it won't allow the interaction to continue, and it definitely won't keep you in an optimal mood to talk to other girls that night. Take the good with the bad and carry on with your approaches until you succeed.

Wingmanship

One way to reduce the negative effects of cockblocking is to have a horny friend with you who is ready to go *all the way* with the potential blocker. I say "all the way" because although it's nice if your wingman can distract the blocker for a few minutes, what will happen when he withdraws? You get blocked. Another benefit of a wingman is that he provides you with social proof that you are not a loner. The third benefit is that you can talk to your wingman to stay in a sociable mood. These benefits are neutralized, however, if you both have the same taste in women and compete with each other, or if your wingman is prone to create drama when he gets drunk. In these cases, it's better to go out alone.

I had the best wingman in the world when I was living in Washington, D.C. We had completely different tastes in women and never once argued about a girl during our many years of hanging out. We also both knew the boundaries of not interfering with an active pick-up by trying to get into a deep chat with each other's girls. Our goals were so aligned that our mutually beneficial relationship resulted in both of us getting dozens of wingman-assisted bangs. I've had many wingmen since, some quite good and some really bad, teaching me that a good wingman is worth his weight in gold because he will sharply increase your results.

Your wingman should liven up your mood and not harm your results. When I go out with a new wing, I don't necessarily expect him to jump on the grenade and distract all the ugly friends of the girl I like, but he should not make my life harder by interfering with my pick-ups or trying to insert himself into conversations I'm trying to have. He should also respect the golden rule of wingmanship that the man who does the approach on any group gets first pick of the hottest girl in that group.

Wingman relationships are most fruitful when they're underpinned by genuine friendship. You can anticipate his needs and moves, and he can anticipate yours. Being on the same wavelength enables both of you to increase your results. But if you constantly have to teach your wingman the rules and tell him to stop cockblocking you, there is a disconnect that you probably won't resolve. My best wingmen instinctively knew how to be a good wing.

The default strategy with a wing is for one of you to approach a set of two or more girls and for your wing to join the group about one to three minutes into the conversation. When the wingman arrives, the approacher should warmly introduce his friend to everyone in the group. The wingman should talk to the target's friends and try to get intimate with one of them while the approacher works on his girl. A variation is to signal to your wing when you want him to join the set. I usually turn to my friend and wave him over when I'm ready for him.

The best scenario is when both of you want to sleep with at least one girl in the set. If not, your wingman should be able to talk to your target's friends for five to fifteen minutes before bowing out. During this time, try to establish strong interest with your girl to prevent a future block. If the block never comes, your wing will be alone and have to fend for himself. I've had nights where I've been at my wing's side all night and others when I talked to him for only ten minutes before approaching a girl I stayed with for the rest of the night. You will encounter a variety of situations, but the bottom line is that if your wing doesn't want to sex up any of the friends of the girl you like, or her friends don't want him, he will be of little use and you'll have to go it alone.

The most common question that girls ask in the presence of your wingman is, "How did you two meet?" This is an opportunity to show humor while conveying that you are not the type of guy who tries to impress women. My default answer is, "Internet sex chat room. I thought he was a girl." If a girl insists on a "real" answer, you can simply say, "Through mutual friends."

You may encounter situations where you are hanging out in groups of three, four, or more men. I find that if you go out with more than two men, you will encounter cockblocking from your own team, or one guy in the group will start hurting sets because he isn't on the same wavelength as the others. When I want to bond with men, I go out with a big group to a bar, grab some drinks, and converse with them without looking at girls, but when I want to meet a girl, I go out with only one or two men who see game in the same way as I do.

Loose Ends

There are a few additional scenarios that I have repeatedly encountered. The first is when a girl is sitting down. A girl who is seated will be less receptive to your approach than if she were standing, and her decision to sit when other people in the venue are standing should be taken as a slight indication that she's not open to meeting a new man. In some cases, she will adopt the attitude of a queen, ready to instantly dismiss any courtier who tries to entertain her.

Understand that there are power dynamics at play in every approach. The balance of power is not in your favor if you have to turn around and move away when the conversation ends, which is the case when approaching a seated girl. This is why I aim to approach girls in situations where *she* has to move away if the approach doesn't go well. If a girl perceives that she has the upper hand and won't have to do a "walk of shame" after a rejection, she will be less inclined to treat you with respect.

Another option is to wait until a seated girl gets up to use the bathroom or order a drink at the bar. A moving target is not ideal, because an object in motion tends to stay in motion, but it's better than approaching a girl who is seated, because it equalizes the balance of power.

If you want to approach a girl while she's seated, sit next to her within two minutes of the approach to get her out of her "queen" mentality. Do a false time constraint by saying, "I can't sit for long," and then sit down beside her without waiting for her to say yes. I do this only if she receives me favorably and doesn't look annoyed.

Another common scenario you'll encounter is a girl dancing, either alone or with friends. Approaching while dancing was one of the first game tactics I tried, but I stopped doing them because it was far less effective than verbal approaches. If you do dance approaches, understand that the only two things a girl can evaluate you on are your dancing and attractiveness. If one is lacking, you will have a high rejection rate. At the same time, dancing can be a great way to start running game if you're not yet confident of your conversational skills, but this assumes you know how to dance, or at least have the time to learn.

When you're ready to do dance approaches, first become a fixture on the dance floor by dancing alone or with your friends. Get into the music and start enjoying yourself to show anyone watching that you're skilled and having fun. You will inevitably spot a girl you want to dance with. Move towards her. When she is facing you, gently grab her hand and smile while continuing to dance (you can also attempt a salsa-like spin move). She will evaluate your offer within one second. If she chooses to dance with you, she'll allow you to continue holding her hand, or she will let go of your hand but remain facing you. In a rejection, she will remove her hand, shake her head, and turn away.

It's difficult to use this approach method on a girl who is dancing in a circle with her friends since she will never face you. One option is to triple tap her on the shoulder and wait for her to turn around before grabbing her hand, but this usually doesn't succeed. You could also wait until she takes a break from dancing to use the bathroom or get a drink.

You don't have to hold a girl's hand the entire time you're dancing with her. It's better to play it "hot-cold" where you give affection with extra touching, withdraw for a bit, and then touch her again. How you treat a girl on the dance floor is a microcosm of the entire seduction. Give her your undivided attention, but also show you're not crazy about her and don't have a problem with temporarily withdrawing by taking two steps back (while still facing her). Don't touch her constantly.

After dancing for some time, you'll want to move her off the dance floor and have a conversation to see whether there's a connection. Say, "Let's go to the bar to get a drink." If you're short of money, or don't want to buy her a drink yet, say, "Let's take a break at the bar." You can also try to start talking to her while dancing, but this will be a challenge because of the noise, so keep your statements short and simple, such as "Your dancing isn't bad" or "You look like you're from so and so."

If she follows you to the bar, you have her interest and can proceed as if you started a standard verbal approach, knowing that she will be fully receptive. After chatting for a while, move back to the dance floor. Approaches that start with dancing usually get physical quite fast, and kissing within an hour is common.

The next situation you'll encounter is girls in motion. I find that people's minds move at a pace that correlates with their movement. When someone is in a rush to be somewhere, they are anxious and their mind is occupied with thoughts about making it on time, what they will do if they're late, and so on. When someone is not in a hurry and is moving slowly, their mind is more focused on what's going on around them. If a girl is zipping through the venue, and you manage to stop her, how much of her attention do you think she'll give you? Not much, and that's assuming she stops at all. But if you see a girl who is trying to find her friend, or is moving a bit slower, she'll pay you more attention.

When I enter a night venue, I scope out the entire space and stand at a central spot near the bar. My decision to approach is based on the following: girls who make eye contact with me (high attraction), girls who are looking around a lot or appear lost (high availability), or girls I'm extremely attracted to. I then wait for an opportunity or create one through boldness. It's rare for a girl I like to pop up out of nowhere. Instead, I will notice when a girl I've already selected separates herself from her group and starts moving. I get into position so that I can intercept her, ideally after she has completed what she set out to do.

One of the reasons I wait for opportunities is because I'm older and more patient, but if you're younger and full of energy, you are free to approach at any moment you see fit, because there is no such thing as the perfect moment. Whichever technique causes you to do the approach should be the one you use. For some men, it's better to approach quickly before anxious thoughts paralyze them, while others approach better if they take their time to plot and plan.

For an approach to work on a girl who's in motion, she has to be alone and not moving *too* quickly. If you suspect she's going to the bathroom, approach her on her way back, and if she's going to the bar, position yourself behind her so that you can approach after she orders. If you're not sure where she's going, or if she will ever come back, approach her right then and there because this could be your only opportunity.

Another situation you may experience is going out alone. I've already pointed out that the problem with this is that you have zero social proof—girls don't see you as well-liked or having cool friends. As a result, your overall game has to be that much stronger. If you have no friends, your game is weak, and your appearance is below average, you will struggle mightily at night and should consider day game instead.

If I go out alone to a bar or club, I choose a comfortable spot near the bar, make small talk with the bartender, and carefully watch the crowd. When I see an opportunity, I strike. If a girl asks me whether I'm alone, I'm honest and say that I wanted to get out of the house and have a drink. As long as you can be sociable when you're alone, your results won't be that much worse than when you go out with friends, particularly if you focus on girls who exhibit high attraction or availability.

It's common to have male friends who may not be free to go out at night, but if you have no friends at all, that's a warning sign that you won't do well with women. If you can't maintain a friendship with a guy, it will be tough for you to bond with women, and you should try to resolve your social issues first. Having friends is a prerequisite to being good with girls, because it conveys your ability to connect with other people.

Chapter Conclusion

I've seen firsthand how night venues have become steadily worse over the past two decades, with no sign of improvement. While bars are better, you'll still face problems such as cockblocking and high ratios of men to women. Night venues that attract a large number of women will always exist, but we may be seeing the end of a golden era for men who wanted to score big after making a small or medium effort.

In spite of the decline, night venues that provide a decent

return on investment still exist, although the window of opportunity may be open for only part of the night, usually before midnight. If you're unable to find such a venue, or are simply not interested in night game, stick to day game.

You may be disappointed that I have not shared an internet game strategy, but I choose not to meet girls online. It's simply too demoralizing. When I use it, I can feel myself turning into a thirsty copy-and-paste monkey, only to be defrauded by "secret internet fatties" who look nothing like their photos. If you have downtime and want to try it, go ahead, but the time you spend online could be better spent walking outside and meeting girls face-to-face, no matter the hour. Websites and apps come and go, and one will degrade as soon as you master it, but having the ability to walk outside anywhere in the world and have a chat with a girl will never die.

Though this chapter is called "approaching," I have covered many of the steps that are designed to lead to sex, such as touching, kissing, and changing the venue to a private room. I included these steps because you may have to implement them very soon after meeting a girl, and they may not be separate from the approach itself, especially when the universe sends you a girl who is ravenously horny and wants you immediately. In the next chapter, I'll slow things down and discuss how to have long conversations with girls, how to go on dates, and how to communicate with girls via phone.

Chapter 7: Dating

The nature of a date means a girl is ready to have a conversation that lasts a number of hours while discovering what type of man you are, instead of simply identifying that you're attractive enough to bed, as is the case with a same-night bang scenario. This means that you'll have to be able to maintain a long conversation.

It's common for men to run out of things to say on a date or not know what to talk about. Besides radio talk-show hosts, who can talk for long periods without prompting, all men struggle with maintaining a conversation, and the girls you date won't have exceptional conversational abilities either. Don't make yourself anxious by thinking that you must be a great conversationalist, something that I imposed on myself in the past. Girls won't judge your conversational skills as harshly as you do, and you only need to do well enough so that a girl's attraction for you doesn't diminish.

Before I get into how to have long conversations, I want to discuss how to get dates by contacting girls who gave you their phone number.

Contacting A Girl

With the exception of approaching, the most frustrating part of game is contacting girls, either via voice call or by texting. Girls no longer have basic manners when communicating with men they've shown an interest in, so you'll repeatedly be disappointed when interactions that seemed to be strong and genuine fade to silence.

The strong connection you feel is fleeting in the mind of the modern girl who wants to continually experience a smorgasbord of excitement and adventure. She will love you one moment and treat you worse than a homeless bum the next. This is why I advise that you push the interaction as far as you can while a girl is in your presence. With night game, we've already reached the point where we have to sleep with a girl in order for her to consistently respond to our first text, and we may not be that far for this being true of day game as well.

The most common stage at which a seduction breaks down is when things move to the phone. The smartphone allows a girl to effortlessly screen and block men who try to get in touch with her and also to "ghost" on men with whom she has had sex. It's therefore a technology that aids a girl's efforts to receive attention from multiple men simultaneously without having to follow through with any of them. Any game strategy that depends on building attraction through the phone, a tool that girls primarily use to gain attention and relieve boredom, will ultimately fail.

While long voice calls can create enough attraction to change a girl's mind about you, text messaging has an exceedingly temporary attraction-boosting effect. Trying to maintain attraction by using witty or funny texts won't work. The best strategy is therefore to maximize the attraction a girl has for you *before* you have to communicate by phone. When that communication is eventually in progress, ensure it is short, functional, and centered on taking her out on a date.

Some guys try to be witty or funny when they text, but this usually backfires when those texts are interpreted differently than the way intended. Although there is more leeway for you to use wit and humor to build attraction if you're doing internet game and the girl feels neutral about your photos (you'll know from her lazy responses), this is unnecessary if you met a girl through day or night game. If a girl is not firmly attracted to you after meeting in the flesh, there is almost nothing your calls or texts will do to change her mind, because a phone will not enable you to surpass face-to-face communication in creating attraction.

A girl has decided whether she wants to go on a date with you before you contact her. In fact, I believe a girl decides as she's giving you her number. You may be thinking, "So why would a girl give me her number if she doesn't want to go out with me?" For attention. Out of boredom. Because it's easier for her to give you her number and then never reply to your messages than it is to say "No." Girls hate confrontation to such an extent that they will rather lead men on and get their hopes up than be direct or honest.

Consequently, your phone communication should merely serve as a bridge that allows a girl to do what she has *already decided* she wants to do. We don't convince over the phone, we don't try to make her like us, and we don't try to entertain her. We do just enough to get her to say yes to a date. Only after a few dates can we begin to text her out of boredom or for fun.

If a girl didn't decide she wanted to go out with you before you contacted her, and acts wishy-washy by stating how "busy" she is, sending her entertaining texts or making her laugh will amp up her emotions only temporarily, and possibly get her to say yes to a meeting, but guess what happens once she calms down and it's time for her to prepare for a date with you that may last several hours? She flakes. She cancels the date, or simply doesn't show up. The more you had to entertain her with texts to get a yes, the more likely she will flake, which is far more annoying than an upfront no.

The only time entertaining her with texts may work is if you capitalize on an emotional high and get her to agree to see you *right then*, but this will happen only if she's fast with her reply times. We actually exploit this principle during night approaches where we push the interaction as far as it can go when a girl is showing attraction for us. This is easier when you're face-to-face with her, but over the phone, the chances of setting up an immediate date before her emotional high dissipates is quite low, particularly if you're in a big city with long travel times.

Once the game has moved to the phone, and it will inevitably have to, a genuine connection is necessary. To get a same-day bang from day or night game, you need a lighter form of attraction since you're taking advantage of a fleeting situation based mostly on emotion, but once you reach the phone stage, she has to *want* to schedule blocks of time to be with you. This means that a girl who goes on a date with you is highly open to the possibility of sex for both emotional and logical reasons.

Girls will give out their number to just about any man, but they'll only dedicate time to meeting men they are excited about. This means that only 5 to 25% of the numbers you get will result in a date. The range is wide because getting a response largely depends on the type of girl you're pursuing, the venues where you meet her, and how far you push the interaction before settling for a number. The hard fact of game is that you won't see most of the girls who give you their number. To prevent yourself from getting depressed about this, take a step back from your failures and keep the big picture in mind: this is a numbers game. Experiencing enough failures means you're statistically due for success.

There's a debate over whether you should call or text. When I started with game, I always called first, but there's a good chance you've never first contacted a girl by calling. Texting is here to stay, but calling should not be written off entirely because it shows that you're bold and helps you stand out from just about every other man she has interacted with. I'll discuss texting before calling.

Text Game

My texting game might as well be locked up in a time capsule because I've barely changed it in ten years. When contacting a girl for the first time, I go right for the date without much foreplay, because I know that she has already decided whether or not she wants to see me again. This makes texting game easy and fast in that you'll know within just a few hours of where you stand. If you try to run a clownish text game, however, you'll think you're doing great because she's responding to your funny and cocky texts with exuberant emoticons, but she'll suddenly disappear when you ask for a date. Entertaining a girl with texts merely postpones the inevitable.

My old advice recommended waiting three days before you send the first text. For example, if you got her number on Saturday night, you would first text her on Tuesday. This guideline was suitable for a more innocent time before smartphones when a girl wouldn't forget about you in a day. Now we have to account for the fact that guys are hitting up girls on their phones a lot more.

You'll be bumped down the queue if you wait too long, particularly if her attraction wasn't strong, which it usually isn't. I now advise that you text on the *following evening*, starting at 7pm or later, or on the second evening. The risk of being seen as needy from contacting her too soon is smaller than the risk of being forgotten. You want to stay fresh in her mind.

In the past, when a girl didn't have a river of men flowing through her phone, we could create some anxiety by delaying our first contact, but now she can alleviate that anxiety by going on a dating app and getting dozens of new prospects within a few hours. Therefore, we'll have to create anxiety in other ways, such as the qualification method that will be discussed shortly.

Aim to set a date for one or two days after the day you contact her. Let's say you meet a girl on Friday or Saturday. Sunday evening would be a good time to contact her between 7pm and 8:30pm. I'd then try to set a date for Monday or Tuesday. If you meet her on Sunday, contact her on Monday or Tuesday evening and set a date for one or two days after that, and so on.

A disadvantage of first contacting girls on Friday or Saturday, the two days when most girls are busy, is that it may make you seem too available. If I meet a girl on Thursday or Friday, I will likely contact her on Sunday and set up a date for Monday or Tuesday. I generally don't like setting first dates for the weekend, because she may think I value her greatly, but I will do so if I need to prevent a long gap of not seeing her. Other situations where I will go for a weekend date are if I've already had heavy intimacy with her, she is showing strong interest and excitement about seeing me soon, she hinted that she is free on the weekend, or she seems to have few friends.

Other men are more relaxed about contacting girls on the weekend, but I find this can easily result in girls putting you in the "needy" box, as if you're overly eager to see her instead of going out and having fun with your friends, as she would expect of a man with some status. Girls are also busier on the weekends, so there's a chance that your messages will get lost in the shuffle. When in doubt, stick to the general guideline of making first contact very soon after meeting her and setting a date one or two days after that.

What should you do if a girl goes out of town before you can get her on the first date? I've tried a few tactics to overcome this problem, such as messaging her periodically while she's away, sending interesting and humorous texts so that she doesn't forget about me (similar to a relationship texting scenario I'll share later), or keeping silent and waiting until she comes back. In my experience, going silent won't give you worse results than when you engage her regularly.

Texting a girl while she's away can give you the illusion that she's genuinely interested, but then she may disappear when she returns and you ask for a date. The tactic I've settled on is to wait until she comes back if she'll be gone for a week or less. If she'll be away for more than a week, I'll text her in four or five days to ask about her trip, and not text her again until she gets back. If a girl likes you, and doesn't have a ton of penis options, she will want to go out with you even if she's been away for a month. There is no need to waste time by constantly texting her while she's away.

I usually meet girls in the second half of the week, which means that I first contact a girl on Sunday or Monday night. If I'm running weekend night game, however, my primary goal is to get a same-night bang. My secondary goal is to get a Sunday night date. This means I push an interaction as far as I can, and if I hit a wall, I will ask her for a Sunday evening date, knowing that she is more likely to be free on this day compared with any other. If she says no to a Sunday date, I'll ask for another day. If she's also "busy" on that day, and doesn't make a counter-offer, I won't even bother to get her number.

If a girl won't agree to go on a date with me while I'm in her presence and she can directly feel my masculine power, she won't agree after we've been apart for a day or more and all she's got is my texts on her phone. Below is my texting script for the first contact.

> Me: "Hey Denise it's Roosh. How are you?" I tell her my name even if she has saved my details in her phone.
>
> Her: "I'm good, just got home from work/school. And you?" If she doesn't ask how you're doing, it's a reliable sign she won't agree to a date.
>
> Me: "I'm reading a book on chinese communism…it's very exciting. So how about we meet tomorrow night at 8pm?" Acknowledge her answer if it warrants doing so, make a short comment about something you're doing, and then propose a time for a date in one or two days.

If you want to appear scarcer, imply that you'll be free on the day you want to meet her.

> Me: "I'm reading a book on chinese communism…it's very exciting. So I'm free tomorrow night at 8pm, how about we meet then?"

The time it takes a girl to respond to your first text is a good indication of how things will go. If she takes less than an hour to respond, you're looking good. If she takes one to four hours, you should begin to doubt that you'll see her again. If she takes longer than four hours, forget it—she has zero respect for you. If a girl really liked a guy, would she risk ruining the interaction by taking so long to text him back, especially when she's never more than two minutes away from her phone?

You can also expect a bad outcome if she says she's "busy" but does not offer an alternative day and time to meet. This means she's not interested. You can try to keep the seduction alive by suggesting another day, but now you're being needy, because you're trying to please someone who isn't making an effort to please you. To mitigate this problem, I often suggest two possible days for the date, particularly if I have no idea what her schedule is like.

> Me: "I'm reading a book on chinese communism…it's very exciting. So how about we meet Monday or Tuesday night at 8pm?"

What I like about this request is that it's harder for a girl to give you the excuse that she's busy. Don't buy a girl's "busy" excuse—if she met the man of her dreams, she would find time for him. No final exam, job, or event would stop her.

A good outcome is when she agrees to your date or makes a counter-offer. Once the date has been scheduled, you can settle the final details, including the venue.

> Me: "I just played frisbee with my friends…it was pretty fun. So I'm free tomorrow night at 8pm, how about we meet then?"

> Her: "Okay sure." Many girls will add, "Where do you want to meet?"

> Me: "Great let's meet at Café Cosi at Dupont." Choose a place to meet or a venue that is reasonably close to where you or she lives to set up a venue change to someone's home at the end of the date.

> Her: "That works for me."

> Me: "Cool." I like sending a final "See you" or "Cool" confirmation to lock in first dates, but I don't send one if her last text was a clear confirmation such as "Okay" or "See you there."

For first dates, I prefer a time of 8pm. Any time between 7pm and 9pm is worth a try depending on your preference, though 9pm dates can be a bit late since they may not leave you with enough time to escalate.

I generally avoid dinner for a first date unless I will be hungry and want to eat, because it can be expensive while not helping with the seduction. By scheduling the date for 8pm or later, the girl won't be expecting food. To make it clear that you're not going out for dinner, you could text, "So how about we meet tomorrow night *for drinks* at 8pm?" Choosing a bar with a food menu can be a reasonable compromise.

If I got a number from a girl that I talked to for ten minutes or less, perhaps because she was in a rush to be somewhere, I sometimes add an extra exchange before asking for the date.

> Me: "Hey Denise it's Roosh. How are you?"
>
> Her: "I'm good, just got home from work/school. And you?"
>
> Me: "I just got home from work… now I can relax a bit. How did your meeting go?" Ask a question about a topic or event that came up during your initial conversation.
>
> Her: "I was late, but everything worked out great."
>
> Me: "That's good. So how about we meet tomorrow night at 8pm?"

All I did was add an exchange that referred to something from our initial meeting. It's fine to throw in a light joke that can be capped off with a smiley, but you don't have to rack your brains to come up with something funny. If you could see my last 100 text exchanges where I set up a date, you'd see very little humor. I add it in gradually over time.

When a girl is interested in you, and doesn't have a social calendar that is stocked with other men, the above texting program is all you need to get dates. It works if the girl's attraction for you is apparent during the initial meeting when she asked you personal questions and made a reasonable effort to maintain the interaction. It also helps that we lay the logistical groundwork for a date by getting a sense of her schedule when asking for the number.

Make sure that you're conscious of your reply times, because you don't want to seem more eager than her by replying too quickly. Sometimes your reply time will be longer than hers and sometimes it will be shorter, but it should never *always* be shorter. If, for example, a girl replies 50 minutes after I sent her a first text, I may take 65 minutes to reply. If she takes 30 minutes to reply to that text, I may take only 12 minutes for the next reply. If her third reply also takes 30 minutes, I might wait 40 minutes. I mix it up so that it's clear I'm not needy while also being unpredictable. It can be frustrating if a girl is taking hours (or days) to reply to a text, but that is a clear sign she has low interest.

Even after you've had sex with a girl, you must regulate your reply times. It's almost silly to have to do this, but girls have antennae that are sensitive to how needy a man is.

If a girl takes a long time to reply, it may get late before you could iron out plans for the first date. If it's past 11pm, should you keep texting or wait until the next day? Take the texting as far as it can go that night, but don't send a text if you're reasonably sure she's sleeping. Wait until after 12pm the next day to resume the conversation. The reason for waiting until the afternoon is that she may be groggy or tired in the morning. I doubt most girls feel sociable when they get up (I sure don't), so it's better to wait until they've settled into their day before communicating with them again.

When a girl agrees to a date that will take place more than two days later, you need to run a flake defense move to prevent getting stood up by informing her that you'll share the location on the day of the date.

> Me: "I just came back from the gym...now I get to eat whatever I want. So how about we meet Thursday night at 8pm?" This text is being sent on Monday. She had told me that she's free on Thursday.
>
> Her: "Okay sure."

Me: "Cool I'll think of a good place and text you on Thursday afternoon."

Between 2pm and 4pm on Thursday, I inform her of the location.

Me: "Good afternoon! So let's meet in front of the big church on the main square at 8pm."

Her: "Okay."

She *must* confirm with a reply. If she doesn't, she's flaking, and you should not show up at the venue. If you're dealing with a girl who seems extra flaky, you may need to run flake defense even for dates that are scheduled for the following day.

An indication that you also need to run flake defense is if you're getting stood-up often. This means there are extra flaky chicks in your local environment. With the type of girl I usually meet in my current location (Eastern Europe), I don't get stood up if I schedule the date one or two days in advance. Longer than that and I need to run flake defense.

Another common situation is when you meet a girl and get her to agree to a date the next day. This commonly happens to me when I meet a girl on Saturday night and she says yes to a Sunday evening date. I get her number, say goodbye, and text her on Sunday afternoon between 12pm and 4pm to finalize our plans.

Me: "Hello Paula it's Roosh. How are you…did you sleep well?"

Her: "Hey Roosh. I slept okay. You?"

Me: "I'm feeling good, just went for a walk in the park. So how about we meet today at 7pm?"

Her: "Okay. Where?"

If she doesn't reply to the first text, there obviously won't be a date. The prospect is dead. It's common for things to go nowhere at the texting stage, and that's simply because you're getting numbers from girls who have weak attraction for you. To check her attraction level, look back at what happened before you got her number. Did she ask you personal questions and pass your compliance tests? Did she compliment you? Did she suggest a future meeting before you did? Did she give you the impression that she has an available schedule? Could you have pushed the interaction further before getting her number? Could the intimacy you had simply been the result of her being intoxicated and horny? You'll find there's a strong correlation between the effort she makes during your initial interaction and how responsive she is when the interaction moves to the phone.

Now that you have an overall texting strategy, below are six more tips to refine your game further.

Don't send a text that contains the phrase "Let me know." This is the most limp-wristed phrase that you can send a girl. You're essentially asking her to treat you like a weak man. Your instinct may be to send a text message with this phrase (or something similar) when she responds that she's "not sure" if she can meet you on a certain date. What she's really saying is that she needs more time to find out whether Chad is going to come through or not. You're her backup option if he flakes.

Her "not sure" response shows that she doesn't respect you, particularly if she doesn't make a counter-offer or say when she will be sure. In my experience, a "not sure" without a clarification *never* leads to a date. It's best to respond with "Whatever" or "Never mind" when she is using you as a back-up and forget her. If she wises up, she will text back.

A corollary to this rule is not to text the phrase "Just kidding." You should not make a joke through text that can be so misinterpreted that you have to announce you were joking. This is one step from saying "I'm sorry," another phrase you want to completely avoid.

Minimize sending a back-to-back text, also known as a "double text." It's okay to split a long text into two replies, but try to avoid sending two unconnected texts in a row. This often happens when you send a short text, she doesn't reply, and you later want to get things started up again by sending another text. This means she has the upper hand in the interaction and you're straining to get her attention. Sending double texts also trains her to think that she doesn't have to reply to all of your texts. Try not to send a double text more than once a month with a specific girl.

It's far more preferable if a girl sends a double text to you. Apart from a date confirmation, if you're about to send a text that you're sure won't elicit a response, it may be best not to send it.

Give her an opportunity to show interest. Many men are anxious that they will "lose" a girl if they aren't fast with their texting or fail to provide a steady stream of entertainment that garners little more than "lol" replies, but this will merely encourage flaking. Don't make it *too* easy for her. Occasionally be distant and silent to give her an opportunity to fill the void with her own effort.

An example is with voice-call game. If I call a girl and she doesn't pick up the phone, I'll skip leaving a message and wait at least an hour to give her an opportunity to contact me before I send a text. That one hour is her chance to make an effort, because she doesn't know that my plan is to text her eventually. You never want a girl to think, "Why should I put in this unit of effort right now when I know he's going to do it anyway?" Create some anxiety in her mind that if she doesn't step up to the plate and put in some work, she may never hear from you again. If she doesn't act on this feeling of potential loss, her attraction for you is weak.

Don't text more exclamation points or smiley emoticons than she does. You will come across as starved for affection if you're trying to be fun and cheery while she's stoic. If she is being fun, you can match but not exceed her, but if her texts are completely flat, with no exclamation points or smiley faces, you should not use them either. Consider sending them as a reward when she displays the behavior you want to see. I put "haha," "hehe," and "lol" in the same category as emoticons.

Assume that she is showing all of your texts to her friends. It may be hard for you to believe that a girl would show your text messages to practically everyone she knows, but this is exactly what she does. Her reasons are to get a reaction from her friends, mock something you said, show off that she's receiving sexual attention, or solicit an interpretation.

This rule is often called the "Jumbotron test." Your texts pass the test if they could be displayed on a Jumbotron screen in a giant sports stadium without the crowd bursting into derisive laughter. Would the crowd think you were needy or confident? Would they think you're a sucker or admire your game? If the texting script I shared with you was displayed on a Jumbotron, the crowd would think my communication was direct and to the point, without any faults to mock. Your texting game is tight if a random person who reads them would not think you have low value.

Mirror her general texting game. A rule that encapsulates the previous five rules is to absorb the nature of her texting game and spit it back at her. If her texts are lively and her responses are quick, your texts can also be lively with faster reply times. If she's being nonchalant and emotionless, you should text the same way. If a girl loosens up with stories or jokes, you can loosen up as well. By mirroring her general game, and not exceeding her level of excitement, you will ensure that she never interprets your behavior as needy.

This rule also applies to getting sexual in texts. I like to wait until she brings up the topic of being horny or feeling lonely. I then find out what she's wearing and tell her (not ask) to send me a picture. If her picture shows a lot of skin, it's safe to assume that she wants to send more explicit photos. I either pretend I'm not satisfied with her clothed photos or use reverse psychology and tell her *not* to send me more photos because I'm becoming excited. It used to be tough to get girls to send nudes, but by the time you meet a girl, she will have sent them to countless other men.

Once you get into a relationship, your texts will go from functional to conversational, where you and the girl text each other because it's a fun way to pass the time, especially on days you aren't seeing her. When texting with my last girlfriend, we sent a lot of memes, inside jokes, and funny pictures that described our days. It looked similar to how I would text a friend or relative.

Although your texts will loosen up over time, don't forget the rules. You must still be careful about sending double texts while monitoring your reply times. You also want to make sure that you're not always the first one to initiate a new text conversation. She should initiate conversations as often as you, if not more. You may be tempted to loosen up on the Jumbotron test, but this would be a mistake. Even in a long-term relationship, a girl will show your texts to her friends.

Except for playful kissy-face emoticons, I *never* show affection in texts with phrases such as "I miss you" or "I can't wait to see you again." It's the girl's job to say these mushy things. Only in person can you once in a while reward her with a reply of "Me too" when she says that she missed you. A girl will say that she wants her man to show affection, but when he does, she interprets this to mean he is weak and starts to look for another man. It's usually a trap when a girl complains that you don't show her enough love.

I am often asked how to revive a solid prospect that went cold. You experienced a genuine connection with a high level of rapport and now she has disappeared. Although a one-night stand can be explained away as the result of being under the influence of alcohol, it's harder to accept when a girl disappears after you felt a real connection. The reality is that the connection was one-sided: your mind missed the warning signs of her disinterest and created a false tale of attraction, because a girl will not go cold on a man she has strong interest in. Girls are fully capable of hotly pursuing men they like, so if a girl is not replying to your texts or coming out on dates, she is simply not interested in you. I can't imagine how much collective time men have wasted trying to revive dead leads on girls who have already soundly rejected them.

For other cases where the lead didn't go completely cold,

meaning she didn't disrespect you by not replying to a text when you were expecting one, you can hit her with a "restart" text. This is most common if a girl was traveling or busy. My favorite restart text is simple: "Hello. How is your week going?" I can tell from how wordy her reply is, and if she asks me the same question, whether or not the lead has gone cold. If her reply consists of one or two words, it's on the cold side, and it's unlikely that she will then agree to a date.

Other restart texts should tie into what you know about her. If she's a student and told you about a school project or exam, ask how it went. If she took a trip somewhere, ask about it. If a girl doesn't reply within a day to one of my texts after I asked her a question or tried to set up a date, I delete her number. I don't waste time on cold leads. You internalize thirstiness if you pursue girls who are treating you poorly, which can convince your subconscious that your value is low. Your time is much better spent gaining new leads than forcing dead ones.

There is also the "nuclear" restart option. Use it when you're *absolutely certain* there was an intense romantic connection, where you stopped one step short of making up names for your future children, and she didn't respond to your first text because of something beyond her control, such as an issue with her mobile network. Problem is that sending a nuclear restart text does cause you to lose the upper hand, at least temporarily. Again, this is something you should only do in an emergency, because it doesn't work on a girl you didn't connect with. I've used it only three times in my entire life.

To do a nuclear restart, send the following text if you didn't get a reply after 24 hours: "You forgot all the good things about me already?" The ideal response is her providing a valid excuse for not responding. If she doesn't even give you an excuse, things will end badly.

At the end of the day, if a girl likes you, it matters little what you text, so you might as well keep it simple and direct to schedule a date as efficiently as possible. As you get to know a girl, you can loosen things up and start to have more fun in a way that matches your personality and sense of humor.

If you're stressing out about how to respond to a text message, you have already put a girl on a pedestal. Whenever you're wondering what you should text, ask yourself whether she's wondering the same thing. If not, her value is higher than yours, and she will inevitably realize it. When you feel that she is privileged to be talking to you, and that she should be worried about *her* chances with you, you're on the right track. Instead of trying to satisfy her by texting the "right" things, give her an opportunity to please you by acting like an adult with setting dates and showing up on time to them.

Voice Call Game

I will consider calling a girl instead of texting under two conditions. The first is if she has saved my number in her phone. When you get a girl's number, one option is to call her immediately so she can save your number. If you then call her and she answers, it's clear that she wanted to talk to you. On the other hand, if she didn't save your number and she answers the call not knowing it's you, and decides that she doesn't want to talk to you, she will abruptly end the call or even hang up on you.

The second condition is if the connection was particularly strong during an approach that lasted many hours. In this case, she may be excited if you call instead of text because she wants to hear the sound of your voice.

When I call a girl, I do it so that I won't be at a disadvantage if she doesn't pick up or call me back. This is accomplished by not leaving a voicemail. If she doesn't answer the phone, I hang up and wait an hour to see if she will call me back. Most girls won't. After one hour, I will then start my standard text game without mentioning that I called her.

If you leave a voicemail, and she doesn't text or call you back, the prospect is dead. If she doesn't call you back when you didn't leave a voicemail, and she doesn't reply to your text within a day, the prospect is also dead. You can delete her number.

Another instance where it makes sense to call is after a date or two. When things are getting comfortable, I may throw out a test by calling her on a random evening to see if she'll answer. If she doesn't, I won't leave a voicemail, and will wait to see if she calls me back within one or two hours. If she doesn't reward my phone call by answering or calling me back, I know that she wants to communicate exclusively through text messaging, at least for the time being.

You don't need special tactics to have phone conversations with girls. My framework is to start by talking about what we're both currently doing and how our days went. Then I have a short chat about related topics until closing out the conversation by scheduling the next date. Let's do a phone call example.

Me: "Hey Laura, what's up? What are you doing?"

Her: "Nothing much, just got home from work."

Me: "Hard day?"

Her: "I had to complete some TPS reports, which weren't so fun."

Me: "Yeah, I hate TPS reports too, even though I'm quite good at them. I just got home from the gym and now I'm cooking some chicken breast because I need protein."

Her: "You're eating late."

Me: "Yeah, I skip breakfast, so I eat a late lunch and dinner. I think breakfast is a scam because you're almost never hungry when you first wake up."

We proceed to have a two-minute conversation about the merits of eating three meals a day.

Me: "Cool. Well how's the rest of your week looking?"

Her: "Pretty good, I'm not doing much."

Me: "I'm free tomorrow night. How about we grab a drink?"

A natural phone conversation involves talking about things that are currently happening, allowing you to hit on an interesting topic or two. Once you are done with that, ease into your upcoming schedules and plan another date. The most helpful tip I can give you is to call her while you're doing something or immediately afterwards so that you have a topic to begin the call with. If you've been sitting at home all day masturbating, you won't have anything to say unless you make something up.

Phone conversations don't have to be long, but if you run out of things to say early on, fast forward to scheduling the date. In the early stages of dating, most of your phone conversations will last two to ten minutes. Be the one who ends the call first. If a girl says that she has to go because she has things to do, you prolonged the call beyond its peak and should've ended it sooner.

As with texting, keep in mind who is initiating the calls. You'll be making slightly more calls early on, but she should also begin to call you. Ideally, you want the relationship to reach the stage where she calls you more than you call her. If you're doing most of the calling, you're showing too much interest, and should dial it down by switching to texting even if you don't really like texting. Personally, I like to mix up calling and texting when I'm in a serious relationship, because doing either one exclusively can get boring. In casual relationships, I rarely call a girl, although I might do so just for the novelty factor or if the girl put out signs that she will pick up the phone.

Based on current trends, talking on the phone seems to be on the way out, so you won't be calling much outside of a relationship. Before the days of texting, you absolutely had to call, so this is one area where technology has made dating easier but at the same time more impersonal.

Dating How-To

Not all first dates conform to a standard format. In some

cases, you'll barely know a girl beyond her first name. In others, you'll have kissed or had sex. These two extremes result in distinctly different vibes. With the former, it may take one or two hours before she gets comfortable, while with the latter, it may take only fifteen minutes. When deciding how to escalate on a date, use your best judgment based on what you've done with the girl so far. The less you know her, the more you should focus on building attraction. If you feel that strong attraction is already present, focus on creating deeper rapport.

The purpose of a date is two-fold. First, it's to re-heat the attraction that was present when she last said goodbye to you. Some of it has been lost while you were apart and must be regained early in the date when she remembers why she came out to see you in the first place. It's for this reason that you shouldn't pull any aggressive moves at the beginning of the date.

The second purpose is to add to the initial attraction through touching, intimate eye contact, and sharing of personal anecdotes, stories, or routines that enhance your value and make her comfortable enough to want to have sex with you. I will first discuss basic date logistics before focusing on conversation, which applies not only to dates, but also when you first meet a girl.

An important consideration is the venue. If you live in a small town, your choices may be very limited, but if you live in a major metropolitan city, you'll have hundreds of options. I select venues based on four factors: lighting, noise, seating, and crowdedness.

With lighting, the darker the better. It gives a sensual mood that makes her feel less self-conscious around other people, and is more conducive for touching.

When it comes to noise, pick a venue that's mid-way between library-quiet and club-noisy, although a noisy venue can be an advantage if you have to sit closer so that you can hear each other.

Seating is the most important consideration, because it determines how close you can get to her. The worst type of seating is a large table where you and your date sit on opposite sides. This is fine for an instant-date venue in day game or the first venue on a date if you will soon be moving to another venue, but touching from across a large table is awkward. If I have to stay in such a venue because there are no alternatives, I excuse myself halfway through the date to go to the bathroom and sit next to her when I return.

The last consideration is crowdedness. The fewer people in the venue, the more likely she will feel comfortable being intimate with you. Ideally, you want to be alone with her in a dark part of the bar that is not visible to anyone else, as if you have your own private room. My overall strategy is to start the date at a venue that may not be ideal in terms of the above criteria and later move to an optimal venue where I get more intimate.

Venue changes during a date are perhaps the most important component of success for the reason you already know: it makes the girl feel she's known you longer than she has. By default, all your first dates should consist of at least two venues that are within walking distance of each other. If you live in a small town, this may be impossible, so you'll stick with only one venue.

Spend about one hour in the first venue and one to three hours in the second venue. A third venue is required if you feel that you're not making much progress with touching or if she's not participating in the conversation. A third venue is also helpful if you're both in a party mood and want to go to a lively club that has dancing. Venue changes are only critical *before* you have sex with a girl. Afterwards, you can have dates where you stay at one venue, or simply invite her straight to your place.

For the first venue, I pick an average bar or café that is not necessarily ideal. Since my focus is to re-heat the attraction with my conversation and presence, I don't need perfect logistics to get physical, and I'll sit across from her even if I can sit next to her. I give her plenty of space at the start of a date so that she sees me as a calm man who is not desperate to jump her bones.

At the first venue, we will likely have one or two rounds of alcoholic drinks, I'll pay the entire bill, and we will move somewhere else after I tell her there is a cool place we should check out. In addition to re-heating the attraction, you'll be building comfort, which is "boring" in the sense that you'll mainly discuss the basics such as family backgrounds, daily routines, upbringings, hobbies, favorite places to eat and drink, favorite books, and so on (the conversational details will be explained below). If she shares something you find strange, feel free to humorously pretend that it's a deal-breaker: "You like cats instead of dogs? I'm sorry, but it's not going to work out between us. We have to break up! I'm sure you'll find another man." Ham it up by acting emotional or feigning to ask the waitress for the check.

A similar tease is saying "Minus 100 points" when she does something you don't like. It's good to touch her when you tease to make it clear you're joking, because many girls have an impaired ability to perceive humor. Be careful about overdoing teases or you will come across as phony. Once or twice on a date is enough.

It's fine to play up differences that don't matter, such as preferences in food, drink, or animals, but gloss over differences on family, relationships, politics, and culture, or she may think you're not even worth a casual sex encounter. I'm not saying you should alter your views or lie, but on the first few dates be vague about where you stand on hot-button issues and deeper values until you can see whether you have an emotional connection that is strong enough to overcome any major differences. Nothing dries up a girl's vagina faster than debates over politics or religion.

While walking to the second venue, do the arm-in-arm move with the standard "I don't want you to fall down" excuse. On most dates, this is the first big touching move besides a few touches on her forearm across the table at the first venue. By the time you get to the second venue, the attraction will be re-heated if you've shown her that you're not an octopus who will grope her or act aggressively.

At the second venue, add more touching and intimate silences while putting in the face time necessary for her to feel that you've worked hard enough for sex to happen. Consider transferring to a third venue if you're encountering firm resistance to minor moves such as walking arm-in-arm, or if she says she doesn't want you to touch her because it's too "early."

It's worth discussing touching in detail because of how crucial it is at priming a girl for intimate contact while announcing your intention of being more than just a friend. It is more powerful than speaking if you consider that you can have sex with a girl you've *only* touched, as in a club pick-up, but you can't have sex with a girl you've only spoken to but haven't touched.

I'm not a naturally touchy guy. I need to know a girl for some time before I instinctively want to touch her. I consciously have to remind myself to do so, particularly at the first venue where the seating may not be conducive to touching. I start with tapping her forearm or the back of her hand while I'm making a funny or interesting point. A single touch will have no effect, but a number of touches will cause a girl to expect your touch and crave it. Imagine how the girl would feel if you didn't try to touch at all and then at the end of the date you suddenly went in for a kiss. She would see your attempt as "weird" or "awkward" without really knowing why. Touching lays the groundwork for intimacy—you simply cannot skip it.

Approach touching as a logical progression from short taps that a girl barely notices to prolonged contact that begins to steer her thoughts into wanting to have sex with you. The opportunity to do this is ripe at the second venue where you sit next to her and have prolonged incidental touching with your legs or the sides of your torsos. Whatever the situation, gradually increase your touching as if you were cooking a frog in a pot of slowly heating water. The first touch may come after several minutes of talking, and then ten minutes may pass before you do a second touch. A few hours later, the touching may be almost constant.

Since I know the touching will be ramped up, I'm not too concerned about touching when greeting a girl at the very beginning of a date. Instead, I stand close to her and give her an opportunity to show interest by leaning into me for a hug or kiss.

It's fine if she doesn't want to take that opportunity, because I'll begin touching her soon anyway. Even if you kissed her beforehand, don't be overly eager to start a date with a kiss. Reheat the attraction and make her anxious about whether your interest in her is still strong.

Intimate touching is easier in a club environment when you're standing and able to touch a girl's hips, lower back, and the top of her ass. On dates when you're sitting, the intimate areas are her knees, upper thighs, and hands, with hand touching being the most intimate. You can touch her hands when commenting on her jewelry, the shape of her hands, or the length of her fingers. You could also offer to "read" her palm, where you pretend to be psychic but make silly or funny comments as you hold her hand and trace its lines with your fingers.

My favorite move while sitting next to a girl is to snake my arm behind her back at the level of the seat so it wraps around her hips. I usually do this when we've been at the second venue for about an hour.

If a girl is not touching you, give her permission. Place her hand on your forearm and say, "It's okay to touch me if you want." A girl doesn't have to be insanely touchy-feely, particularly before you've had sex, but she should participate in the seduction by occasionally touching you. As the dates pile up and you enter a relationship, you'll find that she will touch you far more than you touch her.

Now that you're armed with the broad strokes of how dating works, including touching, I can fill in the gaps when it comes to conversation.

Conversation Framework

Reading books and watching an episode of *Seinfeld* a day are more than enough preparation to get through long dates. Consider, too, that girls love to talk. They will take a load off of your shoulders by speaking at length about random things or events, especially as their comfort with you increases. Before this, however, you may have to put in a bit more work to ensure a smooth conversation.

At the start of the date, when you're at the first venue (or walking to it), you can refer to basic things such as the weather, how she got to the date, and what she has been up to since you last saw her. This is similar to what you do when phoning her: chat initially about what you were doing prior to the interaction. Move on to conversation that is mostly factual in nature where you get to know her and her background, bringing up things that didn't come up during the initial approach. As I mentioned in the previous section, you do this to re-heat the attraction and make her comfortable so she begins to feel that she knows who you are. You want to transition from being a random guy she met on the street or in a club to someone with a unique story that draws her in.

Many of your questions will be direct, along the lines of what she does for a living (and whether she likes it), where she went to school, whether she has any siblings, where she has traveled to, and so on. If you do a search online for "date questions," you'll find dozens of pages of open-ended questions, but most of them train you to interview a girl using a script. Apart from basic personal questions that tell me a girl's life story or provide information that I want to know for my own reasons, there are only six questions that I repeatedly ask.

Question #1: "If you could be any animal, what would you be?" The answer to this question helps me understand her temperament.

Question #2: "If I gave you a billion dollars right now, what would your life be like one year later?" Her answer taps into her true calling or passion.

Question #3: "If you had to leave this country and pick only one other country to live in, which would it be?" This tells you her dream country and lifestyle.

Question #4: "What's the earliest childhood memory you have?" Her answer will enable you to start evaluating the quality of her parental relationships.

Question #5: "How would your life be different if there were no internet or cell phones?" This tells me if she has an internet addiction and how she feels about modern society.

Question #6: "What is your favorite band?" After she answers this question, I tell her what my favorite bands are, including at least one that is obscure. I praise the obscure band as one she definitely has to listen to. Later, you'll see how I use this to change the venue to my place.

After focusing on basic personal information, you'll ease into broadening the conversation so that it's possible to talk about anything. Instead of giving you another list of questions to ask, I'll provide a general framework that can guide you for as long as the date lasts. The framework minimizes script memorization and leads to conversations that are natural. Let's start with the first guideline.

Flip back all her questions to understand her core values. If a girl asks you a personal question, it addresses an issue that is important to her. A good example is when a girl asks, "What do you do?" She considers employment to be important, and has most likely devoted the past few years of her life to landing a good job. Another example is, "Where have you traveled to?" A girl won't ask this unless travel is important to her, so you can guess that she is planning to travel a lot. And consider this question: "What is the craziest thing you've ever done?" Would a girl ask this if she didn't value doing crazy or exciting things? The type of questions she asks are a reliable window into her values.

There are three ways to answer a girl's questions: lie, give a joke answer, or give an honest answer. I don't recommend lying because you will have to remember the lie, which increases your anxiety as you try to keep the truth hidden. For example, if you lie about your age, you will have to make sure she never sees your identification card while changing details about your past so that they match your fake age. This will cause a lot of headache, and is usually not worth it.

A joke answer is a good option, because it shows a girl that you aren't impressed by her, which indirectly does impress her, but be careful not to turn *every* answer into a joke or she will become annoyed and frustrated.

The last option is to be honest and direct. I mix up my joke answers with this option, but if I don't have a good answer to her question, I'll deflect it with a joke.

After I have answered her question, I ask her the same question and relax as she talks about something she's interested in. I may do this relatively quickly if I give a joke answer to prevent her from trying to get a real answer out of me. This is how I temporarily conceal things that I don't want a girl to know (for example, that I write books like this).

Her: "So what do you do?"

Me: "I'm a lumberjerk."

Her: "No, really."

Me: "I make money on the internet. It's too boring to talk about."

Her: "Hmm."

Me: "So what do you do?"

If I pause too long after giving an honest answer, she will dig deeper and ask how I make money on the internet, and be horrified to discover that she's on a date with a "pro-rape advocate," the term the media has used to defame me. By immediately asking her the question back, I interrupt her train of thought and turn it inward. She'll then be happy to tell me about her office job and how she's changing the world.

If she asks you about something that you genuinely enjoy talking about, you can give extensive answers, but do not *appear* to be trying to impress her. Many men I've spoken to have even tried to impress me by listing all the countries they've visited or the exact number of girls they've banged when I didn't ask.

I know that you may be proud of your accomplishments, but it will seem like you're trying too hard if you rattle them off. A girl will pick up on this because it's what men have been doing since she reached puberty. Instead of focusing on the accomplishment itself (for example, the number of countries you've been to, your job title), describe something related to it (the vibe of your favorite travel destination, the part of your job that is the most fun).

Flipping the conversation back not only helps when you don't have much of an answer, it also makes the girl feel like you "understand" her. You seem to know what to ask even though you're merely asking her the same questions she asked you. In fact, you can go on a date without having any potential questions in your mind and simply ask what she asks.

Make observations and comments about the things and people in the environment you're in. This is my favorite tactic, because all it requires is a pair of eyes. When you're talking to a girl, you may be at a bar, park, or city square. What is your opinion of the venue? What do you like and not like about it? What do you think of the people who are there? What do you think of the food or drink? Have you noticed interesting or strange things about the venue, such as a wall painting or decoration? Does the venue remind you of somewhere else?

I'm writing this book in my bedroom. I have a bonsai tree on my left, which reminds me of the movie *Karate Kid*. I have a house plant directly in front of me that is growing fast and which I have named. I think I would like to try gardening one day, because it seems like a peaceful activity. I have a large water jug to my immediate right, because I don't trust municipal water, which may contain chemicals that are bad for my health. To my left is a cup of coffee that I made using Aeropress, a contraption where I push brewed coffee through a filter. I can tell you about the coffee bean I used and the grinding process.

The objects around me open a door to talking about other subjects, and I'm confident I could chat nonstop about them and the things connected to them. When you're in a venue, the things around you will remind you of other things and stories, allowing you to go on for as long as the girl appears interested. If she starts breaking eye contact or stares at her phone, change the subject or take a break and let her bring up a topic of her own.

What I like most with talking about the environment I'm in is that it's relaxing. You're in the moment and not worried about the past or future. You're enjoying your time together and creating a bubble that only the two of you share, as if you've joined forces to discuss the world. For you and a girl to draw meaning from your environment, both of you have to be seeing or experiencing the same thing, creating a subtle level of compatibility.

If I'm in a bar or restaurant, I'll start with observations about the music, lighting, decorations, drinks, or food. If I'm in a café, I'll talk about the quality of my beverage and my experiences with tea and coffee in general. If I'm on the street, I'll make comments about the general demeanor of the people. She might give you a rich response that allows you to take the conversation in a different direction, or you might remember a story or experience that you want to share.

The easiest way to comment on your shared environment is to talk about the people around you. Women are natural people-watchers, so your date will be eager to share her opinion. For example: "That person's outfit is interesting. What do you think?" Or you might see someone with a cool hat: "I've been looking to buy a hat like that." If you see another couple, ask, "How long do you think they've been dating? It looks like they just met."

If you talk about things or people in your environment, try not to be overly critical, or else you may come across as negative. Unless I'm experiencing something that is really making me upset, I don't complain about the little things, such as a bar that's slightly too noisy or a waitress who is too slow. I keep this in mind particularly when I'm commenting about people. I don't point out individuals to make fun of them, and I use neutral words such as "interesting" or "strange" to describe ugly people.

Tell anecdotes. A natural result of talking about your shared environment is relaying similar experiences you've had. This thing reminds you of that thing, which reminds you of some other thing, and from there you can naturally hop from topic to topic. Anecdotes are a great way to show value since they are often based on something interesting or noteworthy you did, perhaps while traveling or seeking adventure.

When I'm in a coffee shop, I can relay anecdotes about how I make my own coffee, or how I was blown away by the coffee I had in Italy. If I'm on the street, I can talk about how the people compare with those in my town or somewhere else. If I'm in a bar, I can talk about how a bar I went to sold a tasty drink that I can't find anywhere else. Or I can just take the type of venue I'm in and talk about my favorite one of its kind: my favorite café, my favorite restaurant, my favorite city, and so on. I can share my reasons and add a story that helps her to visualize my world. Below is an example that combines talking about the environment with sharing an anecdote.

Me: "What kind of drink did you order?"

Her: "Strawberry-infused organic lemongrass whole wheat vodka cocktail."

Me: "How is it?"

Her: "It's pretty good—tastes like a strawberry cupcake."

Me: "Have you been to a bar called Russia House? They have more than fifty infused vodkas."

Her: "I haven't."

Me: "The best is their pepper-infused vodka. You take it by shot. It clears any throat infection you have because it's like putting fire in your mouth."

Her: "I don't like drinking vodka without a mixer."

Me: "I didn't either, but then I went to Russia. If you don't drink shots with the guys, they think you're a weak man and won't invite you to their home."

Her: "Wow."

> Me: "Yeah, the society there is tougher than here. They also have a pro-bullying culture where you're supposed to shame men until they toughen up. Have you ever been to Europe?"
>
> Her: "Yes, but only to Spain. I went alone. The parties were endless. It was the most exciting time of my life."

I started by asking a simple question about her drink and ended up finding out that she banged a dozen Spaniards during a recent trip, telling me it will be safe to go for a fast bang. Note how my anecdotes were quite short, only a sentence or two. If you're not a good story-teller, you don't have to tell stories. Although I'm decent at telling stories, I find that most people don't have the attention span for them, especially in noisy environments. The more deeply you get to know a person, whether a guy or a girl, the longer your stories can get.

Another way to introduce an anecdote is to start with "The other day." Example: "The other day, I was going to a gym and saw a really ugly pug, but it made eye contact with me, so now I'm curious about them." Then I can talk about dogs or pet ownership in general. Usually, at least one noteworthy thing will happen to you every day, whether it's an old lady cutting in front of you in the supermarket line or almost getting into a car accident. Bring these up as springboards to talk about other topics.

It's important to give the girl an opportunity to respond to your statements or anecdotes with some ramble of her own. Otherwise, the conversation will be one-sided. If you give her a chance to respond and she doesn't give much more than a "Cool" or "Yeah," you can try asking a question.

If you've tossed out various comments or anecdotes and she hasn't responded with much conversation of her own, there are a few explanations of what's going on. First, she may not be an interesting person. You'll be surprised how dull girls can be. Their beauty has been sufficient to get hundreds of suitors straining to entertain them without requiring any banter in return, but if she was lively when you first met her, it may have been because she was drunk. On dates, I often have to wait until a girl has had a couple of drinks before she will loosen up again.

Second, it's possible you haven't touched on a topic that interests her. Considering that girls mostly talk about guys, food, partying, and makeup, it can be hard for a man to identify a shared interest that will engage her.

Lastly, she may not like you, but this is the least likely possibility, because a girl won't spend time with you on a date if she dislikes you (unless you promised her a free meal). If she does dislike you, she will make an excuse to leave early, reject your venue change, or be resistant to kissing.

"I read that..." Here, you bring up, or simply invent, a piece of information that will encourage conversation. I touched on this earlier where you refer to an article you read as a way to talk about an interesting topic. For example, say I'm on a first date a few days after meeting a girl in a club. I could say, "I read on the internet that the hardest place for people to meet each other is a club, because it actually promotes anti-social tendencies." I could go on to talk about all the aspects of clubs that limit social interaction, such as the loud music, high-school-like cliques, and so on. If it's an opinion that I genuinely hold, I could introduce the topic with "I think that."

Here's another example I have used: "I read that white tea has 20% the caffeine as a cup of coffee, but everyone thinks it has 0%, so many people who drink only white tea are addicted to caffeine without even knowing it." I could use this during a day approach or while on a date in a café. Another real-life example from a supermarket approach: "I read that supermarkets are modeled after gambling casinos in that they put the big money-makers in the middle. The healthy food goes on the outside while all the junk food is the most accessible." An example where food is being served: "I read that we evolved taste buds that are highly sensitive to salt and sugar, because they were in short supply in our ancestral past. We only got sugar through bee honey, which was risky to obtain, and salt through animal meat. Now salt and sugar are everywhere."

Don't memorize these examples, because I surely didn't—

they were in my head at the time due to my habit of reading articles and books. It's no surprise that girls respond well to interesting factoids. They tend to love listicles, shareable memes, and "Did you know" trivia.

I also use "I read that" to identify where she stands on something controversial. If I sense she is emotionally invested in an issue, and I hold an opposing position, I'll avoid talking about it until I at least get the bang. Modern culture has encouraged girls to believe that their identity is bound up in their political opinions. If you clash with those opinions, she'll feel that you can't possibly be compatible with her. I strongly encourage you to avoid talking about hot-button topics like abortion or gun control before you've had sex, but if like me you're something of an instigator who likes to get a rise out of people, you may not be able to help yourself.

When I'm in the mood to troll, I use "I read that" to indirectly praise masculinity or challenge feminist orthodoxy. Example: "Do you like that woman's blue hair? I read that if a girl has weird colored hair, she is over ten times more likely to be morbidly obese. I wonder why that is." Another example: "I read that men who have tested with lower levels of testosterone are more likely to be submissive in relationships, or even want to watch their girlfriends sleep with other men. That's crazy." If I encounter a danger zone, where she holds a position that I don't, I'll let the topic die or risk losing my attractiveness for her (or vice versa).

"Why do you...?" This involves asking a girl, in a neutral tone, why she does certain behaviors, with the aim of showing her that you're evaluating her worth. This communicates that you believe your value is high and *deserve* a girl who meets a set of criteria you deem important. Posing this question is not an act—you genuinely care about the quality you're inquiring about.

My favorite "Why do you" question is, "Why do you have short hair? I think you would look better with long hair." I think it's a crime for girls to make themselves ugly on purpose, so I am quite direct with expressing my interest in long hair. If the short-haired girl is offended, she can walk away, because in the long run I only want to date a girl who is amenable to having long hair. Most girls with short hair will give me a lame reason that I can counter with a "I read that" statement: "I read a study that showed men rate girls with long hair as five times more fertile." I would have sex with a girl who has short hair, but if she doesn't ever want to grow it out, I put her in the pump-and-dump category.

Another "Why do you" question concerns her footwear. It grinds my gears when a girl wears flip-flops on a date or goes to a night venue in sneakers. In a flat tone that at least partially conceals my true opinion, I ask, "Why are you wearing those shoes?" She'll say that she likes them, and I will respond by asking her why, specifically, she likes them. Then I will reveal my position by saying, "Wearing those shoes in this venue is like saying you don't care about what other people think of you." If that's too heavy for you, point out the appropriate shoes worn by a girl nearby and ask, "Do you ever wear shoes like that? She seems to be putting in a lot of effort."

The last example is asking, "Why are you cursing?" It's become common for modern women to curse excessively in order to appear cool or hip, but I find it distasteful. If I'm talking to a girl who has potential, but she's letting the f-bombs fly, I ask her why she speaks like that, and whether she has some kind of inner rage that causes her to use those words. When I think she's about to get angry, I add, "For the pleasant time we are having, profanity doesn't match the mood."

Don't be shy about communicating your standards and what you expect from a girl. Stop short of insulting her or starting an argument, but understand that if you don't communicate your standards, she may think you don't have any. When you show a girl that you have standards, and you sleep with her, she will feel a sense of pride that she was able to please you. This sets up a frame where she will want to keep pleasing you.

The examples above relate specifically to my standards. Yours may be completely different. If she's not meeting one of your important standards, and you want to investigate whether it's a genuine red flag while conveying your value, simply ask her why she does something. Her answer will enable you to make a well-informed decision about her long-term value.

If you're feeling a bit hesitant to ask about her behavior, understand that she's evaluating you even more harshly—you just won't hear it from her mouth because women are less confrontational than men. At the very minimum, fire off one or two "Why are you" questions to a girl who is especially cocky, because it helps to shift her thoughts from your flaws to hers.

"……………… " The last conversation guideline is silence. As a date progresses, you can begin to relax and not rush to fill in a silence like you did when you first approached her, where a silence could have resulted in her exiting. On dates, when she already has blocked out a long period of time to be with you, she will not leave if you stop talking momentarily. Silences will show that you are calm, steady, and confident. They're also helpful if you're tired of talking or have run out of things to say.

To create an intimate silence, wait for a pause in the conversation, lock eyes with her, and wait until she looks away first. It's unnecessary to have a penetrating stare—simply look into her eyes with a relaxed, warm expression. The girl may blush, a good sign that she perceives your masculinity and feels vulnerable because of it. When you're talking to a girl, eye contact is standard and doesn't suggest attraction, but eye contact during a silence is a highly intimate gesture that is reserved for lovers.

To help a girl become comfortable with eye contact, I sometimes force it by playing a staring game: "I bet I can beat you in a staring contest." If I blink before she does and lose the contest, I will jokingly claim that she cheated in some way.

A girl will increase the time she can maintain eye contact with you as time goes on. It may reach a point where she starts to make *you* feel uncomfortable with how long she can hold a gaze (it's okay to occasionally break eye contact first). If the staring length doesn't increase as she gets to know you, her attraction is probably low. This can be confirmed only when you attempt to kiss her or change the venue.

What would a girl prefer during a date: nonstop conversation that may be boring or intimate silence? Nonstop conversation is better in the first thirty minutes of a date to re-heat her attraction and confirm that you are a man worth spending time with. Starting at about the one-hour mark, silence is better than talking about something you know is boring or lame. At the end of a long date, there may hardly be any talking at all.

When can you remove the chatty clown mask and just be yourself? I am able to play the clown up to the point where I have sex, but then I return to my normal baseline. If she doesn't want to stick around after that, she's telling me that I have to remain a clown for the rest of our relationship, an intolerable proposition. Even girls put on a clown mask when they first meet you by showing their best side. The real magic happens when both of you can be yourselves and enjoy deep compatibility.

If your personality doesn't allow you to be chatty, even temporarily, you will have to find a girl who is not only chattier than average, but who is strongly attracted to you from the beginning. This is usually the case if she makes sustained eye contact before you approach. You may have to fall back on developing a social circle where a girl can discover your value through casual hangouts.

A girl may lose interest and dump you after you've toned down your artificially high chattiness. She was attracted to the high-energy clown who approached her, and now she doesn't like it when you are more or less yourself. We are living in a time when being an entertaining clown is highly valued by women, so you'll have to think deeply about the sacrifices you're willing to make to sustain intimacy with them.

One tactic you should not employ on a date is talking about sex, something that men often do in the hope that it will make girls horny. This isn't necessary because girls come pre-installed with a vagina that is already aching for sex, and trying to force the topic may turn her off instead. However, it is useful to make a comment that implies you don't judge girls for sleeping around (even if you do). This will reduce the time it takes to get a girl into bed while allowing you to understand her true nature. Here's a routine I often use:

> "I think people are too quick to judge these days. I should be able to live my life in a way that I want. If I'm not hurting anyone else then it's no business or concern what I do. It's obvious to me that people judge others just to make themselves feel better."

If you use this routine around the time of the kiss, she will connect it with sexual activity and feel looser. When I'm in a foreign country, I take it up a notch by almost endorsing the promiscuous behavior of women in my home country:

> "One thing we have in the United States is equality, where men and women are treated the same. So if a girl wants to sleep with 100 guys, she can do so, and the culture says we can't judge her for it. People sleep with each other very quickly and it's the normal thing to do. Maybe it's different here."

Apart from these routines, I don't bring up sex during the date, but if she wants to talk about it, I will do so without showing that I'm excited.

Putting anything more in your mind other than the conversational guidelines above risks confusing you and making your vibe robotic, because it would remove you from the moment and get you stuck on how an ideal conversation should go. If you still think you need more help on how to have a conversation, your problem is anxiety, not conversational ability. In that case, reread the chapter on internal game and adjust your autosuggestions. You need to internalize that *she* should be worrying about maintaining a conversation and doing things that please you.

You will have many bad dates, regardless of how much game knowledge you're able to accumulate. Trying to prevent sour encounters is a waste of your energy and will cause you to miss out on interacting with girls with whom you're compatible. The way I see it, even a bad date can be beneficial, because it provides me with useful information about the type of girl I should go for and how to avoid costly mistakes. Every experience you have with girls, whether positive or negative, is important for ensuring greater success in the future.

Always Be Leading

More important than the content of your conversation is maintaining the lead. You should control the flow, tempo, energy, and direction of a conversation. It's okay for a girl to ask questions about you, and discuss topics that interest her, but she should never take over the conversation completely while you wait passively for her to ask another question or bring up the next topic.

Leading the conversation can be tiring, especially when dealing with a girl who doesn't talk much. It can seem like a relief when you meet a "strong and independent" girl who asks all sorts of questions and raises various topics, but permitting her dominance will cause her to lose respect for you. Most girls are not attracted to men who let them lead. If she is comfortable with leading the conversation, it's likely she's not feeling any sexual tension or nervousness, so what you may perceive as a sign of interest is actually a lack of interest. She's treating you more like a co-worker instead of a potential lover.

Even if a girl is chatty, you should control the conversation. To let a girl know the role I expect her to take, I push back against her attempts to lead the conversation by saying: "Are you normally this aggressive? Let's take it easy, there's no rush." Another possibility: "You're asking me a lot of questions like this is a job interview. Slow down a bit."

This principle also applies when making decisions on dates, such as where to go and how long to stay in a venue. I may ask about a girl's general preferences or tastes, but I don't allow her to make the final decision. If she does attempt to pick the venue, I will push back by asking, "Are you paying?" Then I will choose my preferred location. She is free to leave at any time if she doesn't like it.

As with leading the conversation, it can be tiring to always make the decisions on what to do and where to go, but this is what a masculine man does. I've seen many men slip in this area when it comes to relationships. Don't yield the power to your girlfriend because you want to take a mental break from making decisions. Her attraction will decrease as a result, putting the relationship in jeopardy. Strike down a girl's attempt to step out of her submissive role. The reins should be firmly in your hands during the *entire* course of the relationship.

Another sign that you're losing control is when a girl asks nonstop questions and you always answer in a direct manner. If a girl asks you multiple questions in rapid fire, she is testing your masculinity to see whether you will jump through hoops and answer obediently. Even if your honest answers show high value, you're still giving up the lead, which brings that value back down.

Mix up your answering style. For half the time, tell the truth, and for the other half, evade with humor, be annoyingly vague, or tell an obviously exaggerated lie that shows her you don't care about the answer. This strategy will make her expend more energy trying to learn who you really are. You may answer directly more than 50% of the time in traditional countries while less than 50% in degenerate countries such as the USA, Canada, and England.

I'm always experimenting with answers to the most common questions girls ask me, such as "What do you do?", "How old are you?", and when traveling, "Why are you here?" For each question, I test various evasive or humorous responses before using ones that I believe elicit the most attraction based on who I am as a man. If I don't feel like talking about my job, but a girl insists, I will say, "I'm not allowed to talk much about my job." She may think I'm some kind of spy. If a girl in a foreign country asks me why I'm in her city, I respond, "I ask myself that question every day." She'll know I'm not impressed with her country, suggesting that I'm an experienced man. If I feel that a girl has earned a real answer, I will give it, but if she shows annoyance, or even goes as far as to give me an ultimatum, I will definitely not give in to her.

Direct answers are a reward. A girl has no right to them. I learned this in Brazil when I spent time with a German man who never gave a girl a direct answer besides his name. He didn't even say where he was from. At the time, I thought girls would be so turned off by his evasiveness that they would leave, but it actually made them more curious and turned conversations into a fun game where he doled out clues as if he were giving little treats to an eager puppy.

Curiosity is a form of attraction. Giving direct answers removes curiosity. Therefore, always answering directly can hurt attraction. Imagine an interaction where a girl knew all the pertinent facts about your life within ten minutes. She'd get bored and later say, "There was no chemistry."

It's also important to lead if a girl is using her cell phone frequently enough where you feel disrespected. I used to deal with this problem by teasing the girl so she indirectly got the message, but it's better to take a more direct tack by explicitly telling her how you want her to behave.

The most common situation is when a girl leaves her phone on the table with the screen facing up and looks at it constantly. I won't accept this. I didn't go on a date to speak to a girl who is babysitting her phone.

Me: "Are you expecting an important call?"

Her: "No."

Me: "Because I don't want to compete with your phone, and you seem overly focused on it. Can you put it in your bag?"

When you make this request, you must be prepared to end the date if she doesn't comply. It's your way or the highway. If she refuses to put away her phone, or she says it's on silent mode, say once more that you would prefer her to put away her phone because it's not respectful. If she refuses to do what you ask her, find out how much she owes, settle the bill, and leave.

It's even worse when her phone is constantly going off and she's checking it or replying to messages. I may first warn her by saying, "Do you need a break to catch up on your texting? Go ahead, I'll wait." Let her finish the text she has to send. If she grabs her phone again, she is showing disrespect. Say, "I don't like how you're using your phone so much. Can you put it away?" If she continues after this, you should end the date.

It's not fun to scold a girl for her anti-social behavior, but remember that it's entirely your choice whether or not to accept it. If she's making you feel bad, don't put up with it, or you're explicitly giving her permission to treat you like garbage. Nip the problem in the bud as soon as it happens so she understands you have standards that must be met. A girl will either walk away, which means she wasn't that attracted to you in the first place, or highly respect you for calling her out on her shit in a way that no other man has probably done before, which will greatly increase her attraction for you.

My experience shows that most girls will comply with your request because they've already invested time in coming out on a date. Of course, we don't want to be a phone Nazi and forbid her from ever using her phone, but if she's texting more than once every hour, and you're feeling annoyed, you must tell her what you expect.

Leading starts when we make the decisions on where the date should take place, with minimal input from the girl. During the date, we are careful with how much information we divulge while putting the brakes on her attempts to dominate the conversation or interview us. Lastly, we call out any of her behaviors that make us feel uncomfortable, the most common of which is her phone use. Being a leader in these areas will show the girl that we have expectations and are willing to walk away if she doesn't behave properly.

Qualification

Questions or routines that attempt to qualify a girl, where she must prove or justify herself, help to raise your value, because a person who justifies themselves concludes subconsciously that they are dealing with someone who is worth that justification. An added bonus of qualifying is that you will start to know whether she's worth only a quick fling or something more.

Qualification happens naturally if you are a man with standards. You ask questions to find out if a girl holds to the standards you deem important. Problems arise when you are young and don't yet have standards, or when you're so horny that you're ready to sleep with anyone. In these cases, you'll skip qualification entirely, causing her to conclude that you're desperate or that her value is higher than yours.

When I first started with game, my standards were purely physical. I didn't care what a girl was like as long as she could satisfy my boner and allow me to achieve an orgasm. I can only wonder how this made my job harder, because with most of the girls I approached, I must've subconsciously communicated that they didn't have to do anything to receive my sustained attention. This unattractive vibe can easily be squashed by asking a girl questions that evaluate her worth. If you have a list of qualities you want in a girl, simply ask questions related to them. If you don't yet have standards, make them up. Whenever you qualify, ramble about how that quality relates to your life.

The most basic qualification question is asking a girl if she can cook. Even if you don't care that a girl can't cook, it's worth asking. Since most girls lack cooking skills, you will make her feel insecure as she realizes you have expectations besides her merely possessing a vagina.

Me: "Do you know how to cook?"

Her: "Not really."

Me: "So what do you eat?"

Her: "I mostly eat out because I'm a foodie."

Me: "Isn't every human being in the world technically a foodie? We all like to eat food."

Her: "Yes, but I like taking pictures of my food, and I appreciate the art that goes into it."

Me: "I see. So if you ever have children, what will you feed them every day?"

Her: "I haven't thought about that."

Me: "I'm a big fan of home-cooked meals. It's healthier and tastes better. Cooking may seem difficult, but it's just a series of techniques that you can learn. I have a pot roast that I'm perfecting right now."

Without preaching or being overly judgmental, I communicated that cooking is an important value to me, that I'm spending time getting better at it, and that most girls don't know how to cook (in other words, her value is average because she's like every other girl). She will know without a doubt that her value has sustained a negative hit in my mind. I sometimes even jokingly blurt out "Oooh… minus 100 points" when she reveals that she lacks an important quality, a good technique if you think that a girl is too dense to pick up on subtlety.

Another quality you may be interested in is fitness. Ask questions to find out if she takes time to work out.

Me: "Do you go to the gym?"

Her: "I do Crossfit."

Me: "How many times a week?"

Her: "Four times."

Me: "That's good, because our bodies will gradually turn into a soft marshmallow as we get older. I go to the gym twice a week. Are you satisfied with how your body is right now?"

Her: "I could lose about 90 pounds."

Me: "I read an article that stated 95% of girls are not satisfied with their bodies, even if they are at a normal weight."

In this example, I gave positive reinforcement to a girl who is adhering to a gym standard (but perhaps not a weight standard). I still inserted a dose of insecurity by pointing out that girls are never satisfied with their bodies. An effective hot-cold technique is to boost a girl's ego before bringing it back down. It's a sad fact that if you communicate to a girl that she perfectly hits all of your standards, she may think she's too good for you. Be stingy with showing direct approval.

Another qualification is to screen for a normal attention span. Ask, "Do you read?" Let her tell you about the books she reads. You can also tell her about some of the books you've read recently, which is a sure way to bring up many topics to discuss. If a girl doesn't read at all, ask her what she does in her spare time. Other qualification questions can involve whether she gardens, goes to church, plays an instrument (or is otherwise artistically inclined), or attended university.

When a girl fails your qualification test, show disapproval with your body language by frowning, crossing your arms, or leaning back. Verbally, you can use the "Minus 100 points" joke or say "I see" while pursing your lips. This sends her the message that she is not meeting your standards. If she has attraction for you, she will attempt to regain your favor through other means. Either way, it's a great position for you to be in, because you're establishing a frame where she is trying to prove her worth to you.

The flip side of qualification is when she attempts to qualify you. If you remember the strategy of giving 50% humorous answers to show that you don't care about meeting her standards, you'll avoid being sucked into her frame. You can also "agree and amplify," where you accept the negative trait she is trying to pin on you and amplify it to an absurd degree.

> Her: "Are you one of those guys who goes to the club to pick up girls?"
>
> Me: "Yes. I go to the club ten times a week and I pick up 100 girls each night."

Her: "No, but seriously."

Me: "Seriously. Before I talked to you tonight, I already had sex with 30 other girls in the bathroom."

As the term suggests, agree with the negative quality and amplify it until she gives up in exasperation.

Her: "Where do you see yourself in five years?"

Me: "On the streets, begging for beer money."

Her: "No, but really."

Me: "Really, I want to be free like a bird. No worries, no troubles."

Girls are so used to men who immediately fall into their qualification frame that they can't help but be more attracted to a man who doesn't. If you realize that a girl is trying to qualify you, simply do not allow it. Refuse to provide answers. The more she demands proper answers, the more you should agree and amplify. Remember, she must follow your frame and rules, not the other way around.

You will sometimes encounter a girl who agrees and amplifies herself, or fails all of your qualification tests. If she is mocking your standards, or simply doesn't conform to any of them, it's usually a sign that she has little attraction or respect for you. Walk away. If you don't, she will know that your standards mean nothing and proceed to toy with you.

You only need to qualify a well-behaved and feminine girl two or three times before sex. With girls who have a tougher attitude or flakey nature, you may need to hit them with every single qualification in your arsenal. Just remember to spread them over the entire interaction instead of doing them back to back. Also try to match your qualifications with the venue. For example, if you're in a noisy nightclub where everyone is drunk, it wouldn't make sense to ask her if she goes to church or is great in the kitchen. Instead, you could ask her if she's a good dancer.

You can get more creative with your qualifications if you want to evaluate her values and not only her behavior. This is important when you're trying to identify whether a girl is suitable for a monogamous relationship. Here's a value qualification I like:

> "I noticed that most people structure their lives either around seeking comfort or seeking adventure. What are you most interested in now?"

Her answer is irrelevant, since we know that girls lie by giving idealized answers that reflect how she likes to see herself or how she wants you to see her as. The main point of the question is to see if there is a disconnect between her behavior and words. Her answer should match what you've seen of her so far. If it doesn't, you're dealing with a girl who is either deceitful or confused, and you should proceed carefully and ignore most of what she says. We do not trust a girl's words on their own: she must always confirm them with her actions, which tell us who she really is.

The next qualification is one a girl may have asked you before: "What is the most exciting thing you've ever done?" Men do not really want to know the most exciting thing a girl has done, because it will almost always involve a gangbang, but what she reveals can be telling. Mentally multiply her answer by five to know how depraved and slutty she is.

Her answer may also allow you to show approval by saying the following: "You know, at first I thought you were a bit boring or quiet, but now that I've talked to you for a while, you seem fun." If she feigns insult, insist that you "thought" she was boring but no longer think so. In essence, you are communicating that she is gaining your favor over time and that your interest depends on factors other than her beauty.

My favorite part of asking a girl the most exciting thing she has done is when she asks me in return. She will be expecting an answer that attempts to impress her, but I will do the opposite and give a boring answer such as, "I once read a book for five hours straight" or "I made a batch of chocolate chip cookies completely from scratch." If she asks you to be serious, you can provide an even more boring answer: "I once tied my shoes with my eyes closed."

We are not obliged to answer a girl's questions in the way she expects, and the more unpredictable we are, the more attraction she will have for us. If your life really is quite boring, being honest about it may cause her to think you're hiding something exciting. The less you try to prove something, the more it's implied.

Another qualification test covers a girl's internet addiction and attention-whoring: "Do you use Facebook, Instagram, or Snapchat?" You will already know the answer to this question based on how often you've seen her reach for her phone, so what you're really doing is finding out how much she will try to deceive you. If her answer confirms what you already suspect, that she is an attention whore, show disapproval.

Be careful of overdoing qualifications or it will seem contrived. I aim for one or two when I first meet a girl and two more when we meet again. If you exceed that, you may come across as a stern teacher and suck the fun out of a meeting that should lead to intimacy. You may also notice that when you start qualifying, girls will remember to start qualifying you. If she attempts to do so, deflect with humor to establish the frame of her having to jump through hoops for you but not the other way around.

Teasing

It's very important to tease the modern girl to show that you are selective. It also implies that you know, or feel, that your value is higher than hers, because most men are scared to death of teasing girls they like for fear of losing them. When I started gaming back in 2001, teasing was the first tactic I learned that helped maximize the attraction girls have for me while concealing the fact that I intensely valued the chance of having sex with them.

A good tease humorously shows that your value is high *or* that her value is low. You know you deployed it successfully when a girl smiles or playfully hits you. The easiest type of tease is fake boasting, where you brag in a way that is obvious.

The first example involves your build. Unless you're a bodybuilder, you can refer to how your body is so "huge" that you should stop working out. Example: "I went to the gym today, but I think I should stop because I'm getting so huge. Look at my bicep. Does it scare you?" She may play along by saying, "Oh my God, yes, it's so big. Can I touch it please?"

Another example refers to your facial hair. When a girl brings up my long beard in conversation, I say, "The funny thing is I actually shaved today. If you look closely, you can see it growing right now." I insist she stroke it to feel its power.

You can also boast of your intelligence. If you make a witty observation or comment, say, "Sometimes I think I'm too intelligent for this world. It's really hard to get along with everyone else." The format of the fake-boasting tease is to take a quality and amplify it to a ridiculous degree without being self-deprecating. This is a good starter tease because it doesn't insult the girl.

Earlier, I discussed the "We have to break up" tease. A different tease comes after she asks about your past relationships. Say, "I have a very cold heart, and no girl has been able to touch it." You can grab her hand and put it on your chest. This sets up a challenge where she may want to be the one who "warms" your heart.

Invent games and introduce them by saying that you're the undefeated champion. If she wins, claim that she cheated, as with the staring contest. You can do this with simple things: "I bet I can make it to the end of the street faster than you" or "I bet I'm more flexible than you." Physical challenges also serve double duty in providing opportunities to touch her. You'll be surprised how competitive girls are (many will genuinely try to cheat). Even playing a simple game of trivia on your smartphone is an opportunity to tease her about your "unparalleled genius."

The above teases involve either you or your interaction instead of being solely about her, which have a higher chance of going wrong. Girls are so sensitive these days that I've phased out most teases that focus on a girl's flaws, particularly those that concern her appearance or intelligence, although a safe tease I like to do is making fun of a girl for not being as muscular as I am while suggesting an arm-wrestling contest. If I'm going to tease her about a possible flaw, I only do it face-to-face so I can gauge her response. I also don't tease myself in a negative or self-deprecating way unless it's part of an agree-and-amplify tactic to deflect from a girl's pointed questions.

Some girls need to be teased hard to bring down their value, and you'll find this is the case if she's teasing *you* hard. If she's making fun of your shoes, hair, jokes, or otherwise riding you for no apparent reason, she's treating you in the way that she wants to be treated. Dish it right back to her.

Unfortunately, girls are becoming so confused that they're mistaking snarky sarcasm or insults with flirting. If you want to sleep with a girl, you'll have to participate with this type of banter to maximize the attraction she has for you. Otherwise, ask her, "Why are you acting like this? Do other men like you after you act so silly?" Either she will calm down and respect your frame or lose interest entirely.

Teasing is meant to increase attraction, but if the attraction is already high, and the girl isn't teasing you or challenging your frame, you won't need to do it much. I seldom tease foreign girls unless they are Westernized, because my exotic status has solidified a big chunk of the attraction. Otherwise, you need to tease her once every one or two hours. Most guys, when they find out about teasing, overdo it to such an extent that they hurt the connection. Teasing is like the seasoning that is put on the meal of attraction, but it's not the meal itself.

Home Venue Change

Do not show up for a date unless your intention is for it to end in sex. Although this may be unrealistic if you're going out with a conservative girl or if you live with your parents, your goal must still be sex so that your subconscious will help you get as close to it as possible. Always go on dates with a condom in your pocket to prepare for this outcome.

As I have pointed out, a girl may quickly lose interest in a man she hasn't had sex with if she has many other options. The sad truth is that for every date you go on, you must assume that you will never see the girl again. This can be the reality even for dates that go well. You won't feel good when this happens, but you will feel even worse if you know that you passed on guaranteed sex.

We cannot expect a girl to come through simply because she thinks we're interesting or attractive. This is not enough to ensure future dates with her. Instead, she must *invest her body* into the interaction. This means you have to push the intimacy as far as she allows.

Before I discuss venue changing to your place or hers, there is the important issue of paying for dates. I always pay for the first date, because I don't want the issue of money to disturb the seduction. I am the man who approached her, contacted her, and picked the venue, so it makes sense for me to pay. Before sex happens, I don't want to introduce a complication that will change her perception of me as the leader. This doesn't mean I will blow my entire paycheck on a girl in the hope of getting laid, but I will happily spend an amount that won't make me feel upset if the girl disappears or I never sleep with her.

The reason I don't do expensive dinner dates is that I'm unhappy if I shell out a huge amount of money and don't get laid. Additionally, dinner can be formal and stuffy without affording you opportunities for close contact like in a bar. If you're wealthy, you may not mind dropping a lot of money without getting sex in return, so your first date will look different to mine, but even then, you need to beware of overdoing it. You don't want a girl think you're willing to give her a huge reward simply for showing up, which will cause her to postpone sex. Save the fancy dates for when you're in a relationship.

If you don't have much money, do simple dates, such as going for walks or hitting a dive bar during happy hour when the drinks are cheap. I've often had to tell girls that "money is tight right now," and they've understood, even offering to pay. I still insist on paying for the first date, but if she's absolutely sincere, like often is the case with Scandinavian girls, I'm willing to let her do so.

With the bill issue settled, let's review two date scenarios that I commonly face. The first scenario involves a more conservative girl where, because of bad logistics, I'm not able to venue change to a second bar. I also can't change the seating arrangements to sit next to her, and I've touched her only lightly. She's drinking very little—or no—alcohol, and her demeanor is polite but not exactly flirty.

When it's clear that I won't be able to get close enough to kiss in the second or third hour of the date, I suggest a "walk" outside, perhaps to a nearby square, park, or mall. There will be a moment during the walk when I pause to look at a pretty tree or sit down with her on a bench. It's during this time that I try to kiss her using the fly-by strategy. If she pulls her head away, I stop trying. I then walk her to the subway station or to her home and try to kiss again after giving a goodbye hug. If she accepts, and her kissing is enthusiastic, I will try to invite myself to her place. If a girl is not willing to kiss you, or puts up heavy resistance, your odds of sex will be quite low, although you can still try the home venue change. This scenario is more common with foreign, conservative, or sober girls.

The second common scenario is where I have bounced her from the first venue to the second. As the date went on, I touched more, she reciprocated, and I was able to sit next to her. If we're drinking alcohol, it's likely we have consumed at least two drinks each, and are entering the third or fourth hour of the date. We're both feeling comfortable and the silences feel intimate. At this point, I try to kiss her on the lips. If she accepts, I remember not to get too eager, because I want to leave her wanting more. If she doesn't accept, I try again later. She is a prime candidate to get into bed if I kiss her at the venue, and I will aim for a bedroom venue change about thirty minutes after. You are likely to encounter this scenario when you're dating girls who drink alcohol.

It's difficult for me to tell you exactly when the kiss and home venue change should happen. Speaking from experience, if I start a date at 8pm, the kiss will probably happen by 10pm, and I go for the bedroom venue change at about 10:30pm. If I know a girl has to wake up early the next day, or we've been previously intimate, I may try a little sooner. If it's a weekend date, I will go slower, knowing that we have lots of time. It's important that you're not in a race against the clock that causes you to skip the foundational moves of building comfort and touching, because if you do, you'll trigger the logical part of a girl's mind and encounter robust resistance.

It's far better to move too slowly than too fast. If you move too fast, the girl may get creeped out and shut down. If you move too slowly, you may make a girl anxious about whether you'll eventually make a move, which isn't a bad position to be in. There is no recipe that can guarantee success, but I generally take my time by changing venues and waiting for a couple of hours to pass before trying to kiss her. If she's receptive, I attempt the home venue change not long afterwards.

Looking back at my dating history, I've identified clear signs that a girl is likely to accept a home venue change. The biggest is if she consumed at least two alcoholic drinks and allowed me to kiss her, either at the last venue or right outside it. I strongly advise going for the home venue change if you find yourself in this situation. Another reliable sign is if a girl is in "party mode," where she keeps drinking, suggests doing shots, or moves her body sensually as if she wants to dance or fornicate. She may also ask you where you live or make a comment about how she doesn't have to get up early. One last sign is if you kissed her before the date. If a girl goes on a date with a man she has already kissed, it means she is ready to do more than kiss.

There are also signs that indicate you won't get sex or even a kiss. The first is if she doesn't drink at all. It's not that alcohol is essential for intimacy, but a sober girl is mostly thinking logically when deciding whether or not to have sex with you. Since logic is slower to accept intimacy than emotion, the best you can hope for is a kiss at the end of the date. I find that convincing such a girl to drink won't improve your odds, because her decision not to have sex early is firm, but I may tease her with something like, "Are you scared that you will drink, lose all inhibition, and try to take advantage of me?" If logic is what she needs to choose to sleep with me, and it takes more time, so be it. With these type of girls, sex may not happen for several dates.

The second sign that you won't get far is if a girl has other plans for later that evening. If she says that she is meeting "friends" later, she has no intention of going far with you. You must conclude that her attraction is low if she doesn't want to give enough time for the date to proceed naturally. When I find out that a girl has other plans, I wrap up the date quickly so that I don't waste any more of my time, because I really dislike it when a girl uses me to warm up for her main event. If this happens to you often, you may want to set your dates later so that a girl doesn't think she'll have time for anything else that night.

The final negative sign is if she interrupts your touching progression by telling you not to touch her, often at the early stage of light touching. It's fine for a girl not to want to indulge your touching, such as by refusing to put her arm in yours, or to challenge a specific touch by asking what you're doing. However, when a girl says "Don't touch me" or "I don't like it when you touch me," you might as well get up and leave, because you're not getting further. This is the equivalent of a girl telling you that she just wants to be friends.

Assuming you're not getting any bad signs, you've put in the required face time to make the girl feel comfortable, and you've kissed her (or at least know that she is ready to be kissed), it's time to move the date to a bedroom. Your options are to invite her to your place or go to hers. If you want to move her to your place, you should take her to venues close by. If your logistics are poor and you can't take her to where you live, the date should take place in venues close to where she lives. Don't make things difficult for yourself by choosing venues located far from where either of you live.

Your Place

It's ideal when the final date venue is within walking distance of your place. A short taxi ride is acceptable, but try your best to achieve a situation where you can literally point to your building from the venue. The further you are from your home, the more she will resist coming over.

When I travel, I look for apartments that are no more than 0.7 miles (1.1 kilometers) from the main area where I'll be having dates, because that translates into a fifteen-minute slow walk that I can tell a girl is ten minutes away (it's not like she'll time it). It's even better if the walk time is in the single digits, because anything that eliminates the thought in her mind that your place is hard to get to will increase the likelihood she says yes to your invitation.

I like taking a girl to my place because I have more control over what happens and can avoid negative factors such as a cockblocking roommate, bad music, or improper lighting. This home-field advantage also means that a girl knows she has to behave if she doesn't want me to revoke the invitation. Being able to tell a girl "the door is right there" if she starts acting stupid is a powerful way to show your value and get her to behave.

Before going out on a date, I assume the girl will come over, so I ensure my pad is comfortable, clean, and stocked with alcohol (a bottle of cheap wine is sufficient) to eliminate any logistical obstacles towards getting laid. When she walks through my door, she will not see anything that may encourage her to leave, such as dead bodies hanging from the ceiling.

I usually warm up the venue change by telling a girl—particularly if she's conservative—that I don't expect sex if she comes over, as I already explained in the section on night game. Here's the routine again:

"By the way, there is something I want to tell you. If I ever invite you to my apartment for a drink, whether today, next week, or next year, I don't expect sex. I don't want you to think that just because we're going to my place, I expect it to happen and you have to do it. But if you do want it, I may be able to help you out."

This might as well be called the "I'm not a rapist" routine, because you're letting her know that you understand "no means no." It also tells her that you won't immediately turn into an octopus once you get her alone, which is what many guys do when they're under the influence of alcohol. You can also add, "Where I come from, we have an after-party culture where you can hang out in someone's place without expectations." You can use this line even if you're from the same city as her.

The "I'm not a rapist" routine may seem like you're putting your penis in a lockbox, but I find the opposite to be true, because it increases a girl's comfort and trust to such an extent that sex is more likely to happen.

Fifteen minutes after the routine, go for the invite. Do you remember when I advised you to ask about her favorite band, and to tell her the name of one that is obscure? You can use that now. Segue into the invite by asking her if she's tired.

Me: "So are you tired right now or do you have some energy left?"

Her: "I'm just a little tired."

Me: "How about we go to my place and chill a bit? I want to play that band I told you about."

Feel free to swap out the band for something else you discussed that would be cool or interesting for her to see. I have many travel pictures and videos, so sometimes I use that, but over the years I've become lazy and simply sell her on a crappy bottle of wine or a tea with an exotic flavor. I always have multiple reasons for her to come over, because a girl will almost always resist my first invite attempt. I stack on as many additional reasons as necessary so that she will eventually say yes.

Do not allow the fact that a girl rarely says yes on your first attempt to discourage you. It's in a girl's nature to say no to a man she likes to prove that she's not easy. When you first ask a girl for her number, a no is definitely a no, because giving out her phone number doesn't imply she's easy, but when it comes to kissing, accepting an invitation to your apartment, or having sex, you'll encounter many no's. The correct response is to respect the no and try a different angle to make her feel like you've put in a sufficient amount of effort.

In the age of "rape culture," where leftists are trying to redefine sexual consent, we have to err on the side of caution and make sure that a girl is enthusiastic when she eventually kisses us or comes to our apartment. You should never feel like you're forcing her to do anything, especially through grabbing or pulling. Most men naturally know which line not to cross, but I need to emphasize that a physically aggressive "caveman" game that many girls fantasize about could get you into serious legal trouble. If a girl says no, or physically resists you, back off completely until she changes her mind.

If a girl says no to my first invitation to come to my home, I try four more times. I advise that you get at least *five no's* before giving up, especially if you've already kissed her. Here are two examples:

> Me: "So are you tired right now or do you have some energy left?"
>
> Her: "I'm okay."
>
> Me: "How about we go to my place and chill a bit? I want to play that band I told you about."
>
> Her: "I can't. I have to get up early." Her first no.
>
> Me: "That's cool. I have to get up early, too. We can just chill for half an hour."

Her: “Maybe some other time.” Second no.

Me: “But I really want you to listen to this band. I’d feel bad if you go home without hearing their best songs.”

Her: “Hmmm… I don’t know. It’s better not to.” Third no.

Me: “I’m just fifteen minutes away from here. It’s a nice evening to go for a walk.”

Her: “I think I’m going home.” Fourth no.

Me: “Okay, how about we go and play just one song? And then you can leave after that.”

Her: “But only for one song, okay?”

Me: “Yeah, okay.”

Here’s another example where I use completely different reasons:

Me: “So what time do you have to get up tomorrow morning?”

Her: “7am.”

Me: “Oh that’s not too bad. So I live nearby. How about we grab one more drink? I bought a nice bottle of wine that I’ve been wanting to open.”

Her: “I can’t. I need my eight hours of sleep.” First no.

Me: “I understand. I have to get up a bit early myself. How about just one glass?”

Her: “No, I’m not much of a wine drinker anyway.” Second no.

Me: “I bought this wine because it won a competition, something like the best wine of 2017 in Chile. The flavor profile is supposed to be rather elegant. I also want to show you the video I made from my trip to Ukraine. It came out really good." I stack on a second reason because she's not a big wine fan.

Her: "I don't know. It's a bit late." Third no.

Me: "We can have a glass and then I'll drive you home. It's a weekday so I can't party all night anyway."

Her: "No, because I really do have to be on time for my meeting tomorrow." Fourth no.

Me: "It's 10:30 right now. At 11:30 on the dot I'll drive you home, and you'll be able to get a solid six hours of sleep. Cool?"

Her: "Fine, just one glass."

In some cases, a girl will keep her word and leave exactly when she said she would. In other cases, she will get lost in the moment and have sex with you. It often comes down to a matter of luck. Even if I'm sure I won't sleep with a girl, I still like to get her into my home anyway, because it will be far easier to convince her on a future date to come home with me.

Another option if you're getting multiple no's is to stop trying after the third or fourth no and say, "Let's go for a short walk instead." Then walk in the direction of your apartment and try to get as close to it as you can before she asks where you're going. Say, "Actually, I live right there, just five minutes away. You sure you don't want to grab a drink? It's not that late." And then keep trying until you get a new set of five no's. Avoid shaming her for not coming over, and never become desperate by begging or saying something like, "Oh, come on." Be respectful, calm, and sell going to your place as something that would be natural or fun.

An option that requires you to be more assertive involves

assuming that she wants to come over and taking all appropriate action to get her in front of your building. Invite her in only after arriving. This is my preferred strategy for quick extractions from bars when my apartment is within walking distance (it doesn't work if you need to take a taxi or car). When she eventually asks where you're headed, assume the yes by saying, "Let's go to my place and have another drink and listen to music. You're not tired, right?" If she says it's too late, say, "That's cool, let's just chill for thirty minutes. I know you can't stay all night." If she still says no, you have to stop where you are and sell her the idea until she says yes.

A girl's reasons for not wanting to come over may sound sincere, but ultimately they're bullshit, because if she really likes a guy, she will make large sacrifices to be with him. This is why you must ignore her excuses and go for at least five no's. If she refused your invitation to spend only "thirty minutes" at your place, and you persisted until you got five no's, you must conclude that her interest is weak, even if she kissed you. In this case, it's unlikely she'll show up for a future date. Another possibility is that she's genuinely conservative.

If she ever raises a plausible objection that can be resolved, resolve it. If a girl says she's tired, say you have tea or coffee. If she says she's hungry, tell her you have food or know a great take-out restaurant near your place. If she says her phone is about to die, say you have a charger for it. If she says she has to get up early, say you'll kick her out after half an hour. Resolve any objections as you go for five no's. What happens at the end of a date is the moment of truth, so it would be a waste if you give up so easily after spending all that time with her.

Another problem is when a girl says that the bus or subway service is ending soon and she doesn't have enough money for a taxi home, a common situation if she's a student. In my early game days, I had a firm rule of not paying a girl's taxi fare, because I was so scared of being seen as a beta male. This was an unreasonable stance that cost me many lays.

I now price the possible cost of a taxi into the date so that I don't see it as something extra. If I have a budget of $60 for a date, and a cab ride is $20 on average, I will spend about $40 on the date itself and be open to spending more if it means she can come over. If something such as the cost of a ride home is her only objection to coming over, I will squash it.

> Her: "I can't come to your place because the bus service ends in twenty minutes."
>
> Me: "How much does a taxi cost from this part of town to your home?"
>
> Her: "I don't know, maybe $20."
>
> Me: "Well look, I'm having a nice time with you and don't want the date to end yet. I will give you the taxi money when you need to leave. That money is small to me. I wouldn't want to let a great night end early because of it."
>
> Her: "No, you don't have to."
>
> Me: "Let me check if I have cash. Yup, I do, so there's no problem. Come on, let's go to my place."

The advent of ride-sharing apps has made things easier, because you don't have to discuss how much you will pay. When it's time for her to leave, simply order her a ride. Shelling out for taxi fare doesn't automatically mean you'll get the bang, but I see it as the cost of "doing business." As a bonus, since she is depending on you to follow through on your word to pay her fare home, she will be extra respectful while at your place.

She must believe the reason for the venue change is based on your desire to drink, listen to music, talk, watch videos, and so on. Don't say that you want to kiss her more or have sex. While she is certainly thinking about intimacy, expressing it will make her feel pressured while running the risk of making you come across as desperate. You have an irrational desire to listen to music or drink with her at your place, and that's all, even if the mood of the evening suggests otherwise.

It won't help you to memorize the dialogues I've shared. Every time I try to get a girl over, I make up lines on the spot based on the circumstance and what my bait of the evening happens to be (music, videos, wine, champagne, tea, etc.). I remember only that I have to persist calmly until I get at least five rejections, and each of my attempts can differ slightly until I find something that convinces her to say yes. What's more important than the content of the attempts is that you actually make the attempts. Even if your reasons are totally lame, such as asking a girl to see your collection of sports memorabilia, they are better than not trying at all.

Many guys are concerned that they may appear too pushy. Whether this is the case depends on if she had a cold demeanor during the date. For example, if a girl was pulling out her phone often, complaining about the drinks or service, making it difficult for you to touch her, or not maintaining eye contact during silences, she will strongly resist your repeated attempts to get her over to your place. If a girl doesn't like you, she will dislike you even more if you try to have sex with her, but if a girl does like you, she will be charmed that you want to have sex with her and that you're being a man about it.

It's common sense that a girl will reject a bigger move if she already rejected a smaller one. If she wouldn't let you touch her hand, she won't let you put your arm around her. If she wouldn't let you put your arm around her, she won't let you kiss her. If she wouldn't let you kiss her, she won't let you have sex with her. Don't skip steps. There are exceptions to this principle, such as when you're with a girl who hates public displays of affection, or one who has a boyfriend and views kissing as more intimate than sex, but over the course of the date, you should feel that things are moving forward and becoming more intimate. If they aren't, your home venue change is likely to fail.

You need to guard against moving too slowly because you think a girl is "good." It's possible that she is good, but it's also possible that she's putting on a show so that you'll think she's good. Unless a girl doesn't drink, comes from a religious background, is socially awkward in a way that suggests she hasn't been on many dates before, or appears to be genuinely nervous in your presence, you should assume she's a standard girl and run default game.

If a girl is accepting your moves and showing interest, doing a home invite where you keep trying until you get five no's is natural, expected, and won't damage your future chances with her. This type of persistence has many benefits. First, it prevents a girl from putting you in the friend zone, which is commonly the fate of passive men who hope that the girl will make a bold move first.

Second, most girls are not looking for serious long-term relationships, so they appreciate a confident man who is direct about giving her what she truly wants—fun and excitement. If there is no action on the first date, she may conclude that there was no "passion" or "connection," and say no when you try to schedule a second date. Making a move for sex at the end of a two- or three-hour date may even be considered *slow* by some girls, but it's the strategy that will result in the most success.

A third reason persistence doesn't hurt is that, even if she is looking for a long-term relationship, she will be flattered that you are sexually attracted to her and willing to work to spend more time alone with her. It won't cause her to lose attraction for you.

I would prefer not to have to be so persistent, because I'm patient and relaxed by nature, but I've been on way too many first dates where a girl kissed me passionately and told me what a great time she had only for her not to agree to a second date, without any explanation.

We no longer live in an age where you court a virgin over a long period. If you're meeting a girl through a cold-approach scenario, there is a less than 2% chance she's a virgin, and odds are she's already had at least one fast casual sex encounter. Unless you have evidence that she is a fair maiden with the right values, you have to assume she's moderately promiscuous and act accordingly to maximize your chances of getting intimate and seeing her again. Even if she is a virgin, she may want to have sex with you to get rid of her virgin status.

Once a girl walks through your door, the home venue change was successful. You will then move on to the next stage of the escalation, which will be described in the chapter on sex.

Her Place

If you can't take a girl to your place, the next-best option is to go to hers. This was the common scenario for me when I lived in the suburbs of Washington, D.C. and went out in the city. I would select venues close to where girls lived to make it easier for me at the end of a date.

By the time the date draws to a conclusion, you should have kissed her or come close to doing so. Without revealing your true intentions, say that you can escort her home. This will be particularly easy if you have a car. Otherwise, walk with her, take public transport, or hail a cab. Persist even if she says that she doesn't need you to escort her home.

Me: "So that was fun. You live close to here?"

Her: "Yeah, not that far. It's just two subway stops away."

Me: "Well, I have time, so I can escort you so you get home safe."

Her: "That's okay. You don't have to."

Me: "I'd like to. I read recently that there is a surge of crime in the city, so it's safer this way."

Her: "No, really, it's not necessary."

Me: "I insist. My mother taught me to always escort a young lady home. I would feel like a bad person if I didn't."

Once you reach the entrance to her place, you'll need to find an innocuous way to get inside. The best way is asking her if you can use her bathroom at the moment she expects you to say goodbye.

Me: "Can I use your bathroom?"

Her: "My house is messy."

Me: "I'll just be a minute. I should've gone in the bar."

Her: "But my roommate is sleeping."

Me: "I'll be as quiet as a mouse."

Her: "This is not a good idea."

Me: "Okay, well, can you point to an alley nearby so I can urinate in the street like a dog?"

Here I had to overcome three no's. It's unlikely you'll get that many when you do the bathroom move. Once she lets you inside, the first thing you should do is use the bathroom. If you don't really have to urinate, pretend by sprinkling some faucet water in the toilet bowl.

If you shared a taxi to her place, say that you'll get out of the vehicle to say goodbye. Let her exit the car first, quickly pay the driver, let him drive off, and then ask if you can use her bathroom because you "really have to go." I have let taxis go even before finding out whether a girl will let me in, but these are the sort of risks you must take if you want to have sex instead of jerk off.

The downside of the bathroom line is that it will work on girls who don't like you. I know this because girls have left their front doors open so that I could leave immediately after I finished urinating. For this reason, I have used it less over the years and moved to self-invitations that result in more upfront rejections but fewer rejections once I am inside her home.

With a self-invitation, start with the home escort move. When you're in front of her place, instead of asking whether you can use her bathroom, ask if she has any good drink or food.

Approve of one thing she mentions and ask to have it.

Me: "So, do you have any drinks at your place?"

Her: "Not really."

Me: "You don't have anything?"

Her: "Well, I have some old vodka and beer."

Me: "Old vodka is the best vodka. How about we have one more drink before I head home?"

Her: "I don't know if that's a good idea. It's getting late."

Me: "I agree, I have to wake up early, too. So how about we call it a night after twenty minutes?"

Her: "My house is really messy."

Me: "I'm a guy, not Martha Stewart. A mess doesn't bother me."

Her: "But my roommate is home, and I think she's sleeping."

Me: "I can walk on my tippy toes."

As with previous examples, I kept going until I got five no's. Try different angles to squash her objections, but never get into an argument or say she's wrong.

Another option is to go for the invite earlier when you're at the final venue by asking her whether she's tired and wants to hang out somewhere quieter. This move works better on the weekends after a long night of drinking, not on first dates that take place on a weekday.

For weekday dates, I recommend you use the bathroom line. The less certain you are of where you stand with a girl, and the more sober she is, the more indirect you should be. The more certain you are, and the more she is touching and kissing you, the more likely your suggestion to hang out at her place will succeed. If you're a complete newbie, start with the bathroom line and work your way up to more direct invitations.

If your home venue change move gets five no's, it's safe to call it a night. If you have already kissed her, you can give her a final kiss goodbye and leave. If you haven't kissed her yet, this is a good time to do so. Give her a hug, and without letting go, turn your cheek towards her face and say, "Kiss on cheek." She should kiss your cheek. Then turn your other cheek and say, "And the other cheek." After the second kiss, while you're still embracing her lightly, stare into her eyes and smile warmly. Then go in for the lips. If she leans back, she's rejecting your kiss. A variant that I already discussed is asking her to also give you two cheek kisses, but that tends to be overkill after a long date.

What should you do if you can't take a girl to your place and you can't go to hers? I encountered this problem many times in my late twenties when I lived with my father and I met girls who were living in a dorm room or with their parents. My "home" venue change became my dad's car or a nearby park. Because girls think it's exciting to have sex in public, my success rate was surprisingly high. If your only option is a car, suggest a ride.

Me: "So how about we get out of here and go for a ride?"

Her: "Where do you want to go?"

Me: "It's a nice night, so we can drive by the lake/park/boulevard and talk some more. And then when you get tired, I can drop you home."

If she resists, frame it as going for a short ride to show her something interesting. In the middle of the ride, park your car in a secluded area. Then say, "Let's chill in the back seat—it's more comfortable." Getting a girl into the backseat is essentially the same as getting her into your bed.

If you don't have a car, another option is a friend's place. Do you have a cool friend who won't mind if you come over for an "after-party?" This option works best if you're already out with your friend. Go to his place, have a drink, and then use his couch to do the business. Make sure you respect his couch by removing any sex stains afterwards.

The last option is to use a public park or wooded area. You may be surprised how eager girls are to have sex in a park, because they see it as an exciting experience they can share with their friends. To pull it off, tell the girl you want to go for a walk in the park. If she lets you kiss her long and hard in a public area of the park, she's probably open to going further. Say, "Let's go in that area for more privacy." The possibility of park sex is a good reason you should always have a condom with you, but be aware that having sex in public is illegal in most jurisdictions.

Chapter Conclusion

Once you get a girl inside your home, or achieve a suitable level of privacy, you're in a position to have sex with her, which is what the next chapter is about. The tactics I provided in this chapter are the most common ways to get to that point, but as you know, it's impossible to anticipate every type of situation you may encounter. You'll have to adapt by trying something, gauging the results, and then making adjustments. It's okay if you lose out on having sex with a girl here or there to increase your overall knowledge and skill.

There are three major points to understand from this chapter. First, keep your phone communication direct and logistical. Don't try to entertain a girl on the phone. If a girl likes you, she will agree to a date after a few simple text exchanges. Second, ramp up the intimacy on dates. After building comfort with conversation, turn up the temperature by sitting closer to her, touching, and sustaining eye contact when silent. Lastly, when executing a home venue change, persist until you receive five no's.

At this point, I hope you can see that game does not consist of only linear progressions but also interchangeable building blocks. The same-night bang strategy in the previous chapter has many similar components to our dating strategy, and day game techniques can be used on night dates. What's important is that you understand the main concepts. There is no universal law that governs how you should get a girl into bed.

If you're a newbie, you should follow the steps I have described so that you know you're on the right path, but once you get a few notches on your belt, you can start to mix and match the various components to your liking. Flexibility is key: if something happens that I haven't described, choose a plan of action you feel is best and execute it. Whether or not it fails, you'll have gained crucial information that will help you when you encounter a similar situation in the future.

Chapter 8: Sex

The hardest part of the seduction is over. You met a girl, identified that she is attracted to you, allowed her to invest in you, and got her alone in a private home. Your instinct may be to speed things along because you're so close to the prize, but rushing at this stage will damage the trust and comfort you've built up. Relax and take it slow. From this point on, our game is about allowing the girl to convince *herself* that sex is what she truly wants. We do this by creating a calm environment for the seduction to be completed.

Before Penetration

Once you're alone with her, initially be distant by not touching her or standing too close. You want her to know that you're a composed man who doesn't get overly excited or aggressive. If you're at her place, give yourself a small tour by viewing any photos or cool items she has around her home. If you're at your place, give her a tour of everything but the bedroom.

Suggest drinks or food and move to the kitchen where it can be prepared. Don't be in a rush to get out of the kitchen—comment on her kitchen, or if you're in your home, show her how you cook, what your favorite food items are, how your Panini maker works, and so on. If she definitely wants to have sex with you, she may be getting anxious about why you're not grabbing her to push things to the bedroom. This is good, because it will help to reduce any resistance later.

After a few minutes in the kitchen, move to the couch. At this point, you will either allow a girl who wants to have sex with you to have sex with you *or* give a girl who hasn't made up her mind more time to decide whether she wants to have sex with you. We do not convince girls to have sex with us, because they will feel regretful afterwards and possibly imagine that we manipulated or coerced them.

Put on some music and sit next to her on the couch. If you invited her to your place under the guise of showing her something interesting, go ahead and do so. After a few minutes on the couch, move closer for the kiss, which you could initiate in the kitchen if she's being affectionate.

Kissing will escalate the intimacy and lead to touching her torso, butt, and legs. You can also touch her face and hair. There are no rules on how to kiss and touch at this stage. Sense her energy and respond in kind. If you want to kiss her neck, do so. If you want to put your hand on her face as you kiss her, go for it. Just bear in mind that your level of excitement should match hers. If she's lying there like a dead fish and you're doing all the work and breathing heavily, you need to dial it down until she catches up with you. It's okay if you're one or two steps ahead of her in terms of excitement, but not five.

After kissing, the next major escalation move involves her breasts. Cup one of her breasts with your hand to see how she responds. If she doesn't react negatively, squeeze it sensually. If she removes your hand from her breast, respect her wish and continue kissing and touching her elsewhere. Five or ten minutes later, touch her breast again and see how she reacts. If she repeatedly puts a stop to one of your intimate moves, you could have reached the line that she doesn't want you to cross that night.

The hardest question to answer is how many no's you should accept before you give up on a certain move. In my youth, there was no limit. I'd try an infinite number of times until it was easier for the girl to say yes than to resist, or until she asked me to leave. I found that when a girl finally succumbed after resisting me for a long time, she was exceptionally passionate during sex, suggesting that resistance is foreplay for many girls. Judging by the high sales of romance books that feature rape, it's clear that many girls fantasize about a man who aggressively breaks down their resistance.

Unfortunately, the culture had convinced girls that a romantic experience involving resistance is rape. This creates an internal conflict: a girl feels pleasure with a man who persisted, but also feels guilty because the culture told her that she was sexually violated. Therefore, I cannot advise you to aggressively overcome her resistance, even though it's what a girl's nature demands.

At the same time, it's dishonest to say that "no means no," because girls are prone to saying no with their mouths but yes with their bodies to communicate that they want a man to keep trying until they're fully aroused and vaginally lubricated. This creates a dilemma for me as a teacher. I want you to reach your intimacy goals but not be falsely accused of rape. I've settled on a method that might cause you to lose out on sex with girls who need to be bedded by an aggressive man, but that will greatly reduce—if not eliminate—your chance of a false rape accusation.

I recommend you stop upon getting three no's at any particular step while escalating physically, with each rejection spaced about ten minutes apart. Once you get the third no, tell her that you respect her no and she must explicitly give you her consent if she wants you to go further. If you live in a country that is not yet a sexual dystopia, where false rape accusations are rare, you can increase the number of no's that you receive.

Let's return to when you were trying to touch her breast. The first time you try, she removes your hand. Ten minutes later, you try again, and she removes your hand once more. At this point, you should take a break. Get another drink, put a new song on, lean back, have a chat, and assess her mood. If she looks annoyed or upset, her resistance is genuine. This may be underlined if she makes a comment such as "It's getting late," which indicates that she's not being coy and really does not want to go further. A girl who wants to have sex with you after you've made out on a couch for some time and caressed her body will not sabotage things by suggesting the night is over. On the other hand, if she looks calm, relaxed, and happy, she doesn't want you to give up. After a brief chat, resume kissing her, and when the moment feels right, go for the breast again. If she doesn't resist, you're past the barrier and can keep going, but if she does resist, you've hit three no's. Lean back and say the following:

> "I noticed that you don't want me to touch your breast after I tried a couple of times. No means no, so if you want me to go further tonight, you have to tell me. I don't want to make you feel uncomfortable."

If she says, "Yes, I'm feeling uncomfortable" or "It's just too soon for me," I'd stop all intimate activity for the evening. If she says, "I think I just need a little bit more time," it may be worth trying once more after a long break. The best outcome is if she grabs your hand right then and puts it on her breast. Any response that doesn't give you a clear green light means it's best to stop.

If she ever says "Stop," it really does mean stop. If a girl is noticeably uncomfortable after she tells you to stop, you should interpret this as a red light and halt all intimacy for the night unless she resumes it. Do not ignore her negative words and actions. The whole point of intimacy is to experience the joy that comes from a genuine human connection. If you ignore her wishes, you are no longer working within that connection, and are using her as a mere sex doll.

If things are going well on the couch, and she lets you fondle her breasts, it's time to consider taking things to the bedroom. It's easier if you try to seal the deal on the couch, because you don't need the added step of moving her to the bedroom, but if either of you have roommates, it's better to relocate.

After a pause in the intimacy, say, "I forgot to give you a tour of the bedroom." If she resists, which is unlikely, you can add that it has something really interesting you want to show her. If you're at her place, say, "You forgot to give me a tour of your bedroom. I'm curious where you sleep." If she resists, say you need to check out her room so that you can see what type of girl she is.

One move that tends to open the floodgates is the hand-on-cock move. It's exactly what you think it is: you put her hand on your cock while still clothed. I usually do this move after breast fondling but before I start taking off her clothes. I gently grab her hand, usually when it's near my waist, and place it on my erect penis. Ideally, you want the girl to stroke it expertly. This means that she's beyond horny and ready for sex. A neutral response is if she keeps her hand on your cock for a few seconds before removing it. A negative response is if she treats your cock as if it's a hot rod of steel and instantly withdraws her hand, which is a sign that you probably won't get laid.

If there's a hand-on-cock move, there must also be a hand-on-pussy move. This is where you rub her pussy, or just outright grab it. I prefer to gently rub a girl's pussy as if I'm trying to release a genie from its bottle.

Your chance of getting laid after moving a girl to a bed is high but not guaranteed (the biggest reason for failure at this point is if she's on her period). Unless she's in a state of extreme passion where she's ripping off your clothes, continue to take your time. The game is now about getting naked in a reciprocal manner without ruining the mood. Take off her socks then take off yours. Take off her shirt then take off yours. Take off her pants and then finally yours. If you get a no or two, hold off a little, restart from the top of your touching progression, and then work your way back up to the point of resistance.

Removing her pants is usually the most challenging step in the bedroom. I like to attempt this after stroking her pussy and eliciting a pleasurable moan or two. Sticking to our three no strategy, here's an example of how it could happen:

> Me: "It would be more comfortable if you take off your jeans." I then try to unbutton and unzip them.
>
> Her: "No, I don't want to." First no.
>
> Me: "I just want to take them off." My hands are on the top button.

Her: “No.” Second no.

Me: “But I think it’s better if you take them off.”

Her: “Okay, fine.”

This dialogue may seem funny, because I’m essentially repeating the same statement, but I’ve lost count of how many times it has worked for me. Allow the girl to say no to “prove” to you that she’s not easy and then go for three no’s. If you get three no’s at the pants stage or after, take a break. You can start again later or hit her with the no-means-no routine, where she must give you explicit consent to move forward.

Once her jeans are off, you can rub her pussy through her panties before slipping a finger or two underneath to make direct contact with her labia. It may be so exciting for you to feel a girl’s pussy that your primal brain will want to take over and demand you inseminate her, but you must continue to think rationally to ensure you have her consent while being mindful enough to practice safe sex.

If she doesn’t let you rub her pussy, usually while her pants are still on, lay off for a while. Play with her boobs, repeat the hand-on-cock move, and let her put more effort into stimulating you. It’s possible she won’t let you grab her pussy because she’s on her period. In this case, she’ll usually tell you while things are starting to get hot and heavy.

Based on the length of the female period, there’s a 10% to 20% chance that a girl will be on it when you get her in bed. This will happen to you repeatedly and be the source of great frustration. I used to give up when a girl told me this, but then I meditated about the issue and decided that a little bit of blood should not stop me from achieving my sexual dreams.

Decide right now if you will sleep with a girl who is on her period. If you do, there will be blood, and it may get everywhere. You’ll need an additional layer of game to make a girl comfortable enough to sleep with a man while her pussy is leaking blood, an embarrassing scenario under any circumstance. Make a joke about her period then nonchalantly tell her that you don't mind the blood.

Her: "We can't have sex. I'm on my period."

Me: "I don't care, I'll drink the blood."

Her: "Ewww."

Me: "Are you in the middle of your period? Is it heavy?"

Her: "Yeah, it's heavy."

Me: "That's fine if you don't feel comfortable having sex while on your period, but it's a natural thing that doesn't bother me. I'd of course use a condom, and we can get a dark towel."

Her: "I don't know, it's kind of weird."

Me: "No big deal. It's not weird to me, but whatever you want."

Drop the issue, take a break, and continue with your escalation program. If she's down for sex, she will excuse herself to the bathroom at some point and remove her blood-soaked tampon. If she doesn't, sex will not take place.

Many girls are lying when they say they're on their period, so I act skeptical and ask to see the evidence. If she's unable to prove it by showing you the tampon string hanging out of her pussy, she may be lying.

If she's not on her period, and has allowed you to take off her pants, she will have on her bra and panties and you'll be in your underwear. It makes sense to remove her bra next. I sometimes prefer to lift it off like it's a t-shirt, because it's easier and usually gets a laugh from the girl, but if you know how to unclasp the mechanism, you're free to do so.

Try to take off her panties after that. If she says no, try to rub her pussy. At this point, I may put my cock through the pee hole of my boxers to stimulate her visually. Dry humping on top of her is also an excellent move since it will make her think more strongly of sex.

A good indicator of her arousal is how wet her pussy is. If it's not wet, it will be difficult to put your cock inside it. You should therefore focus on arousing her and then check periodically to see whether she's getting wetter. Without going too deep into vaginal anatomy, it's possible that her juices are trapped below the surface. Insert your finger about an inch to check, and if you feel moisture, scoop out the juice and spread it around so that your cock will slide in easily.

My fingering technique is basic. I insert my finger in and out several times at a moderate speed while rubbing the juice on the outside to facilitate penetration. Use her moans to guide you. If you can't find any juice at all, even after inserting your finger deep inside, she's not aroused, has a medical problem, or has lost consciousness. If a girl is unconscious, you cannot have sex with her, because then it would be rape.

An alternative to the no-means-no routine, particularly with foreign girls who have not been brainwashed with rape culture hysteria, is to take an extended break of half an hour or more. If you've hit a solid wall, but she has not shown discomfort or a desire to leave, it's possible that she simply needs some more face time. Stop touching her for a while and focus on something else, like listening to music or sharing stories. You don't have to be physical with her all the time, especially if you've received more than three no's at a certain step.

During an extended break, I monitor the girl to see whether she snuggles up next to me and resumes kissing. If she does, she wants you to continue and will likely let you pass the previous point of resistance. It could be worth starting from the beginning of your intimacy program with kissing, touching, boob fondling, and so on, making your way back to the wall to see if she will open the gate. If not, it's safe to accept that you won't get any further that night.

An extreme variation of the extended break is the hard withdrawal, which works best if she's at your place. When you've hit a wall you can't pass, say the following:

> "It's fine if you don't want to have sex, but it's hard for me as a man to get so aroused and then suddenly stop. It causes physical pain for me. So it's best we don't do anything else that turns me on."

Halt all affection, touching, and even conversation. Get up from the couch or bed and do something else, such as reading, working, cleaning, or cooking, all without giving her much attention or displaying any anger.

If she tries to fill the vacuum by kissing and touching you, resume your intimacy program, but now with added intensity. You'll likely barrel through the previous wall of resistance because she fears that if she doesn't give you the sex you desire, you will remain cold towards her, and maybe not even see her again. I admit that this technique involves a degree of manipulation, and I won't try to justify it morally, but as a man who genuinely does experience physical pain when intimacy doesn't result in an orgasm, it's also honest. A girl has every right to say no, but men also have the right not to get blue-balled. If she doesn't try to fill the vacuum after you withdraw, the night will soon end.

The hardest withdrawal is asking her to leave. I often have to do this if a girl combines rejections with disrespect or mocking comments. It's fine for a girl to say no to sex, but if she tries to put me down, or makes fun of me while doing so, I'll withdraw all my affection and say, "Maybe it's time for you to leave."

Being asked to leave a man's place immediately forces a girl to reflect on her behavior and decide whether she really wants to sleep with him. Allow her to gather her things and put on her shoes. If she appears upset or regretful, and doesn't increase her bitchiness, offer a redemption as she's about to walk out. Sometimes I wait until she has completely walked out the door.

Me: "Hold on. I think this is a bad way to end the night, because we did have a good time up to this point."

Her: "Yeah, I thought so too."

Me: "We should end the night on better terms. How about we have one more drink before you head out?"

Because the feeling of rejection is too painful for a girl to handle, she will often do anything to relieve it. In this situation, it means coming back inside your home, having another drink, and sleeping with you. You should not pull this move on a nice girl who didn't do anything wrong, but on girls who treat you unjustly or have a bitchy attitude. Rejecting someone, making them feel the pain of that rejection, and then offering a way to relieve the pain is a powerful manipulation tactic that girls use on men all the time, and it has probably been used on you. It's no surprise that it works on them as well.

I don't want to put too much emphasis on moves designed to break down resistance, because it will make you focus on last-minute tricks to get her legs open instead of nurturing the connection you have. Any move to squash resistance must be done on a girl who genuinely wants to have sex with you.

Penetration

I highly recommend using a condom. The type of girl who is willing to have sex without one has almost certainly done so with multiple men before, putting her at high risk of having a disease. I prepare for safe sex at about the time she's in her panties and I'm in my boxers. I grab a condom from my pants pocket or night drawer and say, "I have a condom just in case." Then I leave the condom at the edge of the bed or on the nightstand.

Note the "in case" phrasing within the announcement. It clearly lets her know that she can say no at any time, but that if sex does happen, you're ready to do it in a way that won't expose her to potential diseases. If a girl was concerned that it won't be safe to have sex with you, getting out the condom before both of you are fully naked will remove that objection.

The final barrier before sex is her panties. If she allows you to remove her panties, she wants to have sex. Of course, she is allowed to change her mind at any point after that and tell you "no" or "stop," but in my experience, panty removal is the defining event that precedes sex. Once her panties are off, do a moisture check with your fingers and spread her juices around the outside of her labia to facilitate penetration. Then take off your boxers and grab the condom package. Remove the condom from the package and put it on your cock. Start slow so that you don't hurt her, but once you can insert your penis completely, thrust as you like.

Many men get hung up on sexual performance, worrying about what girls think of how they're doing in bed. To address this concern, I ask the following: how can you possibly know what pleases a girl if she hasn't told you? Until a girl tells you what she likes, which often comes much later, do what you want in bed as long as you're enjoying it and not causing her pain. If she desires something specific, she will let you know, and then you can adjust your technique to provide more pleasure. If she says nothing at all, assume the customer is satisfied. The problem with trying to mind-read and guess what a girl likes is that it may result in neither of you being satisfied with the sex.

What most girls want from a man is for him to have his way with her. She does not want you to ask for permission every step of the way or constantly solicit her opinion—she wants to be dominated. She wants to submit to a being more powerful than herself. This is why she has a vagina that receives and you have a phallus that is meant to pierce and thrust.

I stick to my selfish sex program until I have been with a girl long enough to know what adjustments I can make to please her, but I definitely don't do this the first time I have sex with a girl unless she's a virgin. In that case, I go extremely slow to reduce the pain she's experiencing.

The only goal I have during sex is to last at least three

minutes. If I can last that long, and I experience a nice orgasm, the sex was a great success, and she is more than welcome to give me her input afterwards. Since condoms generally make it difficult to orgasm quickly, especially thicker condoms, you probably have what it takes to meet this benchmark. If not, I'm sure you can find a condom that dulls your sensitivity enough to do so.

Having a low goal for first-time sex eliminates most forms of performance anxiety that affect men who think they're obligated to give a girl an orgasm. The more you care about her pleasure, the more likely you'll stress yourself out. Focusing solely on your orgasm is the best way to reduce sexual anxiety. Ultimately, there is no right way to have sex with a girl, and giving you a manual for life's most intimate activity will only deaden the experience. Do what feels good while using her moans and gyrations to help you adjust in a way that you think is best.

There is also the issue of oral sex, either eating out a girl or getting a blowjob. Personally, I don't eat girls out. Some men swear that it makes a girl hungrier for vaginal sex, but the disadvantage is that it could satisfy her sufficiently enough that she doesn't need you to penetrate her. You may have to experiment to find out whether you prefer doing it, but I have not found eating a girl out to be necessary or helpful.

When it comes to blowjobs, I find that girls either love to do them or not. If she loves them, she will start sucking your dick without you having to tell her. If she doesn't take the initiative, say "I want you to use your mouth" while holding your penis close to her face.

It may take some time before a more conservative girl will give you head, but sluttier girls will probably blow you quickly since they see it as little more than kissing. With these girls, you can be bolder and put your dick right in their mouths and they'll happily oblige. As long as you don't weakly ask for permission, there is no right or wrong way to go about it, because even if a girl rejects you when you command her to suck your dick, she won't lose respect for you like she would if you were to politely ask. Blowjobs in general are fun to receive, but you don't have to incorporate them into your bedroom game before having vaginal sex.

Let's talk about two negative things that could happen to you during sex. The first is having an orgasm too quickly. When this happens, you'll feel insecure and be tempted to explain your performance, or suggest how you'll do better next time. Don't! Instead, remain silent, take some deep breaths, and remember that a single sex episode does not define who you are as a man. If the sex really bothered her, she is free to bring it up, but odds are she won't say anything and will see how things go during the second round.

Most girls' expectations of your bedroom performance aren't such that they will easily write you off. If she does make a comment about how quickly you came, simply say, "Sometimes that happens. Second time will be longer." You don't have to explain yourself further or apologize.

The second problem is having trouble maintaining an erection. This is most common if you drink excessively or think you have to be the perfect lover. If you lose wood, simply say, "Let's try later." When you eventually get a full erection, put on a condom and try once more. Again, you don't have to explain yourself, give excuses, or apologize.

Even if you perform badly in bed, girls don't have a right to mock you or question your masculinity. I swiftly respond when they try to put me down, because I believe that only a rude person would try to shame a sexual partner after such an intimate moment. Here are three different responses you can give to such a girl:

> "I'm flesh and blood, not a robot. If you want more then maybe you should go buy a vibrator."

> "You're starting to be rude. If you're not satisfied with me, go find another guy."

> "You're more demanding than a terrorist. Why are you acting so rude? You're not perfect either."

Sadly, I'm sure you'll have to use one of these comments during your lifetime. As long as you refuse to accept insults, you'll be in a good position to stop a girl from trying to shame you for whatever happens in the bedroom.

After Penetration

Once you're finished with sex, either after having an orgasm or because you've realized you won't, lie on the bed and relax. Slowly and calmly process what happened. This is one of the few pure moments with a girl where you don't have to run any game or be concerned about what she thinks. There is also no need to touch or get close to her—when she's ready and has come down from the sex, she will get close to you.

A benefit of your relaxing vibe is that it makes her wonder whether you liked the sex, putting her in a state of mild anxiety. She may ask, "What are you thinking?" She wants you to pay her a compliment or confirm that everything is okay, but don't take the bait. Either say "nothing" or give a funny response such as, "I'm thinking of mermaids and leprechauns." The more she is wondering what you think, the less she is judging your flaws or failings.

As you start to regain full consciousness, you can begin to observe her behavior and demeanor. A positive sign is if she's affectionate and nurturing. She may cuddle up beside you or place her head on your chest. A bad sign is if she's whiny, negative, or starts sending text messages to her boyfriend or beta orbiters. There's no need to take action if she's being anti-social as long as she's not insulting you—simply monitor her behavior so you can understand what type of girl she really is.

If you're with a girl you want to have sex with only once, or she becomes so negative that you can't stand to spend more time with her, eventually suggest she leave by asking, "Do you need help getting home?" Be gentle, respectful, and polite when doing so, because if you make a girl feel overly rejected, she may conclude that she didn't have consensual sex with you. I often let girls hang out in my place for a while until they get bored and suggest leaving themselves. Before you have sex, you can kick a girl out more rudely, but use a soft touch after sex.

One of my friends once kicked out a girl harshly after she gave him a blowjob. She then called the police and made up a story about how he assaulted her. Don't give girls an easy excuse to get angry. Even if I don't like a girl, I tell her I had a nice evening and that we should hang out again. If I'm at a girl's place, I'll lie down for a while, perhaps get another drink, and then make an exit with an excuse about having to get up early.

It's more likely that you'll want her to stick around and have rounds two or three of sex. She may fish for you to say you want her to stay, perhaps telling you, "Don't worry, I'll leave soon." She hopes that you'll answer, "Oh, no, I really want you to stay." Instead, calmly state that it's her choice and that she's not imposing on you: "You're free to stay for longer. I don't mind hanging out more." If you really don't want her to stay, you can reply with a simple, "You can stay a bit longer, but I really have to get up early tomorrow." If you want her to spend the night in the hope of having morning sex, you should first find out if she likes morning sex.

When you're dealing with a same day or night bang rather than a date, you won't yet have her number or a way to get in touch with her. Upon saying goodbye, if you think you want to have sex with her again, get her number. The only issue is that you don't know whether she truly wants to see you again. One way to find out is by asking her: "Do you want to hang out again?" Most girls will say "Yes" or "Sure," but read between the lines and sense her excitement. If she hesitates before answering or sounds reluctant, she probably won't even reply to your text. If a girl really likes you, and imagines herself being with you again, she will reply enthusiastically. You can end things with a simple "I'll get in touch soon" or "I had a nice time."

Future Dates

Whether or not you got laid, contact her within one to four

days and schedule another date. The aim is to have the second date within a week. Your texting script can still be simple, although now you can loosen things up a bit by having longer exchanges before going for the date. This will be easier because you'll now have many things to reference. Just don't refer to the sex, because that will show her you deeply care about it.

Me: "Hello. How is your week going?" Or "Hello. How was your weekend?"

Her: "Pretty good, and yours?"

Me: "The usual. Did your work project go well?"

Her: "No, it didn't go so well."

Me: "That sucks. I'm watching a funny video." I send her the video link.

Her: "Haha"

Me: "Yeah, it was a good laugh. So you free tomorrow night to get a drink?"

Her: "Yeah, what time?"

Instead of sending a video, you can send a meme, funny picture, or joke. You can also refer to something that happened on the first date. You don't need to use a rigid template. See what she's up to, tell her what you're up to, share a light-hearted thing or two, and go for another date. Keep it simple and use her responses to guide you. If she's replying quickly and being especially fun, chat for a while, but if her replies are short, curt, and slow in coming, you might as well go for the date faster.

As you enter a relationship, the texting conversations will get looser and be full of funny pictures or emoticons. This is fine, but remember to monitor your reply times and take longer than her about half the time.

One trend I've noticed over the years is that girls are increasingly comfortable with having text-messaging dialogues that go on for hours. Because it's unlikely that a girl is busy with actual work, she can fill in the gaps of her day by texting friends and men while keeping up to date with what her favorite celebrities are posting on social networking. As a result, girls now expect men to relieve their boredom with texts. I've resisted this development. I don't like being tethered to my phone to maintain superficial conversations for extended periods, so I usually move quickly to the logistical side of scheduling dates, at least until I'm in a serious relationship.

If you don't want to participate in long texting conversations, move quickly into planning dates and send only brief responses to her jokey texts. If you like doing it, and you're not showing more eagerness than she is, just keep in mind that your participation creates the expectation of daily texting marathons.

When it comes to picking a venue for your second date, stay within your budget and resist trying to impress her. If I'm in the United States, I may pick an average bar for a couple of drinks. Abroad, I would do a dinner date since they are relatively cheap. If you've already had sex with her, you don't need to do multiple venue changes. Otherwise, two venues may be helpful if you suspect that you'll still receive some resistance to sex.

By the second date, you'll have used up your best game material, so let your natural personality shine through, and remember to qualify and tease her occasionally. She'll be chattier than she was on the first date because she is more comfortable with you, relieving you of the burden to perform.

If you're feeling anxious about not having anything to talk about, show her interesting photos and memes on your phone. You can even set up the routine beforehand by creating a folder of images you can share on dates. This is most useful if you have personal photos that show value. When I was in the middle of my travel phase, I saved up my top fifty travel photos and showed them on dates to convey how I'm spontaneous and adventurous.

When there is a genuine connection, the conversation is effortless, and the silences only enhance that connection further, but when you don't have deep rapport with a girl, and you're interested in her only for sex, you will spend most of your energy on simulating a connection. If you really have nothing to say, it's better to keep silent and allow her to see you as mysterious. If she comments on your silence, be honest: "There's nothing on my mind." Since girls find us more attractive when we don't try to impress them, you may even say something like, "I have nothing interesting to talk about right now." This works because it's the very opposite of what every other man has done, which was to blab endlessly about whatever entered his mind so that she didn't think of him as boring.

What you should do on future dates isn't much different from what you did on the first date: set up a meeting, re-establish comfort and intimacy by venue changing as many times as necessary, enjoy your time with her, and try to go to a private room for sex. If you've been on a date with a girl and haven't had sex with her yet, your goal should be to overcome the wall of resistance she put up on the previous date.

Many girls have arbitrary rules on how many dates they must go on before they will sleep with a man—sometimes it's as many as five. As long as the trend is in the direction of greater levels of intimacy on each date, and you enjoy her company enough that you want to stick around after sex, hang in there until you're rewarded. On the other hand, if you only want to have sex with a girl once, and it's clear she won't put out soon, I advise you to jump ship so that you don't feel awkward or guilty for putting in so much time for a single sexual encounter.

If you failed to secure a home venue change on a previous date, either use the same excuse from the last attempt or try a new one. Tell her that you've bought a new type of tea or alcohol that you would like to share with her. If she has already come over, it may be sufficient to say, "Let's go hang out at my place for a bit and have a drink," perhaps adding, "I forgot last time to show you so and so." You can also suggest watching a movie.

When a girl has a formidable wall in the bedroom after multiple dates, ask her if she's a virgin or has rules about when she can sleep with a man. If a girl tells me on date four that she can't sleep with a guy before date five, and she seems sincere, I'll wait until date five, but I've had many experiences of a girl saying she'll have sex with me "next time" and then disappearing. You will get burned repeatedly by girls you spend hours with who eventually decide not to sleep with you. Learn from the experience and move on instead of taking it personally.

I've never had to wait more than five dates to have sex with a girl, including virgins, but I've heard many stories from men who needed more dates to seal the deal. I don't want to lay down a rigid rule you must follow, but it is rare to find a non-virgin who won't sleep with a man by the third date. If a girl hasn't slept with you by then, she should provide evidence that she is a virgin, extremely religious, or has values that are higher than those of normal girls her age. If she drinks alcohol, has a dating history that includes casual relationships, travels to foreign destinations for fun, or values her education and career, it's impossible that she has not slept with a man quickly in the past.

I find it unacceptable if a girl makes me wait longer for sex than the other men she has been with. It would be like going to a store and paying double than what a previous customer paid for on the same item. I can deal with a slut, but not a "reformed" slut, a trait that is common among women over the age of 25.

When a girl is delaying sex, and I want to hint strongly that I'm not going to wait forever, I tell her that I'm concerned we have a weak connection. Here is what I might say if I'm hitting a wall in the bedroom on date three or later:

> "So this is the fourth date and I noticed you still don't want to have sex. That's your choice, but in my past relationships that lasted a while, things started off very passionately. We couldn't keep our hands off each other, and sex came quickly. I don't know if you have rules about sex or what, but I'm starting to think that maybe our connection is much weaker than I thought if you still don't want to do anything more."

You're essentially telling her that you're ready to give up because she's not putting out. If a girl likes you, she'll sleep with you that night or on the next date. If she still resists without giving you a reason, either you're being played or she's wife material.

Until you have sex, the girl has the upper hand, because she has yet to give up the main thing you desire from her. Some girls use this fact to manipulate you, knowing that you won't be willing to walk away from your investment as long as they dangle the sex carrot above your head. This is often the case if a girl is flakey by canceling dates at the last minute or disappearing for a day or two when it's her turn to reply to a text.

No matter how much you have invested in her, walking away is the correct response when you're repeatedly being disrespected. If you don't, you internalize bad game that pedestalizes girls who are treating you like garbage. No matter how much time you have devoted to an interaction, you must reverse directions if you're not getting close to your destination.

Chapter Conclusion

The more a girl is attracted to you, and the emptier her penis pipeline, the more likely you'll bang her. You'll experience few barriers and get sex in a mostly straightforward manner. She may hit you with a few obligatory no's, but they will not be insurmountable. If her attraction or availability is low, she will flake on you, play games, delay sex, be aloof, and treat you like a toy. You'll see barriers spring up out of nowhere to block you. The interaction will have no sense of urgency.

The secret is therefore not to waste time on girls who have weak attraction for you or a full penis pipeline. When you're starting in game, and haven't yet maximized your value, the girls who want you may be ugly or fat, but these girls are a reflection of your initial sexual value in the modern dating market. For game newbies, it may be wise to focus on average or below-average girls before aiming higher, to see firsthand how "easy" it is to sleep with girls who genuinely like you.

Chapter 9: Relationships

Once you've had sex with a girl on at least five different occasions, I consider you in a relationship, no matter how casual. You have conquered her body, repeatedly thrusted inside her, and have shown enough value for her to donate a big chunk of her free time to be with you. This doesn't mean she loves you, but you have done what less than 1,000 other men, and likely less than 100, will do to her during her lifetime.

It would be nice at this point to drop all game and "just be yourself," but unless being yourself got the girl in the first place, you have to be strategic to maintain the relationship. Don't forget why she chose you in the first place out of hundreds or even thousands of other suitors who wanted a level of intimacy you have achieved. This means you have to keep monitoring her behavior and analyzing what it says about her attraction level, which will ebb and flow. Although you won't have to run game as hard as you did when you first met her, you still have to be conscious of what's going on and not fall into the many traps she will set to test whether you're really the strong man she expects you to be.

A girl's love for a man depends on her attraction level. Imagine that a girl writes a diary entry where she professes her everlasting love for you, and then the next day you call her twenty times to say that you will commit suicide if she breaks up with you. You show up at her front door with a dozen roses and declare she's your only reason for living, and you get down on your knees and beg her to stay with you for eternity, saying you'd rather poke your eyes out with a blunt knife than look at another woman. I guarantee she will then rip that page from her diary, burn it, and say to herself that she was mistaken about you. This fictitious scenario illustrates that her attraction depends on the choices *you* make.

Usually, a girl's attraction changes subtly over weeks or months. The change can be so subtle that even she doesn't know why she is starting to feel "bored," "weird," "unsure," or "confused," code words for decreasing attraction. All she knows is that she wants to go out more with her friends while wearing her sexiest outfit, and then when the hammer finally comes down and she breaks up with you, she won't even be able to logically explain why the "feeling" is no longer there, but make no mistake that the lost feeling is the loss of attraction.

The way you treat a girl will do one of three things: decrease her attraction for you, increase her attraction for you, or maintain her existing attraction. At a minimum, you want to do things that won't cause a decrease in attraction. As you enter relationships, your game moves from tactics designed to create attraction to *maintaining* that attraction. In other words, you're going to the gym not to get stronger, but to maintain the muscle you already have.

Relationship Game Theory

There are three kinds of relationships you'll enter after having sex with a girl five times: casual, mini, and long-term. Casual relationships are predominately about sex. You enter a "booty call" frame where she goes straight to your place or you go straight to hers without much in the way of dating or seduction. There is a mutual understanding that you are using each other for sex until something better comes along, and neither of you makes much of an effort. It may also happen that you had a serious relationship with a girl but now see her once in a while to have sex.

Mini relationships are where you go on regular dates with a girl and spend a lot of time with her outside of the bedroom, but because you haven't yet entered a committed relationship, you're willing and able to sleep with other girls without a guilty conscience. The girl may be sleeping around on the side, too, or keeping her eyes open for a better prospect who is more willing to satisfy her or make a full commitment. A mini relationship can last a long time, but it ends before you're able to see her as a potential wife or the mother of your children. Breaking up from a mini relationship is often not emotional.

A long-term relationship continues to progress over time. You go on vacations, engage in mundane tasks such as shopping for groceries and clothes, develop inside jokes, meet both sets of parents, pledge faithfulness to each other, make declarations of love, brainstorm names for future children, and so on. The girl will also take on a more nurturing role by cooking you meals, doing your laundry, and giving you emotional support. The ultimate function of a long-term relationship is to create a family, but if there are obstacles to achieving this goal, the relationship loses its purpose and ends in an emotionally painful way.

Mini relationships can sometimes make the jump to long-term relationships, but it's more likely that you'll decide soon after meeting a girl whether she is worthy for something serious. If a girl is cool or cute enough for the moment, you will subconsciously put her in the casual or mini relationship box and resist her efforts to escalate it into a long-term relationship without caring whether she sleeps with other men, but when you meet a girl who impresses you, you'll subconsciously seek to progress the relationship over time and want her to be dedicated to you alone.

Girls don't understand that men categorize them based on the signals they put out. When a girl drinks excessively, brags about all the "fun" she has had in life, or displays an over-confident attitude, you'll instinctively put her in the slut box and insist on booty calls instead of long dates. If a girl acts like a girlfriend, on the other hand, you will start fantasizing about having a future with her. It's also possible for a girl to see you as nothing more than a booty call, just one of many men with whom she is having simultaneous mini relationships. Ironically, the more of a "relationship vibe" you put out, where you appear loyal, honorable, and dedicated to your family, the less likely a non-traditional girl will consider a relationship with you, or even have sex with you.

When it comes to commitment, a girl wants to feel that she is winning over a man and taming him. We automatically take care of the former feeling with our game methods, particularly when we qualify her. The second is accomplished when a girl thinks that, although you could sleep with other pretty girls, you chose her specifically, and did so upon realizing she has value beyond sex. In more practical terms, the more a girl invests in you, and the more she feels that she's successfully seducing you with her femininity, the more likely she'll want a mini or long-term relationship.

If you show a girl that you really want a relationship with her, will she feel that she won you over or tamed you? No. This insight provides the basis for our relationship strategy: the girl must work harder than you in pushing for a committed relationship. This is often displayed in her concern about the status of the relationship ("Where do we stand?"), and anxiety over whether you're seeing other girls. It's the girl—not the man—who decides if the relationship goes deeper.

If we try to deepen the relationship first, the girl won't fully experience the feelings she needs to be secure in her choice. She'll have doubts about the relationship and then sabotage it, most likely by entertaining other suitors or outright cheating. This tells us why a girl will get into a relationship only to cheat on the weakest of impulses: her boyfriend is not making her feel like she has to win him over or invest in him to retain his affections. She seeks out men who can stir these feelings within her, or she is simply a raging slut who can't keep her legs together.

The good news about relationship game is that we don't have to do anything to get into a relationship—it's the girl's job entirely. Unless she says she wants to meet your parents, is worried that you might be seeing other girls, expresses her interest to go on trips with you, or tries to monopolize your time by seeing you multiple days a week, she's nowhere close to wanting a serious relationship. The girl not only chooses who she gets to have sex with, but also who she wants to have a relationship with. As men, our best strategy is to maximize our value and run game that increases the odds of both outcomes, but because we're living in an era where girls call the shots, any attempt to short-circuit their choosing will lead to disappointment and failure.

The modern age has somewhat inverted the paradigm of men hunting for women and dragging them back to a cave. It's true that we do hunt through approaching, showing value, and making bold moves, but because a woman can say no at any time, we need her to feel like she's hunting us as well, especially when it comes to securing relationships.

Imagine you're in a nightclub and meet a girl who you consider one of the hottest you've ever seen. Because you were there at the right time, had the right game, and happened to have a quirk that she liked at that moment, you were able to take her home and bang her. Since she's the best you've ever had, your instinct is to lock her down, but you will fail because you have already accepted that her value is higher than yours. You'll unconsciously leak neediness and anxiety. She'll sense that you over-value her and choose not to upgrade from casual sex to anything more.

In contrast, imagine you meet a shy and boring girl who doesn't go out much. You have sex with her on the third date and she lovingly cuddles up next to you while you're thinking of an excuse to get her out the door. She will do most of the work in advancing the relationship while always feeling that she has to win you over. Your reluctance causes her to *perceive* your value as far higher than hers.

These two examples illustrate that value is not objective—it is what you believe it to be. Outwardly, you can increase your value by working on yourself and becoming experienced enough with women that you no longer get excited when you meet a hot girl, but because you're the same man from the universe's point of view, any change you feel to yourself is an illusion. Your value is whatever you can convince yourself of, not what it actually is.

Philosophical issues aside, the question is not how to get into a relationship with a high-value girl, but how to get a high-value girl to want a relationship *with you*, and that will involve her believing your value is not only higher than hers, but that you're the best man she thinks she can get in the sexual marketplace. This is exactly why a hot girl in her prime is so hard to lock down beyond a mini relationship: she has so many options that she will not be convinced you are the best she can get until she has confirmed it by doing more cock exploration.

A girl must be the one who first asks if you're seeing other people. She must be the one who first says "I love you." And she must be the one who first gets jealous because she doesn't know where you are or what you're doing at a certain time. To an outside observer, it should appear that you are resisting her efforts to lock you down due to being uncertain of her value, even if you really are happy with her and can't wait to marry her.

When you're sleeping with a promiscuous girl, a bit of deception on your part will go a long way if you can temporarily convince her that your value is high through teasing, qualifying, or social proof, but when it comes to a relationship, your value must have a firm foundation, because a girl will *endlessly* test you to uncover your true worth. If you slip up on these tests by qualifying yourself weakly, she will smell a rat and decide to keep things casual or terminate the relationship, even if she can't logically explain why. You need value to get laid and even more value to get into a relationship, where her incessant testing is sure to expose a fake.

It's also important to be careful about telling a girl that you are eager for a relationship. Her mind will interpret this to mean you are trying and failing to get girls to be in a relationship with you. On a first date, when a girl asks what you want from a woman, be vague and say you're open to a great connection. If you're dating a girl and you desperately want her to commit to you, show only mild satisfaction when she tries to lock you down. Paradoxically, the signal to girls that you are worth a relationship is that you don't want a relationship.

Spend time with a girl you like, fuck her good, and buy modest gifts for her birthday and Christmas, but never show more affection and care than she does. Never be more eager than she is. Never show you're more invested in the relationship or that you're more concerned about the future. If I happened to drop in on one of your dates, I should notice that your girlfriend is aiming to please you much more than you're trying to please her. If I don't, how can I not conclude that the relationship will soon end by her hand?

The principle is easy to understand: to get into a relationship with a girl, don't try to get into a relationship with a girl.

Training Girls

Girls are reluctant to publicly admit it, but they crave being led by a man whose value is higher than theirs. They have a lot to say about equality, but when you look at who they're dating in their youthful prime, and who they have the most attraction for, it's clear they respond most favorably to a strong, attractive man who leads the way. A girl who dates such a man will be somewhat anxious that he may leave her for someone else. This is a better outcome for him than her being so secure in the relationship that *she* wonders whether she could do better. Some anxiety should be present in a girl's mind to banish thoughts about upgrading.

One way to show a girl that she needs to put effort into pleasing you is by training her on standards or behaviors that are important to you. This will be most effective if a girl is already somewhat close to fulfilling your needs, not when your standards are totally contrary to her character. You can train a girl who likes to cook how to prepare your favorite meals, but you can't teach cooking to a girl who hates to cook. You can train a girl who believes in monogamy what your specific rules of monogamy are, but you can't teach monogamy to a slut. What you're training a girl to do should agree at least partially with her character, or the training won't take.

Modern culture interprets a man training a girl as oppressive, controlling, and "emotionally abusive," while saying nothing about the never-ending games and manipulation girls subject men to. Any attempt by you to level the relationship playing field with game or training will result in your girlfriend's friends labeling you an abusive chauvinist, but you have no choice if you want the relationship to succeed and satisfy your most important needs. It's only a matter of time until *anything* a man does is considered abuse, so don't waste time convincing others that your relationship methods are righteous. Do what you have to do to ensure the relationship's success and your happiness.

Even if a girl is "perfect" in your mind, attempting to do some light training is healthy from a game perspective because it shows you're a confident man who knows what he wants and isn't scared that a girl may walk away. If you can make requests of a girl when it comes to her looks or behavior, she will interpret this to mean you have had exceptional women in your life, implying that you are capable of getting *another* exceptional woman who can meet your standards. Without being a dictator, simply convey to a girl that you expect certain things from her, and that if she does not adhere to them, the relationship will not be worth the trouble. My standards are such that if a girl doesn't follow them, I would rather be single or have only a casual relationship.

You started to train a girl on the first date without realizing it through the "Why do you?" question, where you ask her why she behaves in a certain way that insinuates your displeasure. For example, I'll usually ask a girl why her hair isn't longer, even if it's quite long. I ask her to show me a photo of when it was longer and then I practically make love to that photo by complimenting it and asking her how much time is needed for it to grow to that length again. I also ask if she has plans to cut her hair anytime soon, and express strong disapproval if she says that such a plan is in the works. Before either of us have considered a relationship, I'm already conveying the fact that I have standards and expect to be pleased.

For example, one thing I hate is bright red lipstick. It makes a girl look like she's auditioning to be a circus clown. To show my disapproval for such an abomination, I say, "I noticed you like bright red lipstick. Why?" She will give an unsatisfactory answer and I will reply, "Well, I think a natural color is much prettier on you." I'll never see bright red lipstick on her again, and if I do, it means she doesn't see my value as high enough to respect my preferences.

If a girl cuts her hair short even though you explicitly told her you dislike short hair, she's saying that she doesn't care about your opinion, and is essentially daring you to break up with her. You then have grounds to downgrade the relationship, but her insolent act indicates it's likely that she has already downgraded it. If a girl does something she knows you don't like, she's essentially slapping you in the face. You must not ignore it.

Another area of training concerns how a girl treats my home. Younger girls tend to be messy. They don't put away dishes or the items they use after hanging out in my apartment. This annoys me because I don't want to clean up after them. If I don't want to see a girl again, I will not bother saying anything, but if I do, I insist that she not treat my apartment like a hotel. Instead of showing approval or disapproval as in the previous examples, we can use a more direct "I would like you to…" or "Can you…" request so there is no ambiguity. For example: "Before you leave, can you clean up after yourself?"

If she's starting to spend a lot of time at your place, you may want her to do more of the housework. Say, "I would like you to help out more around the apartment by making the bed and doing the dishes after we eat." If she asks you why, your answer can also be direct: "Because that's what I expect from girls I date who enjoy the comfort of my home."

To train a girl, show approval or disapproval for something with the presumption that she will comply *or* convey a direct request. Choose the method you feel best matches the situation and your personality. It's easy to train a girl using one of these two methods when it comes to simple behaviors, such as cleaning and looking a certain way, but it's hard—if not foolhardy—to try to change behaviors that are deeply entrenched in her character.

If a girl is a jealous person, you won't be able to train her not to be jealous. The same applies if she's greedy, has a short temper, or is narcissistic. The best you can do is slightly modify the most visible consequence of the adverse behavior. For example, if a girl curses a lot because she has a negative attitude, your disapproval can decrease her cursing in front of you, but her negative attitude won't change.

Training works only when a girl is already *close* to your ideal. It isn't about transforming a girl who is not your type or does not have the character you want into the perfect woman. Training is like putting icing on a cake, but it's not modifying the cake itself, which is already baked. If you need to change something that's deeper than the flavor of the icing, it's best you find another girl.

It's also important to be careful while training not to inadvertently reveal you're needy or have low value. For example, say your girl is taking an hour on average to respond to your text messages. If you tell her that you don't like her long reply times, this may imply that you feel discomfort or insecurity when she doesn't text back promptly. The better strategy is to hold a mirror to her behavior by taking even longer to reply to her messages until she confronts you about it. Then claim that you take so long because you thought she was indifferent about text reply times. She is then likely to reply faster.

A sign that you should not confront a girl about a behavior is if it's merely making you anxious or nervous instead of making you less attracted to her or less eager to be in a relationship with her. The line is crossed when she's being outright disrespectful or treating you in an intolerable manner, such as taking a day or two to reply to your text messages. In that case, a confrontation is justified.

There is a fine line between training a girl to uphold your standards and being nitpicky, whiny, and obsessive, because for everything you want to train her to do, you will constantly have to observe that behavior to ensure she is complying and confront her when she doesn't. If you don't confront her when she doesn't comply, she will assume that your standards mean nothing. What would your opinion of a policeman be if you flagrantly broke the law in front of him and he did nothing about it? You'd probably see him as weak and less deserving of respect, and contemplate breaking an even bigger law.

As you can imagine, ensuring compliance takes effort, so you should maintain only a handful of critical standards. If you have too many demands and preferences, she will see you as heavy-handed and authoritarian, and the relationship will degrade as you put more effort into securing compliance than enjoying your love with her. Don't try to polish a turd by getting into a relationship with a girl who is too far from your ideal.

To prevent yourself from enforcing trivial standards, mentally codify the standards that are important to you either before entering a relationship or after weeks of careful consideration, instead of merely reacting from date to date, often at the whim of your mood. If you attempt to train a girl on something that suddenly bothers you while you're feeling upset, angry, or anxious, you will cause unnecessary conflict and have to enforce that standard even when it becomes obvious later that you don't really care about it. This is why I begin training on something only if I'm convinced it'll be worth upholding during the *entirety* of the relationship, which, in the case of marriage, could be several decades.

A young man in his first relationship will probably have no standards besides the girl being pretty and having a vagina that doesn't smell. It will take time for him to learn specifically what he wants, and this is the joy of self-discovery. When you're older like me, your standards become far clearer. I have three categories of standard that I expect a girl to maintain in a long-term relationship: how she interacts with other men, how she maintains her appearance, and how much effort she puts into homemaking.

The first standard concerns her interactions with other men. In a committed long-term relationship, the default expectation is that neither I nor the girl cheat by having intimacy with other people, but there are steps before outright cheating that I expect a girl to avoid. I expect her not to meet one-on-one with other men, even for coffee. I expect her not to meet her ex-boyfriends or be overly friendly with them in texts or on social networking. I expect her not to go out with her single girlfriends to bars or clubs that are known meat markets. And I expect her not to flirt with other men or give out her contact information, whether online or in person.

If a girl doesn't want me to sleep with other girls, and I wouldn't mind having a long-term relationship with her, I will relay these expectations before we commit to each other. She can disagree with them and scream at me for being controlling until she loses her voice, but my standards are non-negotiable, because I would rather be alone than with a girlfriend who doesn't comply with them. Your standards may not be as strict as mine (or they may be even stricter), but whatever the case may be, you should not compromise. If she doesn't want to adhere to your standards, do not commit to her.

The second standard concerns my girlfriend's appearance. I expect her to keep her hair beyond a certain length and to maintain the weight she had when we initially met. When you first meet a girl, casually find out what her weight is. If you suspect she is gaining weight, and this is confirmed with a scale, show disapproval, and help her lose the extra pounds.

The weight standard is very important to me, and during a relationship I will not hide that fact: I mock men who have huge girlfriends and remark how I would never stay with a girl of such immense proportions. I also state that although I may not leave her if she gets fat after having children, I may sleep around discreetly. If she gets fat before having children, or cuts her hair in a way that is contrary to what she knows I want, I will downgrade the relationship by removing my promise of monogamy. If she fixes the problem before I am able to find a new girlfriend, I may upgrade the relationship again.

The third standard concerns homemaking. I expect her to help around the house and occasionally cook meals. If I'm using a girl primarily for sex, I will not expect much in this regard, and want her merely to clean up after herself, but if she desires a long-term relationship, which implies the possibility of creating a family, I want to see her begin to behave like a wife who is eager to take care of the home, because I know that if she doesn't do the things I want when she's young, full of energy, and eager to impress, there's no way she'll do them once I sign a legal marriage contract that will make it much harder for me to downgrade the relationship in the event of non-compliance.

Personally, I like to cook, so my kitchen demands are light, but most men don't cook as much as me and may expect more in this area. You should also involve her in the cleaning, especially if she's spending a lot of time at your place. On the days you normally clean, ask her to come over and help you out. She can also help you with chores, whether it's making photocopies, setting up the Christmas tree, or running small errands.

When it comes to homemaking, you don't need to command her like you're some sort of macho man. Use a respectful tone: "I would like you to…," "When you have time today, can you do so and so?" "Honey, when you go to the kitchen, grab me so and so." I'm also not stingy with saying "thanks" to show my gratitude, especially if she completes a task without attitude. Having standards and enforcing those standards is enough to derive the full benefits of training—you don't have to sound tough unless that toughness matches who you are. The only exception to this guideline is during sex, when you should give commands instead of make requests.

A possible fourth standard concerns how often you have sex. This is not a problem with younger girls who are horny, but in longer relationships she may not be "in the mood" more often than you like. You'll then have to set a standard, stating that you expect sex a certain number of times a week, with the insinuation that if you don't get it from her, you will get it elsewhere. Girls tend to put out less when there are attraction problems, so if you tighten your game by being less needy and more masculine, the sex frequency problem should resolve itself.

You may be wondering when you should begin relaying your standards. In many cases, it happens naturally. Your appearance standards will become clear from the first date, when you indirectly share what you like about her. How much sex you want per week is also conveyed early on by how often you contact her to meet. You can reveal your additional standards in your conversations about other people, where you discuss their physical or behavioral flaws. In other cases, the standards will be revealed as the relationship deepens. For instance, you may reveal your homemaking standard after several months when she starts spending more time in your home.

A possible strategy is to teach her one standard, and once she has mastered it, teach her another. I'm not a pet owner, but I believe this is similar to how dogs are trained. The problem with this is that a girl may see no end to your training, and become frustrated that you keep adding standards as time goes on. To avoid this problem, I advise you to convey your standards naturally as the relationship deepens, and then unload any remaining standards when she wants to make the relationship monogamous.

The standard you will probably convey last is how you want her to interact with other men. Before a girl seeks monogamy, I reveal the gist of how I believe a girl should be faithful, often indirectly by telling stories about other people's relationship difficulties. Your girl will probably have no shortage of tales about her slutty friends and how they are behaving dishonorably towards their boyfriends, giving you opportunities to reveal your standard.

It's when a girl wants monogamy that I am as specific as possible about this standard—and all the others—so there is no ambiguity or confusion. She can choose to accept my standards, in which case we enter a monogamous relationship, or not accept them, where we keep things as they are or break up. In one relationship, I made the mistake of relaying most of my standards *after* we were monogamous. I had less leverage over her during that time and it also made me come across as capricious, as if I were making up standards out of thin air. I now see the moment of monogamy as entering a trial marriage, so I ensure she completely understands all my standards from the first day of the committed relationship.

The problem with not relaying all of your standards before commitment is that she will interpret any future standard as an ultimatum. This will lead to arguments and put a lot of strain on the relationship. You can use ultimatums if you never bluff or waver, but you want to avoid them because the girl may think you are looking for arbitrary pretexts to leave the relationship.

Whenever a standard is conveyed, and I strongly recommend you convey all of your standards before you commit to her, remember to always uphold that standard. Think of standards as a weight on your shoulders that you have to carry throughout the *entire* relationship. Keep the load as light as possible while allowing the integrity of the relationship to be maintained.

Beware that a girl will expect you to uphold your own standards or accuse you of being a hypocrite. Men and women are different, and should be held to different standards, but chances are your girlfriend was raised on feminism and thinks that both sexes are the same.

For example, most of a girl's male friends would sleep with her if given the chance, but most of your female friends would not sleep with you. Therefore, if you tell a girl she should not meet with a male friend, you're forbidding her from spending time with a man who is courting her in order to have sex, but if she wants to hold you to that same standard, she would be forbidding you from spending time with a woman who would never sleep with you. There is no equality in this scenario, but your girlfriend will be exceedingly resentful that you hold her to a standard that you don't hold yourself, even if it's based on biological fact.

Another example is if you gain weight but expect her to stay thin. Men are more visual than women, but she may call you a hypocrite if you plump up while not allowing her to. Yet another example is if you go to a crowded bar to have drinks with friends but forbid her from doing the same. No woman would approach you, whereas many horny men would approach her.

The ideal solution is not to commit to a girl who believes that men and women are the same, and who understands that it's 100 times easier for a girl to get laid than a man, but it will be exceedingly difficult to find such a girl. To maintain the moral high ground in a relationship and prevent your girlfriend from resenting your standards, I recommend that you adhere to the same standards you give her. If you're not ready to quit going to singles bars with your buddies, don't tell her that she can't go to the same bars, but be watchful when she does.

At times during a committed relationship, a situation will arise that you hadn't anticipated. For example, your girlfriend may suddenly decide to travel to a foreign city with one of her slutty friends. I find this to be grossly unacceptable. A girl who seeks a long-term relationship with you should not act like she's single by going to an exotic location that most other people visit for fun and casual sex. I would tell her that she cannot go even if it wasn't one of my existing standards. She can cry, pout, and fight with me all she wants, but she is not going on that trip. I would not tell her that the relationship will be over if she goes, but I would certainly imply it.

Even when you prevent her from acting in a certain way, you haven't solved the underlying problem of her wanting to break the spirit of her commitment to you. Unless she stops trying to push against your standards, cheating will be inevitable. In a perfect world, you would commit to a girl of upstanding moral character who instinctively knows how to behave properly, but most girls today have a promiscuous nature, totally unsuitable for long-term relationships.

If your girl repeatedly challenges your standards, the problem is not her, but the fact that you chose her for a relationship when she was far from your ideal. The beginning of any training program will be difficult, because it's likely that you will be the first man she's met who has any relationship standards at all, but she should grow to love the fact that you also live by these standards. Remember that there can be no compromises. Once you lay down your standards, it's the same as Moses bringing forth the Ten Commandments. Be diligent in upholding them for the duration of the relationship.

A huge red flag is when a girl upholds your standards, you make a large investment in the relationship (for example, you move in with her, buy property together, propose marriage), and then she violates them. Once she feels that your commitment to her is secure, she may loosen her behavior, gain weight, seek exemptions to meeting other men who are "friends," insist on eating out more instead of cooking you meals, or party harder with her slutty girlfriends. Some women will pretend to uphold your standards for months, even years, until their true character reveals itself. This is why I don't like telling a girl what my ideal type of woman is early on in the dating stage so that she doesn't fool me by acting it out, which has happened to me in the past.

Not only must you be ever-vigilant with your standards as long as the relationship lasts, you must never let a girl gain leverage over you to the point where you can't walk away when it's clear she no longer wants to comply. In other words, don't let a girl have you by the balls. Don't mix your finances with hers or become legally obligated to her unless you're in a position to kick her out if she fails to uphold your standards. This makes it difficult for men who want to get married and have children, but even in that case, you should have an escape hatch so that you still have the option of ending the relationship while doing yourself as little harm as possible.

Resisting Her Training

Girls are better at training men than we are at training them. Their training is not based on objective standards, as it is with us, but on subjective feelings. If they *feel* something is off, they exhibit the training technique of showing disapproval, otherwise known as nagging. Their nature causes them to break down a man's will by constantly showing disapproval of things they think they don't like, often in a passive-aggressive manner. Girls usually complain about you because they're in a bad mood or dissatisfied in some way, not because they're upset about what they're complaining about. This is why complying with a girl's requests does not end the complaining—she will simply find something new to complain about.

Compare this to our training program, where we have a finite number of standards that we want upheld. If a girl meets all of our standards, and remains in a state of compliance, there is nothing for us to complain about, even if we happen to be moody. This is not the case with a woman. She nags not because she wants a standard to be met but because she doesn't feel right and is unsure why. I first experienced this phenomenon when I was a child. My mother would come home after a rough day at work and complain to me about my behavior on things she would never mention when she was having a good day.

Even if you eagerly comply to a girl's complaint, she will quickly devise another complaint. Therefore, there's no use in complying to the first complaint. Think of a girl as being similar to a terrorist: complying with the smallest request will simply tell her that she can extract further concessions from you. It starts with her telling you to wear a certain shirt, and next thing you know, you're paying for vacations to cities that you don't even want to visit.

Once in a blue moon I'll throw a girl a bone and wear an article of clothing she likes, or I'll go with her to see a band she's a fan of, but there will be no end to the sacrifices you'll have to make if you try to make a girl happy. The end result of compliance is becoming a weak husband who serves his wife like a slave. His enslavement didn't happen immediately but over the course of hundreds of nagging episodes that he never stood up to.

I remember when a girl I was dating complained that I was leaving hair on the soap bar—*my* soap bar. Did I comply by removing hair from the soap? No. In fact, I laughed her off, and said that she didn't have to use my soap. She did not bother me about it again. If I had complied with this trivial request, the next request would have been bigger.

Another example is when a girl asks you to hold her purse while she ties her shoe. I absolutely refuse. I'm a man, and part of being a man is not holding a purse. She can say "Are you serious?" repeatedly, but I will not be swayed. I truly believe that a girl innately knows she must start with small requests before moving on to bigger ones. Say no to the first request to stop the chain. Anything you do for her should be something *you* want to do, not something she's making you do.

When a girl is hit by your stubborn resistance and realizes her training won't take, she will throw a temper tantrum or begin making threats, just like a terrorist would, but you must stand firm knowing that she cares less about the request itself than exerting her will over you. Here are some replies you can give when a girl tries to modify your behavior:

"No."

"I don't want to."

"I'm not the type of man who does that."

"You can't teach an old dog new tricks."

"No thanks, mom."

"You're not my boss."

"I'll change because I want to, not because you tell me to."

"I am who I am."

"Nag, nag, nag. You're worse than my mom."

Understand that the dynamic we're setting up is where she must uphold your objective standards, but you don't have to comply with any of her subjective complaints. In fact, the only standards on which she can legitimately challenge you on are the ones you make her uphold, which is why you must be careful about implementing a standard that you don't adhere to yourself.

A girl must accept you for who you are, warts and all. She does not have your consent to change you in any way, shape, or form, and if she is dissatisfied, she can meet a new man. If a girl gets too pushy, I point to the door and tell her to find a man who does what she wants, because I am certainly not going to comply. Strangely enough, the more I resist her nagging and fail to do what she wants, the more attraction she has for me and the less likely she is to leave, although she will *never* stop trying. I win most, if not all, of the battles, but her war to change me will not cease, and I must always resist her training, no matter how old and feeble I become.

Apart from nagging, a girl may make mildly insulting comments in an attempt to lower your status or hurt you. If a girl says something that causes you to feel bad, stop and think about what she said. Was it an attempt to shame you? Is she emasculating you? Did she try to lower your value in front of other people? If you can answer "yes" to any of these questions, or you otherwise feel that she took a dig at you, you must reprimand her immediately, regardless of who may be listening. Here are a few examples of how you can do that:

"Do not insult me again."

"Do not talk to me in that way again."

"You are not allowed to talk to me like that."

"Do not try to embarrass me in front of other people."

"Are you trying to make fun of me? I don't accept that. Don't do it again."

Impose a verbal punishment that is swift and clear. You should not mock her back, because this would reward her for the insult by accepting her frame and treating her as an equal. Squash her behavior right then and there in the most direct manner possible. Remember that no one has permission to make you feel bad unless you give them permission.

Another response you should avoid is mopey silence. This type of "silent treatment" is the feminine way of dealing with problems. You're hoping she will ask you if anything is wrong only so you can deny there's a problem and continue moping because you fear direct confrontation. Nothing will change if you respond in a weak manner. Communicate directly so that she knows exactly what she did wrong, and tell her not to do it again.

After you communicate that a comment or behavior of hers was unacceptable, she may attempt to get into a drawn-out argument with you. I don't see the point in arguing, because she will merely try to persuade you to accept disrespect. If you believe that she did insult you, and you don't want to be insulted in that way again, telling her to stop is the law of the land. It's fine for her to tell you that she was mad at you because of something else you did, but the fact remains that she must treat you in a respectful manner, regardless of what she thinks you've done wrong.

The belief I endorse is, "It's my way or the highway." I actually say this to women when they try one of their terrorist tactics. If they ask why, I simply reply that I am the man, and I have the final word in the relationship. This will come as a shock to a girl raised in an egalitarian culture. She may even threaten to leave you, and if she does, she has done you a massive favor, because a future wife of yours ultimately has to bend the knee and respect your authority if the relationship is to proceed on your terms.

A woman will test you constantly to find out whether you live up to your image as the king of the castle, so always be prepared to face spontaneous temper tantrums. Do not compromise when she tries to assert frame. On the other hand, if you believe that both partners in a relationship are equal, you're free to do what she says and follow her commands, but don't be surprised if she starts going out more frequently at night and comes home late and disheveled. If you're not treating her in a masculine manner, she will find another man who will.

It may happen that a girl insults you but you don't realize it until hours later. Your options are to bring it up belatedly or ignore it. If you do eventually bring it up, it will not seem as visceral and powerful as it would be if you had brought it up when it happened, but if you feel that the insult was severe, and you want to put an immediate stop to it happening again, tell her that what she did was unacceptable and you don't want her to treat you that way again. If you ignore it, you forfeit the opportunity to communicate your displeasure, but it's almost guaranteed that she will make a similar comment in the future.

It may also happen that you accidentally comply with one of her demands without realizing it, such as fetching items for her when she could have done it herself. A mistake here or there won't doom your relationship, but be careful not to make the same blunders in the future.

I don't mind going out of my way to make everyone around me happy. Doing this for women in a traditional age may not have resulted in punishment, but in the modern age, overly pleasing a girl will put you on the road to her losing attraction for you. If your girlfriend is behaving traditionally by cooking for you daily and cleaning your apartment, occasionally making her feel like a princess won't hurt your relationship, but if she's not nurturing you outside of sex, be careful with trying to please her by being compliant or doing nice things. Both of you should make the same sacrifices and put in the same amount of effort to keep the relationship balanced.

A girl's game is naturally tuned to getting a man who is physically stronger than her to do things that he wouldn't on his own. A girl even knows how to use your previous compliance against you if you suddenly refuse. A common example is her trying to get you to watch yet another romantic comedy film.

When a girl tricks me into watching enough of her stupid movies, I draw the line and tell her that I can't watch her movies anymore, but that she is free to watch her movies at my place while I do something else. This always leads to an argument. I stand firm, because the alternative is being trained over the long term to do things I simply don't like. I'll even ask her, "Why do you want me to do things I don't want to do?" Otherwise, your life becomes nothing more than doing what she likes at your expense. If you don't resist early on, it will just get worse over time.

Many men are nervous, scared, or averse to getting into arguments with women, because they think it will destroy the attraction and cause a woman to leave. It turns out that the opposite is true. Not getting into arguments means that, outside of the bedroom, there is no way for a girl to know if you're truly the dominant man she seeks. While having too many fights may suggest incompatibility or make her feel insecure about the relationship, allowing her to dictate the terms will lead to an equally miserable result. Don't start fights over nothing, but always be ready to state your preferences clearly or simply tell a girl no. Her ensuing anger is merely a test to see whether she is stronger than you. When it's clear that she is weaker, she will feel a spike in her attraction, even though she may continue to complain.

A girl will never stop testing your dominance. This makes sense from the standpoint of self-preservation, because she needs a way to uncover her man's true power level, but if you easily submit to her silly demands, she will know that you won't be able to protect her from more serious threats. When your girlfriend senses that you're weak, her eye begins to roam, and she will start putting herself in a position to cheat on you.

Standing up to a girl's training attempts may sound easy when you read about it, but women have a lethal weapon to ensure your compliance: tears. A girl will cry her eyes out when you challenge her. Her tears will make you feel sympathetic, since in the male world, tears mean that someone is in real pain. Think of the last time you cried in front of someone else. I'm sure it wasn't because of something trivial, and it also wasn't a tactic to convince other people of your argument, but this is exactly what a girl's tears mean, even if she doesn't realize it.

Girls cry more often than men, not because they experience more pain or suffering (apart from childbirth), but because they need a strategy to control the bigger and stronger sex. In other words, when a girl cries in front of her man, either she is losing an argument or wants something from him. God gave men logic to persuade others. He gave women tears.

If you're like me, you'll think that your girlfriend is in serious pain when you see her cry for the first time during an argument. You'll be tempted to soften your position and decide—at least temporarily—to comply with her request. This is foolish! Behind these tears lurks the terrorist whose aim is make you submit to her. Unless her relative died or she sustained a physical injury, her tears should be ignored. Stick to your argument and let her cry. Once she sees that her tears will not move you, she will become a blubbering mess and increase her volume, similar to a child throwing a tantrum. You may even encounter a girl who stomps her feet.

I let a girl cry for as long as she wants, but if she insults me or my mother, I command her to stop. If she doesn't, I ask her to leave or I remove myself from her presence. If a fight gets out of control, and she begins to get physical, record at least the audio with your phone so that you have evidence in your favor in case she calls the police. (Be sure first to check the audio recording laws in your jurisdiction.)

I approach a fight with a girl in the same way a father deals with a daughter who gets angry when she doesn't receive the toy she wants. She can cry and yell "I hate you" or "I'm running away," but the second she uses insults or physical violence, the line has been crossed. A girl who does this will have to make amends with at least a sincere apology for me to continue the relationship.

Until you've seen a girl cry in your presence for no reason, you may be under the impression that women and men are somewhat equal, but female tantrums reveal that the empress has no clothes. All their power is simply the result of men complying with their requests. If you decide not to comply, a girl's only options are to accept your position or leave you, but the odds of the latter are quite low, because you've shown that you are indeed the dominant man she wants. Within a few days—or hours—she is more likely to reward your stance with explosive sex than anything negative.

Tactics

Most of the time, all you need to maintain attraction in a relationship is to uphold your standards, resist her training, and continue to be the high-value man she liked enough to get into a relationship with in the first place. As long as you don't soften and make her doubt your strength, the relationship should continue for some time.

I don't like running much more relationship game than what I've described, because the point of one is to relax and enjoy levels of comfort and intimacy deeper than those you can get from casual sex, but if this comes at the cost of having to run hard game all the time, you might as well focus on casual sex instead where at least you get the bonuses of novelty and excitement. If a relationship requires more game than you're willing to put in, it may be in your best interests to downgrade it and keep an eye out for a girl who has lower maintenance costs.

It's worth sharing a handful of minor relationship tactics that should not be too taxing for you to use. The first is to be more aloof and evasive than her. Earlier, I shared how we should evade some of a girl's questions to show that we're not trying to impress her or become her dog. Extending that principle, a man who puts out signs that he doesn't overly care about a relationship reveals that he's definitely worth locking down for a relationship.

To verbally show that you care less than her, make statements praising her or the relationship half as often as she does. Your praise should be sufficiently infrequent so that when you give it, she gets especially excited and loving. Spend time with her and make love to her passionately, but don't verbalize the joy she gives you, because this could be interpreted as weakness and make her think that she has won you over and tamed you.

It's inevitable that you'll encounter a girl who insists that you make verbal declarations of your affection for her. The correct response is non-compliance. This commonly happens when a girl says "I love you" and expects you to say it back immediately. The last time a girl said this to me, I waited four months to say it back, and when I did, it was in a distorted voice that sounded like Darth Vader. Even if I had wanted to say "I love you" to her after the first time she said it, which I did not, I wouldn't have done so, because it would've sounded too eager and not allowed her to feel at least some anxiety for the following four months.

You can also show aloofness through your behavior by unexpectedly displaying anger, allowing other girls to flirt with you in her presence, or taking a long time to reply to random texts. The problem with these tactics is that they come across as passive-aggressive and could escalate into ways you don't except. Direct communication is the preferable way to convey your dissatisfaction with what she's doing or saying, as long as your complaint doesn't reveal any innate neediness.

Although aloofness, sometimes called "dread game," will put her in a general state of anxiety and maintain her attraction for you, it does not convey clear information about how she must please you. It can also boomerang. If your dread game is effective at making her feel anxious, she may copy you to make you feel anxious as well, and you may find yourself in a passive-aggressive arms race that consists mostly of silence and frustration. I find that dread game is best used on random sluts you're banging, not on girls you're in a long-term relationship with.

My criticism of dread game doesn't mean that you should never vary your routine to the point where she knows the exact minute when you'll respond to a text, but aloofness should be used sparingly compared with directly stating what you like or don't like.

The opposite of dread game is showing that you are content with the relationship, often by giving gifts. While it's fun to give a girl small tokens of your affection, particularly if they are inexpensive, be aware that giving her things can be interpreted as neediness. If you buy your best friend or sibling a small gift from the shopping mall, they will be appreciative and not over-analyze the gesture, but if you buy your girl a small gift, she will analyze what exactly the gift means in context of the relationship, and then ask her friends what they think the gift means. She will inevitably conclude that you are falling deeply in love with her and that she needs to withdraw some affection because she's not yet deeply in love with you.

There was a girl I went on two dates with. I gave her a free travel booklet from the tourist shop after she expressed interest in knowing about the city. She disappeared after that. The fact that I thought about her enough to get her something useful caused her to conclude that I was ready to marry her, so she ran away.

Let a girl do things for you first, and only then can you do something comparable for her, but never in a way that exceeds her initial gesture. If she buys you a novelty gift, you can buy her one too, but one that isn't significantly more expensive than the gift she bought. This is more important at the beginning of a relationship before a girl has fully committed to you. Buying gifts, flowers, and chocolates will more likely than not push her away, contrary to what you see in the movies, even if she's complaining that you don't buy her things.

You are sure to find exceptions when it comes to gift-buying, such as in Russia, where men regularly buy flowers for their girls from 24-hour florists, but understand that most girls don't interpret gifts as mere gifts, and the shorter the relationship has lasted, the more likely she'll misinterpret your gesture and withdraw affections. Unless a girl is buying you many gifts spontaneously, save gift-buying for holidays and birthdays.

Another tactic is to inoculate your girl against negative advice or influence from her friends. Earlier, I discussed how to inoculate a girl you meet in the club against a cockblock by saying that her friends are jealous that she has met a cool guy (you). We take this to the next level in relationships by bringing down the value of her friends over time through remarks about how their approach to men and life is causing them pain, loneliness, and unhappiness. Your girl will then become skeptical of advice that tells her to become more independent or do adventurous things that increase her access to other men. If your girl's friends tell her something that will put her in a position where she could cheat, your remarks about how those friends will die alone because they can't get men to love them will hopefully pop into her head.

Every girl has at least one friend who is a slut. You won't be able to avoid this. (If *all* of her friends are sluts, you may want to re-examine your girlfriend's sexual history with a powerful microscope.) Even if you happen to be in a conservative town where feminism has yet to take hold, your girl will have at least one feminist-minded friend who thinks there's nothing wrong with getting drunk in a club where horny men are ready to pounce. Instead of trying to control which women she hangs out with, simply be blunt about the reality: her friend is not good with men, is jealous of friends who have steady boyfriends, and is unconsciously trying to sabotage their relationships because she needs a wingman to go cruising for cock.

I've painted my girlfriends' friends as being unrealistic about relationships because they are shallow and have ridiculously high standards. After an inoculation campaign that lasts for many months, my girl will be inclined to accept at least some of my truth. Here are some of the things you can say in the course of your inoculation:

> "Your friend doesn't want a relationship, she wants a fantasy. She doesn't want to put in the work for one man."
>
> "Looks like your friend is getting addicted to the party life-style. By the time she gets tired of it, she won't be able to get the type of man who is giving her attention now."
>
> "So your friend is just sleeping around now? Aren't you concerned that she has no respect for her body? Do you agree with this?"
>
> "It's obvious she's jealous of our relationship, because it's what she wants. But she's too lazy and selfish to be a good girlfriend to a good man."
>
> "She's living in a fantasy world where she thinks that all she has to do is go to the club, get drunk, and take selfies to meet her Prince Charming. She's delusional, and should stop watching romantic movies."
>
> "I know your friend hates me because you're here with me instead of partying with her. Her dream is for us to break up. She's jealous and wishes to have what you have."

Be careful about calling her friend a "slut" or "whore." I've tried this and all it does is to make your girl defensive and want to side with the friend, because there is no greater insult to a woman than calling her promiscuous. Insinuate it, but don't use the label outright.

You want your inoculation to portray her friend as clueless with men to the point where she is hurting herself, which implies that anyone who follows her advice about men is an idiot. I don't care about a friend's position on applying makeup, cooking, and so on, but I shine the spotlight on her behavior towards men. By the time a friend tries to sabotage the relationship, I will have devalued her to such an extent that my girl will ignore her advice, and may even tell me about it.

You need to use the inoculation tactic only on friends who are sleeping around, exceedingly liberal, or living the party lifestyle. If you find a girl with good values, she shouldn't have more than two friends like this. At the same time, show approval of friends who are in long-term relationships or who don't sleep around. Share how these friends have the correct mentality that will eventually land them a good husband who cares for them. While her good girlfriends may trash you at some point, at least they won't encourage your girl to have "fun."

Except for these tactics, I don't micro-manage a relationship. Instead, I stay alert to understand how the power dynamic is developing. Is my girlfriend showing more interest and effort than me? Is the comfort between us increasing? Is the bond strengthening? If she starts pulling away, I also pull away. If she pulls in close, I will reward that closeness by doing the same. I let my girl lead the way when it comes to deepening the relationship, because I know that she highly values a man she has to tame, not a man who tries to tame her.

The mindset I like to have in serious relationships is that I'm doing my own thing in life and she is free to hang with me because she's nice to be around. She's the comfortable furniture in my home that doesn't intrude on my existence or define it. This may be too detached for your taste, but I believe it's important for a man to have his own life that isn't only about his girl if he doesn't want her to lose respect for him. It's like the age-old complaint by a woman that her man is "working too much," but a man's job has to be more important than his girl, because if he didn't have a job, he wouldn't have money, and if he didn't have money, he would have no home, no food, and soon enough, no girl.

My approach to relationships gets harder to pull off once you have a family, but until then I treat my girl as secondary to what I have going on, because if I had nothing else going on, she wouldn't be with me.

Boredom

In relationships that last more than six months, your biggest problem will be boredom, both in the bedroom and out. You'll find that there isn't much to do with a girl except eat, drink, talk, watch movies, and have sex. It doesn't help that most of her conversation will not be stimulating, because a girl doesn't have the ability to tell interesting jokes, stories, or anecdotes like a man does.

Women were put on Earth not to entertain us but to provide us with sex, children, and a comfortable home. If you ask anything more of a girl, you're asking for too much. It's simply not in the nature of a girl to constantly provide entertainment, excitement, or even fulfillment.

In an ideal relationship, the man does what he prefers and the girl decides to join him. You eat the food you want, watch the shows you want, read the books you want, do the work you want, and your girl either joins you or hangs around in the vicinity. Any "sacrifices" you make should involve things you wouldn't mind doing anyway.

For example, I don't mind having my girl around as I work. When I take a break, I can have a chat with her, make a few jokes, or allow her to show me a funny meme before returning to what I was doing. She can hang out as long as she doesn't bother me or interrupt. At night, we'll go to dinner, take a walk, and return to my apartment where we can relax and have sex. Although I may do things that I feel neutral about, I avoid doing things that I really don't want to do, but in the rare case I do, it won't be because she has browbeaten me but because I'm throwing her a bone as compensation for neglecting her.

You will run into problems if there isn't much going on in your life besides your girl. Your dependency on her will become so strong that you won't even notice you are being trained by her and complying with things you shouldn't. Your love for a girl should never blind you to the game she's running on you, because it's in a female's nature to never stop running game. You have to read a book like this to know how to handle her whereas she is naturally born with the power to handle you.

Understand that most girls have nothing going on in their lives except work and their social networking feeds, and believe that men exist to entertain and serve them. This means that, as your relationship proceeds, your girl will try to spend more and more time with you. She'll want to see you just about every day and expect that you'll have lined up some entertaining activity. Even on the days when you don't see her, she may want to have extended phone or text conversations that go over the minutiae of her day.

If you want to spend only a certain amount of time with her per week, you'll have to convey that expectation to her at some point, along with how you would like that time to be structured. She may cry and accuse you of not caring about her, and may even start window shopping for another man, but if you don't stick to your guns, she will own you in the relationship.

One way to alleviate boredom is to travel or attend events, but you can't do something fun every day or travel every week. Therefore if you are bored in a relationship, it's because you're allowing her to monopolize too much of your time. The solution is to do things that don't bore you. If you like history books, and want to read them every day, do so. She is welcome to read alongside you, but that's what you'll do. If you want to binge watch your favorite show while she sits next to you, do that, without caring whether or not she's enjoying herself. If you want to go for a bicycle ride in the park, and she doesn't want to, you'll be doing so alone, because for a man, the key to a happy relationship is to do what he wants while having his girl nearby when he wants to talk or be intimate. It's definitely not about being her babysitter or personal clown.

A relationship is when a man invites a girl into his world to be with him, not the other way around. A girl may resist this approach if she's so used to men who constantly entertain her, but this type of relationship is not sustainable for a man, because it causes him to compromise on what he loves. I'm sure at some point you've met a husband with an empty look in his eyes. He has this look because he has made too many sacrifices to keep his wife happy at his expense. He has allowed the terrorist to make him a hostage in the relationship.

A harder problem to solve is when you get bored with the sex. After six months, you will know every nook and cranny of her vagina, and will have established such a regular sex routine that one night's sex will hardly look different from another. While it's healthy to try adding variety through role-playing, wigs, or different sexual positions, you will inevitably become less excited at the prospect of sleeping with your girl. This is the biggest complaint I hear from men who have been in relationships spanning many years.

One way to avoid sexual boredom is not to enter a relationship during your sexual prime when you get a boner for half the girls walking down the street. You're inviting conflict if you do, because not only will you get bored quickly with any girl, you're also likely to act on that boredom. I won't get into the moral issues with cheating, but you will feel guilty and paranoid afterwards. There is also the possibility of getting caught and dealing with the dramatic fallout.

I wouldn't enter a relationship with a girl I think I'd cheat on, but this is an issue you have to decide for yourself. The attraction of new pussy, particularly *easy* new pussy, is hard to resist, suggesting that long-term relationships are for the man who has passed his sexual prime and no longer has the energy or motivation to chase new lays.

It's normal to have sexual thoughts about other girls while you're in a monogamous relationship. You may fantasize about random girls you encounter or your previous sexual partners.

Even if you try to suppress these thoughts, you'll end up dreaming about other women. They are not a sign that there is a problem with the relationship. A man's nature is to desire variety even if we happen to be with the girl of our dreams, so don't feel depressed or ashamed that you're thinking of sex with other girls. The best course of action is not to add fuel to the thoughts by acting on them, and wait a week or two until they fade away. When they come back, repeat the process of not acting on them until they fade away once more.

I don't have much in the way of advice if you want to cheat on a girl besides being discreet about it. If your cheating is a result of sexual boredom, usually because you've been with a girl for a year or more, I can understand your motivation, but if it comes before sexual boredom is reached, it may be that you're in a relationship with the wrong girl or not ready for a relationship. Another possibility is if you're married with children and your wife failed to maintain her weight, causing you to lose sexual interest. If there is a root cause to any sexual problem, you should address it first, but if it's simply because you desire variety, that's quite normal, and something every man faces at some point.

Creating A Family

By the time you've been with a girl for a year, you should know whether or not she's the one. If you're in a monogamous long-term relationship with a girl you *don't* want to have a family with, you're wasting your time by continuing it, because you'll have less motivation to meet a new girl than you would if you were single.

As you already know, the institution of modern marriage confers all the upside to women while transferring all the downside to men. With no-fault divorce, a woman can walk away at any time for any reason, even when she cheats, and collect alimony and assets from you, not to mention get custody of your children. Signing a marriage contract gives a woman huge amounts of leverage over you, though it can be reduced if you draw up a prenuptial agreement. When you throw in anti-male domestic violence laws that always take a woman's word over a man's, a husband's position is that not that much better than that of a male college student who is falsely accused of rape by a deranged feminist and kicked out of school by a kangaroo court.

By taking financial precautions with a prenup, and also applying game in the way I teach, you will lower your risk of a negative outcome because your wife will remain attracted to you and want to comply with your standards, but you can't eliminate the risk entirely. If you're sure you want to have children, you don't have time to wait for the culture to change in your favor, and must work with what you have and accept the risk. The fact that you're reading this book shows that you are ready to make the right moves to avoid a catastrophic divorce.

A big problem is that most men don't properly vet girls for marriage. They believe the lies that a girl tells about her sexual history, miss out on warning signs of promiscuity, and fail to uphold the standards that are essential for long-term relationships, not understanding that girls are far more skilled than men at concealing their behavior. Common sense tells us that a girl who's had many sexual partners has an impulsive nature that indicates she is more likely to cheat than a virgin, but this doesn't mean we can slack off our relationship game with the virgin either. A girl's past behavior is *usually* indicative of her future behavior, but it doesn't guarantee it.

I look for warning signs that could spell trouble. They start with a girl's appearance. If she has unnaturally colored hair, excessive tattoos, ear gauges, or body piercings, she's exhibiting a high level of impulsiveness that will translate not only into a high notch count, but also into getting bored with a stable relationship. In extreme cases, where a girl is using her body as some sort of mutilation experiment, she may be insane and more likely to falsely accuse you of rape.

A more common warning sign is if she's a heavy drinker, which often goes hand-in-hand with having many slutty friends and going out regularly to bars and clubs. Alcohol is the drug of choice for a slut because it lowers the barrier to sleeping with men she barely knows. To receive validation for her bad decisions, often done while under the influence, she will have a support network of other sluts who are making the same bad decisions as her. Keeps things casual with this type of girl.

Another warning sign is if she sleeps with you before the third date. I would like to think that a girl I slept with on the first date did so only for me, but it's almost always the case that she has also done so with other men. If I liked a girl who slept with me quickly, I would heavily screen her sexual history before thinking about a serious relationship with her.

Other warning signs will reveal themselves if you've known a girl for a while. The first is if she's popular on social networking or has dating apps on her phone. This usually means that the attention you give her is not enough, and she can't help but put herself in a position to be hit on by other men.

You will also have the opportunity to learn about the sort of relationship she has with her parents, especially her father. If she doesn't treasure her father, it may be because he did not give her the love she needed while growing up. A girl who doesn't know what it's like to receive unconditional love from a man often resorts to using her body to feel a mere simulation of love from multiple men through casual sex, and will therefore sabotage a stable relationship.

The last warning sign is how she treats your home. If she's a slob who refuses to make you a sandwich, what kind of mother or wife do you think she's going to be? Girls don't instantly change for the better on their wedding day. If you notice a girl showing you warning signs, it's best not to ignore them.

Regardless of the warning signs I share, always listen to your gut instinct. If you suspect foul play with either her past or current behavior, investigate it thoroughly to save yourself a lot of heartache down the line. As long as you understand that a girl will lie to the man she supposedly loves, and continue lying even when that man presents evidence of her lies, you'll know to ignore what a girl says and instead focus on what she does.

There's nothing you can do to stop a woman from becoming a

different person over time, which is common if you get into a relationship with a younger girl. While you believe in self-improvement, and have attempted to change for the better, girls don't have this ethos. The sad fact is that most girls start to degenerate after twenty years of age, particularly if their only "relationship" experience consists of casual sex.

I've seen firsthand how girls become more bitter, cynical, and immoral as they age, in a way that makes it harder to bond with them. Regardless of what type of girl she is today, there is no way to guarantee who she'll be tomorrow. Take precautions, but don't get so hung up on the future that it sacrifices your pleasure in the moment. If she's not exhibiting warning signs, and you're enjoying your time with her, it may be worthwhile to accept her request for a committed relationship or family.

Whatever relationship you get into, you should enter it from a position of strength, not weakness. Commit to a girl because she is your best option and you feel confident about your odds with her. If you commit because you fear eternal loneliness or not becoming a father, you'll blind yourself to the warning signs a girl may be displaying.

I'm sure you don't want to play the game when you're old or find yourself single after a long relationship has ended, but avoiding being single at any cost will push you into bad situations. If I don't want to approach girls when I'm 50, or it's something I fear, my future is already written: I will wife up a girl I shouldn't because fear is driving my behavior. Instead, I prepare myself to be ready for any outcome, and no matter my age when I'm single, I will face the issue to the best of my ability. If I'm 50 and single, so be it. I will do what must be done at that age to resolve any girl problem I have, because if I let fear dictate my decisions, it will just lead to disaster.

I don't want to come across as pessimistic, but we live in a unique age when there is no push from the culture to make women value long-term relationships before they've sampled a dozen or more penises. The media, government, and universities promote homosexual coupling more than heterosexual, shame men for being men, and glorify a woman's pursuit of career and independence, all of which inhibit family formation. It's not your fault if you struggle to meet the right girl because, objectively, there are fewer good girls today than there were a few generations ago.

If you go out there with an intention of meeting a wife, I think you will be disappointed to see that there are few women who can meet even the most basic wifely standards. I'm not saying it can't be done, because I know many men who are doing it, but stay realistic. The best thing you can do is set yourself up for success by maximizing your value, implementing game, and carefully screening out girls who aren't wife material. Whether you find a wife and have children will then be up to God.

I have one last piece of advice when it comes to finding a wife: be the best man she thinks she can get. If not, she may wonder if she can do better and then increase her access to other men. Unless the girl I'm dating is head-over-heels in love with me, clearly doesn't have eyes for other men, and is afraid that her world would crumble without my love, I wouldn't consider marrying her, because when the relationship gets a little boring after a couple of years, as all relationships do, she is more likely to act on that boredom.

Breaking Up

Things may go south with your relationships, leading to break-ups. The less intimate your relationship, the easier the break-up will be. If you're in a casual relationship where she's coming over only for sex, you can probably break up simply by not contacting her anymore.

In a mini relationship, you can give her a reason of some kind. An easy one is, "This relationship isn't what I want right now, so I think we should go on a break." You can make up any reason and it's unlikely that she will cry about it since she probably knows other guys who can pick up the slack.

Long-term relationship break-ups are more complicated and painful. You have shared a deep connection with a girl and may have exchanged vows of love. These break-ups are usually done in person, and there will certainly be tears.

When a girl decides to break up with you, there's nothing you can do to convince her to change her mind, and the fact that she is breaking up with you probably means she has already started seeing another man, because a girl doesn't let go of one man before having another lined up. At a minimum, she has lost so much attraction for you that she doesn't even want to bother trying to change or train you—she has given up on you entirely.

This will feel like a punch in the stomach, particularly if you thought things were going well, but it's rarely a complete surprise when a girl terminates a relationship (she will withdraw emotionally beforehand). The best thing you can do is to resist her efforts to put you in the friend zone where she can receive the emotional benefits of knowing you without having to give you any sexual benefits. It has to be a sexual relationship of some sort or nothing.

A girl's loss of attraction for you is often an irreversible process, but an exception is if you only *temporarily* became too needy or started acting differently to the way you were when she first met you. Simply revert to your normal self to reverse the slide.

On the other hand, if she's slipping away even though your game and demeanor are stable, the loss of attraction is out of your hands. Perhaps you wanted a deeper relationship than she was able to provide, or perhaps she's convinced that she wants to be "free" and "independent" instead of carrying on with a relationship that isn't satisfying her needs. Either way, this is one of the few problems that can't be solved, and any attempt to solve it by promising her you'll do better will cause her to lose even more attraction for you until she pities you, which is the biggest attraction destroyer of all. In fact, if you want a girl to dump you, simply be extra nice and pathetic. A break-up will soon follow.

There are two benefits to a girl breaking up with you first: you'll have only slight regret about what you could've done differently and she won't cause additional difficulties by stalking you. The situation is tougher if you decide to break up with a girl due to an acute crisis like discovering she has been lying or cheating (often both).

Cheating can be not only sexual but emotional, where a girl hides her interactions with other men who are trying to sleep with her. If a man is pursuing my girl and she knows it, her claim that he's a "friend" is a lie—he's actually a suitor. Entertaining a suitor is opening the front door to the house of cheating. Relationship standards have degraded to such an extent that many men tolerate a girl spending time with various suitors, but I refuse to accept this because it puts me one step closer to being a cuckold, a man who encourages his girlfriend to have sex with other men.

Girls love to have their cake and eat it too. They want the stability and comfort that a relationship with a high-value man provides while receiving sexual attention from multiple suitors. Every man has his own line that, when a girl crosses, will cause him to end the relationship instead of trying to fix it. I can only tell you my line: emotional or physical cheating. In my experience, it's pointless to try to change a girl's character flaws that could lead to cheating as opposed to something trivial such as how she makes your morning coffee. Just like how many men go through a "player stage," so do many girls, and they will not be faithful until they consciously decide to be faithful.

It's worth discussing how you can find out if a girl is physically or emotionally cheating. Before the age of the internet, the most common way was through a friend or family member who saw your girlfriend spending time with another man or doing an activity that she hid from you. You would have had to evaluate the credibility of the source before deciding whether to end the relationship. In the internet age, discovery usually involves her activity on social networking. Another way is accessing her phone and computer communications, either because she left them unprotected or because you installed a keylogging program that reveals her account passwords.

I've encountered many men who advise using a keylogger program to vet a girl before a serious relationship. Setting aside the legal and ethical issues, a hypothetical way to do this is to install a keylogger on your computer and wait until a girl uses it to log into one of her accounts (you can persuade her to do so under the guise of wanting to see her pictures). After she leaves, retrieve her password from your keylogging program, log in to her account, change any relevant security settings to stop her from being notified, and view her chats. Note that accessing another person's account is illegal in most jurisdictions, so consult your local laws before attempting it.

My last relationship ended when my then girlfriend left her laptop open before stepping outside. I looked through her Facebook and found out that she was chatting with a man and meeting him without telling me. Generally, when a girl starts getting away with cheating, she becomes overconfident, starts making mistakes (such as leaving her computer open), and may even start accusing you of cheating to take the spotlight off her behavior.

At the very least, consider demanding at least one full social networking audit before you move in with her or get married to confirm she's the good girl you believe her to be. You have only one shot at this, because after an audit she will know that it will not be safe to leave damaging chats on her account in the future.

The problem with using keylogging as the sole means of identifying foul play is that it's easy for a girl to cheat without leaving an electronic trail. A girl can step inside a bar tonight, meet a sexy man within a few minutes, and have sex with him in less than an hour. Since there is no way to make absolutely sure that a girl is faithful, don't allow having access to her internet accounts make you complacent about other warnings signs.

If you discover foul play, the decision to break up should be *independent* of a girl's explanations, tears, or counter-arguments. The reason is that even when a girl is confronted with definitive evidence of cheating or lying, she will deny it. She'll gaslight you, making you doubt the reality of what you know to be true. She'll point to the sky, say it's purple, and shed copious tears, swearing to you that the sky is purple until you actually start seeing shades of purple, even though you've known your entire life that the sky is blue. If you haven't experienced this before, you may think I'm exaggerating, but understand that the weapon nature gave women is emotional manipulation. She will swear to her mother and to her god that the chat transcripts that show she was cheating are false, and then attack *you* for not trusting her.

An alternative to confronting her is asking only for objective facts, such as where she was on a certain day, how long she was there, and whether she has any text messages that can prove her story. If you go beyond the facts and ask her to "explain" things, she will concoct a fantastic tale that makes you doubt you're doing the right thing. After she's done, you won't be sure of up from down or left from right. Once I let a girl explain away her bad behavior with buckets of tears. It weakened me to such an extent that I took her back, only to be burned a few months later. Trust your gut, collect evidence, and issue a verdict of guilty or not guilty as if you were a courtroom judge.

Break-ups that come when a relationship was dying a slow death are less traumatic and may even be cordial, but break-ups that result when cheating was suspected can be explosive, requiring an additional self-protection move. When you break up with a girl, I advise you to record it with at least audio, because a girl you've just dumped is like a wounded animal—ferocious and more likely to attack. One of the most common times for a girl to falsely accuse a man of hitting her is when she's been dumped, and you may be shocked to discover that your "nice" girlfriend is fully capable of getting physical with you. She may also stalk you afterwards. Dealing with stalkers can be difficult, but the best advice is to record all instances of her stalking and consider obtaining a restraining order if she doesn't cool off within a month or two.

After a tough break-up, you will feel vulnerable and emotional, regardless of how masculine you are. A vacuum is created where a piece of you that was cultivated with another person has been lost. It's natural for you to think that you will die alone and never meet a good girl again, and you will constantly doubt your decision to break up. These are faulty thought patterns because the decision to break up with a girl should be based on her worth, her behavior, and whether she's the right girl for you. If she doesn't have what you want, a future that includes her is bound to create more pain than what you're experiencing at the time of the break-up. If you logically decided that she was not the right girl, ending the relationship is the best option before you get attached further.

No matter how great a girl is, there are others like her, and if you were able to meet her, you're capable of meeting another. If a break-up was particularly traumatic, you'll have to take a complete break from girls for a few months and busy yourself with other activities. It may take you the same amount of time that you were in the relationship to fully get over it, but such is the nature of love.

Once the worst of the break-up is over, and you've stopped feeling sorry for yourself, call up your single friends and hang out with them to ease back into approaching and dating. It may be a long time until you replace your girlfriend, but it will happen as long as you do the same type of work that led you to meeting her in the first place. If you don't want to replace her with another girl and simply want to have fun or try new hobbies, that's fine too.

Chapter Conclusion

I have taught you methods for approaching and dating based on my experiences with thousands of girls, but my relationship advice is based on a much smaller sample. The problem with giving relationship advice is that a man can have only so many successful relationships to base his advice on, and while there are millions of men who are happily married, their advice may be so specific to their unique situation that it can't be much help to others.

This doesn't mean there aren't universal guidelines that can help: let the girl seek a relationship with you, maintain the value you had when she first met you, convey standards and uphold them, resist her training, be more aloof than her, beware of giving gifts and tokens, inoculate her against her toxic friends, and do at least one electronic audit before signing on the dotted line. Outside of that, a successful relationship often comes down to keeping your eyes open, being yourself, and not letting your anxieties or insecurities disrupt an otherwise healthy bond.

I wouldn't advise you to "be yourself" when first approaching a girl, especially if you're not normally chatty or interesting, but a relationship involves such huge quantities of time that being yourself is the only way you can truly enjoy it. If being yourself with a sprinkling of game thrown in isn't enough for a girl to stay with you then she can fuck off, because there are two individuals in any relationship, and both of them have a right to be happy in it.

Maintaining a relationship isn't as hard as cold approaching, but it's a challenge to keep one going in an age where monogamy is not cherished. We need a bit of luck to meet a girl and have sex with her, but we need to hit the lottery to find one we can be with for the rest of our lives.

Chapter 10: Conclusion

It will happen that you go on a date with a girl and everything is going great. The conversation is flowing, the mood is right, and the hours speed by. Then you contact her a couple of days later and... nothing. She completely disappears from your life without an explanation or a hint as to what happened. The opposite will also occur, when you're struggling with your game and having what you think is a bad date, but the girl essentially seduces you into bed.

As men, we often try to decode the complexities of the universe, but women don't operate like us. Using logic to decode female illogic will give you a headache and you'll walk away from an interaction more confused than before. Not everything concerning women can be explained, and if you're encountering something that seems illogical, accept that female nature is a phenomenon we can't completely understand.

We must be skeptical when a girl tells us what she desires from a man or why she's acting in the way she does. She's not operating on logic, so why should we accept an answer from her that sounds logical? Her decisions will always be driven by her emotions in ways that she can't see or comprehend. Remember that the truth about women will always be found in their actions and behavior, not their words.

Our grand game strategy is not to listen to women or put them on a pedestal while optimizing our value and game to the point where they choose to be intimate with us. It's a simple concept on paper, but it takes a huge amount of humility to make your ego accept that more than 99% of girls in the world want nothing to do with you, and to carry on anyway to achieve your sexual and relationship goals. The quicker you can get over the fact that most of your interactions with women will go nowhere, the faster you will find a woman who does want to be with you.

When a girl denies you intimacy and doesn't change her mind, move on. It would be nice to learn something from failed interactions, but even if you don't, odds are another girl will respond favorably to the exact same game. Persistence and raw masculinity will always trump analysis and perfection when it comes to success with women.

Game Problems

If you have done at least 500 approaches and don't have much to show for your efforts, you may be experiencing chronic failure. Although it's impossible for me to diagnose a chronic problem without knowing your specific situation, it's likely that either your standards are too high for your environment or you have a social dysfunction.

To solve the first problem, simply lower your standards. The girls you encounter will fall into two categories: those you want to sleep with and those who want to sleep with you. The wider the gap between these two groups, the more you need to do a reality check. Sometimes we have to start from rock bottom until we have built up our value through experience. Unfortunately, in some cities even ugly girls have gained such an attitude that things may not be significantly easier when you lower your standards, which is why so many men hit the road and try their luck in foreign countries (see Appendix 2), but if you're not approaching girls who are giving you eye contact or showing signs of high availability, you will experience chronic rejection.

Social dysfunction or awkwardness is more likely to be reasons for failure if you have a problem with maintaining normal friendships. If you have no friends, or don't have anyone to talk to, your problem is basic sociability. You have to learn how to be a friend and how to maintain normal platonic relationships with men before you can maintain an intimate one with a woman. Once you're able to maintain friendships, you should see more success with a game program.

I've had many cold streaks in my game career where I was

upset and dissatisfied that I could not get the girl I wanted. This dissatisfaction motivates me to keep trying, because without any frustration, I become complacent and don't even bother. We all have to face hurdles and demons during our game journey, but I'm confident that with each passing year you'll be able to look back and see an improvement in both your value and ability to meet girls. However, even if the level of your game becomes high, you'll still have to grind out your approaches like a beginner would and experience the occasional cold streak where it seems like nothing is going your way.

Always be realistic about what game can and can't do. You already know that it can enable you to meet girls anywhere and take them to bed, but the weaknesses are worth discussing. First, it's energy and time intensive. As you can tell by now, game is not a trivial pursuit that can be mastered quickly—you'll have to put in work to become good at it.

Second, it depends heavily on pre-minute attraction. Your appearance plays a much larger role in cold approaches than in social circle game (see Appendix 1). Approaching will be harder for you if you're genuinely ugly.

The third flaw of game is that there are no passive results. The minute you stop approaching girls is the minute your pussy pipeline starts to dry up. There will be many times when you must start from scratch with rusty game and zero prospects, especially after a failed relationship.

The fourth flaw is that, because of the nature of the cold approach, we have to do most of the work from start to finish, and a girl's investment in us starts to increase substantially only *after* having sex with her. A girl is also more likely to abuse a man who cold approached her than one she met through a social circle where she aims to maintain a high reputation. For many girls, the men she meets through cold approaches are like toys to play with, unlike the men in her social circle whom she's actively scheming to lay.

The last flaw of cold approach game, and the one that men complain to me about the most, is the difficulty of landing really hot girls. This often stems from the misconception that you need "advanced" game to date hot girls. If you meet men who are dating girls in the 8-to-10 range, you'll be surprised to find that their game level is *lower* than yours. The problem that these men have solved is not game but access: they were able to play the numbers game in a pool of talent that is far higher than what you encounter.

For example, how many girls in the 7 range do you need to approach until you bang one? Let's say that it's fifty, so if you approach fifty girls who are a 7, you're likely to sleep with one. If you approach a 7 every day, you'll lay one within two months. Now let's say that you need to approach one-hundred 9's to sleep with one. That's double the number of 7's, but still doable. The problem is that you will not encounter many 9's unless you are a fashion photographer or own a nightclub. If I'm lucky, I'll approach one 9 *per year*. Statistically, it would take me decades to sleep with one.

The odds get even worse when it comes to long-term relationships. How many 7's do you have to bang to get into a relationship with one? If it's three, you need to approach one-hundred fifty 7's to have one long-term relationship. Do the math with a girl who's a 10 and you'll see why most guys simply have no chance. Hot girls are surely harder to attract, but if you had an unlimited supply of them, you'd get lucky with one eventually. The main problem is therefore one of access.

The key to succeeding with girls in the 8-to-10 range is inserting yourself in social groups or occupations that give you access to them. Try to become a yoga instructor, university professor, club promoter, DJ, bar owner, popular musician, model photographer, film director, or a celebrity. You could also try to insert yourself into a high-level social circle or hit the road to find a country that has lots of beautiful girls.

If you do eventually sleep with a girl in the 8-to-10 range, you may find the experience disappointing. Your ego will be pleased at the score, and you'll be eager to show her off in public, but the overall experience may not give you the lasting happiness you had expected, especially if she is less pleasing than a girl with average attractiveness. Since people treat a hot girl so well during her lifetime, she's never had to learn how to develop humor, charm, empathy, or even basic bedroom skills. It also doesn't help that your ego will quickly become accustomed to her beauty, and demand you find another hot girl to maintain its high.

The "Good" Girl

All girls have the same hardware, no matter where they are in the world, but not the same software, which results in differences with presentation, character, and behavior. A "good" girl is still capable of evil, since she possesses the hardware to rip your heart out while laughing maniacally, but she'll be far less inclined to do so than a girl who is obviously bad.

Outside of religious communities, I don't know where to find a good girl. Even if you think you've found one, your default assumption should be that she's pretending to be good in order to impress you. On a long enough timeline, most good girls reveal themselves to be quite capable of negative behavior. With every girl you sleep with, you roll the dice on sexually transmitted diseases, even if you use a condom, and with every long-term relationship, you roll the dice on having your heart crushed. To avoid this risk completely, you would have to become a monk, an unacceptable outcome if you desire sex and intimacy with women.

If you do pursue a long-term relationship, understand that your needs will be different to hers. You will desire comfort, stability, routine, and access to sex, with infrequent urges to sleep with random girls. Your girlfriend will tell you that she also desires comfort and stability, but if she perceives *too much* comfort and stability, she will crave discomfort and drama. She will either create this drama with you or find it with another man by cheating on you. Be perceptive of her needs so that you provide them instead of her seeking to fulfill them elsewhere.

Being an alpha male, having tight game, and maintaining attraction will greatly increase the likelihood that a relationship will succeed, but men also need the support of a healthy culture that promotes monogamy to shame or control a girl into being faithful and submissive. Western culture does the complete opposite, so you're on your own when it comes to taming female nature, a task with which men of the past had societal help. Don't beat yourself up if a relationship fails because your girl decided to misbehave.

What may be even more important than finding a good girl is avoiding the bad girl. You'll meet many girls who are mentally unstable or have been taught by the culture to hate men and masculinity. In your game journey, I'm sure you'll encounter a girl who cries after consensual sex or insinuates that you hurt her in some way. After such an encounter, take note of her character to avoid all girls with similar traits in the future. If you're ever falsely accused of rape, do not try to talk your way out of it to the police or even admit that you had sex with her. Hire a lawyer and gather all the evidence you can, including text messages and recordings, to refute the claim.

The sad fact is that the golden era of being a player is over. You can no longer sleep with any willing girl, because many of them have internalized an anti-male political agenda. The less feminine a girl is, the more likely she will cause you problems and anxiety after sex. The more feminine she is, the more likely she will pose a danger to your heart instead of your freedom.

Society is heading in the direction of a full-blown sexual dystopia, so you must be smart about who you bang. If you insist on sleeping with a girl who is showing you warning signs, consider recording the sex. Find out what the laws in your area state about making recordings, though I would rather be convicted of recording illegally than rape.

If you told me in 2006, when I was writing *Bang*, that I would one day advise men to consider recording their sexual encounters with questionable women, I would have said you're crazy, but that's how quickly the world has changed. Keep your eyes open for a good girl who will meet most of your needs, but beware of the bad ones who subtract value from your life and sour your attitude towards women in general.

Sustainable Game

If you want to stay in the game for the long run, and receive its benefits even in old age, you must take long breaks. Each man is able to interact only with a specific number of girls in his lifetime. When he hits that number, he will feel tired and burned out. Game then becomes a chore. Don't hit your number too soon by making game a full-time job year after year, because I guarantee that you'll get sick of girls while you still have many decades left to live.

Men were simply not designed to devote so much time and energy to girls. You may love the idea of eating pizza every day, but if you actually do it, eating pizza will soon feel like torture, and you won't even be able to bear the smell of it. The same can happen with girls. I dedicated most of my life to pursuing them, understanding them, and teaching men all that I've learned, but as I finish this book, I have practically no motivation to go out and meet girls. While my excessive pursuit of game has produced wisdom I can now share with you, it's not likely to lead to happiness unless you're getting into relationships with girls you care about.

A major problem with a constant focus on game is that you're exposed to more female bullshit, flaking, insults, rejection, and attitude than any man has had to face. In the past decade, girls have begun to outright abuse men they're not in relationships with, and this will take its toll on your soul over the long run. You may be strong enough to deal with female abuse, but you will reach a point where you'll seek to avoid this abuse entirely by not interacting with women.

Imagine that you have a big jar of pennies. Every time a girl rejects you, insults you, or flakes on you, a penny is removed. Every time a girl treats you well or makes love to you, a penny is added. If at any point the jar is empty, you will feel the urge to give up. This suggests we must achieve a balance by holding on to girls who treat us well so that we can fill the penny jar. If you do what I did, and focus only on casual sex for many years, you'll wake up one day and find that the jar is empty, and that you'd rather just get a dog and call it a day.

However, don't confuse burnout with laziness or anxiety. It's normal to not want to put in the work or experience bouts of nervousness as long as you still genuinely desire meeting an attractive girl. Burnout is when your testosterone level is healthy but you don't care for the company of girls, not even sex, because you've played the game for a long time without a break.

Most cases of burnout can be resolved by taking a break for a few months, but if you overdid it, or were hurt badly in a long-term relationship, you may have to take a break for a year or two. Once the pain has healed, and you've forgotten about the negatives of women, you can return with a healthy outlook and the primal motivation to have sex restored. Also understand that as you get older, you won't have as much energy, so you'll need to take longer breaks in between bangs before you are ready to chase women again.

During your game journey, the world will continue to change, moving towards light at times and then shifting back to darkness. These shifts are beyond your control. What is within your control is the ability to face your intimacy goals with masculinity, strength, intelligence, and effort. Whatever happens beyond that is out of our hands and should not be lamented.

The last problem you may face is the urge to quit. Game is hard. A book this long wouldn't be necessary if it were an easy task. You'll experience numerous moments of frustration and anger when dealing with girls, and at times you'll feel that you're not receiving a worthwhile return for your efforts. Don't be discouraged. There are numerous obstacles to overcome when you learn anything new, whether it's game, a language, or a sport. When you're in the middle of a cold spell, you'll be tempted to quit and take the path of least resistance, soaking in entertainment, paying for prostitutes, or giving up on girls entirely. Resist those urges, which give you zero chance of experiencing genuine intimacy or love. Take breaks, curse females as much as you want, but stick with it. Once you get over a hump, you solidify a skill that will aid you for the rest of your life, not just with girls, but also with business and nonsexual relationships.

Fin

I predict that game will get harder over the next few decades until male-female relations hit rock bottom when the comfort level of society decreases to the point that girls once again need strong provider men to survive. While the theory behind the game I've taught you in this book will continue to hold true, tactics may change. There will be new inventions that alter how we communicate. There will be new types of venues where people congregate. There will be societal changes that require you to be more (or less) masculine. There may even be changes in laws that criminalize the behaviors I've shared in this book. Always be ready to adapt your tactics to your changing environment.

It's up to you to infuse your intelligence, character, and creativity into what I've taught to achieve your goals. Let your personality naturally customize the lines I've shared instead of memorizing them word for word. Create custom routines that cater to the unique type of girl you prefer. Find a golden goose by experimenting with venues and endeavors that give you better access to women. I've known men who have started fake modeling businesses, designed computer programs to mass-message girls on the internet, worked as waiters to bang hot waitresses, and taken seasonal jobs on cruise ships and at resorts to meet girls on vacation. Find out where the girls are, gain access to them, show value, and escalate to the bedroom.

You may wish that I end this book on an upbeat note, but I trust that you can handle the truth. We live in a dark age when it comes to relationships with women. The values of society have inverted to the point where any girl you meet is empowered to make decisions that directly harm her ability to bond deeply with a man and create a family. The fact that girls are now scared to death of being impregnated in their prime years, and think they can sleep around and have fun for decades, tells me that we live in an unusual time. I can only hope that in the future men will study our plight and use that knowledge to organize their societies so that they are full of life, love, and meaning instead of sterility, vulgarity, and cheap thrills.

Despite everything I know about game, I still have to play the numbers game. I still get flaked on. I still get abused by girls who see me as nothing but a target for their anti-male rage. I wish I didn't have to be conscious of my text reply times or regulate how much attention I give to a girl I like, but I won't deny reality. I've accepted that life is far more painful without sex than when I have to use game to get it.

The fact that you need to learn game as if you were studying a subject in university says that who you are is not enough to get the girls you want in a degenerate society. Your character traits, which probably include aspects of loyalty, politeness, fairness, fidelity, and justice, are not highly desired by girls who have an unbridled choice of men, and only by applying game can you unleash the type of man who will be favored in a society that's broken.

It will be easier to change than you think. After internalizing the best game practices over many years, I learned that for every "nice" character trait I had, the opposite was also within me. I was capable not only of loyalty but disloyalty. I was polite but also rude. I was stoic but also full of anger. I was anxious but also courageous. I was fair but also unreasonable. Within everything that made me unattractive to girls was a seed of something that made me attractive. You will find that the same is true of the girls you interact with. They'll display one trait to you most of the time and then suddenly unleash the opposite. Deep within the nurturing feminine is a seed of destruction, and deep within the nice guy is the asshole who women want to sleep with.

Being able to act on a trait that you read in a book means that it was within you all along. The clash between the extremes of your nature, your original niceness and your post-game persona, will create a synthesis that makes you a man of your time. You will be self-aware and skilled to meet the women of today, but conflicted and nostalgic for the women of yesterday. How we are able to deal with this paradox will be a matter for commentators of the future to discuss, but I'm alive now, and I still crave the embrace of a beautiful girl, and so I submit to the way of game.

Appendix 1: Social Circle Game

In the unlikely event that all types of cold approaching are banned and the internet permanently goes down, one of the few remaining ways to meet girls will be through a social circle, a defined network of people who know each other. The encounters you have with girls in your social circle are warm instead of cold, creating dynamics that are different when compared to a standard approach.

First, a girl you meet through a social circle doesn't see you as a random stranger she can immediately reject. To maintain the peace within her social circle, and not be seen as rude, she will be friendly even if she's not sexually attracted to you. This means the rejection will be softer than ones you'll get while cold approaching.

Second, you are mainly competing with other men in the social circle instead of potentially every other man in the world. For each social group a girl is involved in, she gives greater weight to the highest-status man within that group than to a random high-status man who approaches her outside of it. This means that if you are the number-one or number-two man in a social group, it will be easier for you to build attraction with most of the girls within the group.

Third, you have to play a more drawn-out game where you don't escalate as quickly as in cold approach scenarios. In social circles, the seduction is spread out: you hit a girl with flashes of game to build attraction and then withdraw in a process that could take several days or weeks until you get clear signs that she's interested. There is less urgency to escalate on a girl when you're guaranteed to see her again.

Fourth, your reputation within the social circle is king. If one person in the social circle knows about your past, or whom you have dated, everyone else will soon know as well, which means that much of your game is about maintaining an attractive image to every member of the social group instead of only your target. Most of the attraction you build is therefore reputational, where girls within the social circle like you even before you have a chance to meet them. This is different from a cold approach scenario where you can invent an identity out of thin air and completely shape how a girl sees you.

Fifth, social circles give you access to girls who would never consider dating a man who cold approached her. Some girls have a high need for comfort and will only date men who know someone she knows. This is less common than in the past, thanks in part to the normalization of casual dating, but it may hold true in more traditional countries where it's considered "weird" to meet a random man on the street.

Sixth, the benefits of one social circle extend to at least two nodes outside of it, allowing you to cast a wide net. For example, imagine your social circle contains twelve individuals, and each of them knows, on average, six other people, and each of these individuals knows at least six other people. Within the first node, you have the potential to meet 72 people and be warmly received. Within the second node (the friends of a friend), you can potentially meet 432 more people. This means that knowing only twelve people can allow you to meet over 500 more during the lifetime of that social circle. You don't need to have a huge social circle to access a large number of girls connected to it.

Lastly, social circles create a fragile situation where your standing can be harmed if you're the target of malicious gossip. At worst, you can be exiled from the circle entirely. If you get banned from a nightclub, you can simply go to another one down the street, but if you get ostracized from a fruitful social circle, it may take months to establish yourself in a new one. With social circles, you need to be aware of any Machiavellian power struggles, gossip, and backstabbing.

From the perspective of how much time and energy you have to invest, social circle game is about equal to cold approach game. With cold approach game, you spend hours approaching girls and dealing with rejections and flakes, but your success depends less on other people. With social circle game, you spend hours hanging out with people you may not like, and who can exile you if you displease them, but you can meet girls with a lower level of game.

If you're more of a loner like me and are not particularly enthusiastic about sustaining friendships with more than a few people at a time, maintaining a social circle may be harder than going out and walking up to random girls. The more of a loner you are, the harder it will be to attach yourself to a social circle.

As you climb the mountain of life, you'll find that it gets lonelier, because fewer people will have traveled the same path as you. This hints that social circle game is suitable mainly for young men in their teens and twenties. Once you get into your thirties, it's unlikely you'll have the energy to maintain a fertile social circle.

Social Circle Theory

Think of your three closest friends. Why are you friends with them? What do they bring to your life? You've met hundreds, if not thousands, of people, so why did your three closest friends beat out all the others? It's likely that they are funny, interesting, similar to you, trustworthy, and loyal. The reasons that people are friends with you won't greatly differ from why you are friends with them.

You are closest to people who contain a part of yourself, whether it's how you used to see yourself, how you see yourself today, or how you wish to see yourself in the future. I subconsciously see a part of myself in my best friend, so my bond with him is a form of self-love and a desire to interact with myself. In a friendship that is aspirational, I'm bonded to a man because he is who I want to be or is doing what I want to do, and he's bonded to me because he sees his younger self in me. I'm often friends with younger men who are one or two steps behind me in life because I enjoy seeing my previous journey in others.

Within any social circle you're a part of, you'll be strong

friends with at least one person who forms your anchor to the group. He is the person you trust and will contact first when making plans. Technically, you're also "friends" with the other people in the circle, but for the sake of this discussion I'll call them acquaintances, because it's unlikely that you would keep in contact with them if you left the group.

It's best to run transactional game with acquaintances, where you give or display value so that you receive value back. The most common forms of value you can give to acquaintances are entertainment, fun, and logistical aid, such as providing venues for parties, buying drinks, or otherwise helping to keep the good times going. This will make your social circle acquaintances more eager to introduce you to their female friends, invite you to parties, and help you maintain a positive reputation in the circle.

This may sound easy, but chances are you're an introvert. If you were an extrovert, providing value to a social circle would come naturally, and you wouldn't need instructions on how to do it. Introverts are rarely the highest-value members of a social circle, and are often members of groups that are not bursting with attractive girls. Not only do extroverts effortlessly reap most of the social rewards, but unlike introverts, they also don't see maintaining relationships with friends or acquaintances as energy-draining "work."

If you do see maintaining a social circle as work, you run the risk of failing in your attempts to use it as a reliable way to meet women. With cold approaching, I need to show only bursts of extroversion, perhaps for a few hours a week, which is far less than I need to do to sustain my membership in a good social circle. I'm also more than capable of creating an "instant social circle," where I show a surge of value to a group of individuals in a bar or club by buying them drinks and being cool, while deferring to the apex male of the group, so that I can either attract a girl in the group or show high social value to other girls in the venue. This works well in foreign countries, where your value is already high because you're regarded as exotic.

Men with good social circles aren't conscious of the effort they put in to maintain them (although they may be conscious of the value they give). Since a social circle can only provide you with girls indirectly, don't kill yourself maintaining one if you can get girls directly by walking up to them.

Pulling

The easiest way to sleep with a girl in your social circle is to be the apex male, who the members generally agree is the highest-status man in the group. No girl in a social circle wants the bottom male, and even the bottom females want the top male. This fact alone should push you to invest only in social circles where you can be the apex male, or at least among the top three.

Even if the girls in a group where you're the apex male are not that good looking, you'll get significantly better results than if you're ranked in the middle of a group with hotter girls. In other words, be the shark of whichever social circle you swim in instead of a measly goldfish. Your ability to get laid is therefore mostly determined by your place in the *hierarchy*, not your external game as with cold approaching.

If you have to put on a show in an attempt to be the apex male, you're in the wrong group, because who becomes the apex male is decided through unconscious cues such as body language, frame, and tonality. Regardless of your value as a man right now, there is a group out there where you will be the apex male without trying. This group may be a Dungeons & Dragons meet-up, and the girls who belong to it could be unsightly, but you will have your pick of the girls in that group. I would rather be at the top of a hipster group, where I have a choice of girls with silly tattoos and piercings, than at the bottom of a social circle with supermodels. The latter group will be torture as I watch all the girls sleep with the photographers, celebrities, and business owners while I'm left with nothing.

Over a decade ago, I was part of a group of Washington, D.C. bloggers who would meet for a happy hour every month. Because I had the most popular blog and wrote about controversial topics like fucking girls, I was the apex male in a group of about thirty individuals. I slept with at least ten girls who were either in the group or one node away, and since I had the most power in the group, no one could blacklist me for being a sexual deviant. Although the top girls weren't that hot (this is Washington, D.C. we're talking about), there were multiple 7's who pleased me and were easier to lay than if I had met them through cold approaching. Instead of being attracted directly by my stories, jokes, or attitude, they were attracted by my status in the group, which presupposed that I possessed attractive traits.

If you gain apex status within a social circle, a question that comes up is whether you should select girls in the group or let them select you. With cold approaching, you pick the girl and apply optimal game until you fail, but in social groups it's better to display value to everyone in the group and then allow the women to invest in you by taking the initial steps to gain your favor. When a girl in your social circle likes you, she will flirt openly, ask questions to get to know you on a deeper level, and allow you to isolate her. You'll also notice that she treats you more favorably than other men in the group.

In a social circle, you "game" everyone by being an attractive, fun man while keeping your antennae up for girls who select you for romance. You then use standard game to convert a girl's interest into sex, keeping in mind that everything you do with her will eventually be broadcast to the entire group. This is not necessarily bad, because rumors of you sleeping around will serve as confirmation to the other females that you are indeed the apex male. In fact, you'll be able to sleep with most of the girls in the group and not damage your reputation as long as you're not accused of abuse, lying, or manipulation. You may even be able to get away with pumping and dumping them, but generally it's best to be polite when it comes to break-ups.

Having a "player" reputation can be both good and bad. If girls who are new to the social circle are warned about you, they may see you as a "bad boy" and be inclined to sleep with you to see what the fuss is all about, but this can morph into you getting a reputation as "abusive," which will be spread by the group's beta males to make a power grab for your apex status, or by the fat girls who are jealous that you don't want to sleep with them.

If this happens, you'll have to hurt the reputation of your enemies so that they are ostracized instead of you. In the end, you'll find that there isn't much difference between a social circle of adults and one of high school kids.

When you strongly suspect that a girl likes you, start planning to get her alone. The first way is to get her number and take her out on a date. The date should progress in a similar way as if you had met her through a cold approach, though it should be easier because you've already confirmed that she strongly likes you. The downside of this method is that as soon as you get her number, the interaction goes from her chasing you to you chasing her, giving her the ability to play phone games or flake before the date.

The second method is to make a move towards the end of one of the social circle's gatherings, usually a night party. As the evening goes on, and friends start leaving, attempt a venue change by telling the girl you want to hang out at another bar, her place, or your place. Avoid heavy touching or kissing while your friends are watching. Once you get her alone, seal the deal as you would with a random girl who was with you on a date.

You may encounter verbal resistance along the lines of "We should just be friends," even though her body language is giving you the green light. Agree with her ("You're right, we should just be friends") and try again later. One additional step you can take to build trust is to tell her that you like keeping your personal life private, and you don't want whatever happens between you two to be gossiped about later. Of course she'll still end up blabbing to others, but saying this reduces her fear of looking like a slut to the group.

Whether a girl is in my social circle or a few nodes away, I prefer to establish some intimacy before even thinking of getting her phone number. Girls in your social circle may be very attracted to you, but in the end they're still girls and capable of flaking. It's best to strike when the iron is hot during a face-to-face interaction while under the influence of alcohol. There's no sense ending the moment artificially by getting a number instead of probing her resistance wall. If a girl is not willing to kiss you after showing signs that she's interested, she could be wasting your time, especially if no other members of the group are around.

Most of my success with social circles has come when I went for sex at the end of group meetings, after I was reasonably sure that the girl was attracted to me. If I get a number before making a move, I often encounter flaking. Whether it's a cold approach or a warm social circle lead, you lose ground if you allow a girl to decide when to meet you again in the future. If she likes you, and she's in front of you right now, go as far as she lets you.

If a girl rejects you, get ready to tell other members of the group that you pursued her only because she showed strong indicators of interest:

> "I thought she liked me because she did A, B, and C. She was giving me green lights, but it's okay if she's not interested. No big deal."

Always have in the back of your mind how you'll look to other members of the social circle. Stay out of trouble by acting with plausible deniability, and be sure the leading female of the group, the "mother hen," eventually comes to believe your side of the story.

I generally advise against being friends with girls, because most men try to use friendship as a stepping stone to intimacy and instead get stuffed into the friend zone, but in social circles it's worth having strategic friendships with "connectors" like the mother hen, who knows most of the other girls. As long as you're not sexually interested in the connector, and don't supplicate by tying her shoes or carrying things for her, she will likely help you meet other girls as long as she's not the jealous type. At a minimum, you'll have to be on friendly terms with the mother hen of the group. She is the central node through which all gossip flows, meaning she is capable of hurting your reputation in a way that may result in exile.

In my Washington, D.C. blogger group, I was close to the mother hen. She would tell me which girls liked me and I would give her advice when she needed it or feed her any juicy gossip that she happened to miss. At the same time she was giving me value, I helped to boost her status by making it publicly clear that she was my favorite female in the group. Without the information she gave me, I would have slept with far fewer girls. If a girl you are friends with is being stingy by holding back on gossip or not inviting you to events that you know she's going to, you should pursue another group female for a strategic friendship.

A common problem is having guy friends who don't know any girls. This happened to me in college when I had a group of friends who only played board games and poker. I added a new group of friends who liked going to clubs and drinking, but they didn't know any girls either, though I could at least use them as wingmen to cold approach. If your friends don't know any girls *and* don't want to meet girls, you may have to cool off these friendships until you reach your sexual goals. Branch out and make friends with men who have wider social circles or who at least can serve as wingmen. Your old friends may resent you for trying to improve your sex life, but they're more than welcome to join you at any time.

If you're in high school or college, social circles will be the defining feature of your life and the primary way to get laid. Even though you're younger, the concept is the same: enter a social circle, become the apex male, give value to the group, and make a move on girls who are showing you interest. At this stage of your life, you should be focusing less on mastering the cold approach than being friendly and entertaining so that you are invited to parties and other activities where girls are present.

Appendix Summary

As long as you're sociable and make an effort to add value, you should find yourself naturally entering social circles. If this is not who you are, or you're not up to the task, it may be better to adopt a cold approach program or pursue social circle alternatives, such as being a regular at a small venue (for example, a café or bar), taking part in activities where girls are present (yoga, dancing, co-ed sports), or participating in language exchanges and meet-up groups organized on the internet. While these options are not traditional social circles, they can increase your access to girls and make interactions feel warm instead of cold.

If you have a social circle that is fruitful, enjoy it while it lasts, because they tend to have limited life spans. When you find yourself without a social circle, you can use cold approach game, particularly when you're older. Even when your social circle is productive, it wouldn't hurt to develop a basic cold approach game that you can use in the future when you don't have much choice.

Appendix 2: Love Tourism

If you're from a Western country, it's almost certain that you will derive value from visiting more traditional countries for "love tourism." Women of the West will continue to degrade for years to come, suggesting that a wait-and-see attitude is not a viable strategy for men who are alive today. I started as a love tourist and gradually morphed into a full-blown love migrant after accepting that the grass for me is greener abroad.

The most common mistake men make before traveling to meet girls is thinking that their game will magically improve after they get off the airplane. Yes, girls will treat you differently, but this doesn't mean they will throw themselves at you, and I find that foreign girls tend to put out slower than Western girls. Therefore, I strongly advise you to achieve a competent level of game *before* you start traveling.

At least for your first few trips, you are unlikely to do better than you would at home. There are some exceptions, such as if you're a white man who goes to Southeast Asia, but if you're unable to meet girls in your country because you can't approach them or maintain a conversation, it will *not* be easier for you elsewhere. Whatever problem you have in your home city will simply travel in your luggage to a new location.

Only travel once you have a firm understanding of all the skills that are required to sleep with a girl, such as approaching, maintaining a conversation, going on dates, and sealing the deal. Rack up a few notches in your home city before going elsewhere, because then it will simply be a matter of running your tried-and-tested game on a slightly different audience. On the other hand, if you've never tried to kiss a girl, or you have hardly any dating experience, prepare to endure deep struggles abroad.

Not only will your game not magically improve, but it will slightly degrade because of language barriers and logistical difficulties you never had to deal with at home.

Where To Go

Love tourism is a different beast than general tourism, so ignore the mainstream tour guides and books that do not take your sex goal into account. Also ignore the minimalist traveler who brags about going to foreign countries with only one pair of cargo pants.

For your first trip, pick a country that has the type of girl you're most attracted to while avoiding countries that are Westernized, particularly those in Western Europe or the Anglosphere (United States, Canada, UK, Ireland, and Australia). If you like white girls, go to Eastern Europe. If you like Latinas, go to South America or Central America. If you like Asian girls, go to Asia, especially Southeast Asia, where it's easier than in countries such as China and Japan. If you like black girls, go to Africa.

It's hard to advise you on which specific country to visit within a broad region. Because of your unique appearance, personality, game, and taste in women, a country that is good for one man may be awful for the next. Just as it took you time to find the best venues in your city for running game, it will take time to find the best countries for meeting girls with whom you are most compatible, so get ready to take multiple trips abroad to find your "poosy paradise." You can prepare for your trip by using a resource such as the travel section of the Roosh V Forum (rooshvforum.com), but understand that there is a hit-or-miss element to international game that can't be avoided. You must risk venturing into the unknown to reap big rewards.

Once you decide on a country, the next step is deciding which city or cities you want to visit. You can focus either on the country's biggest cities, which often include the capital, or the lesser known "second-tier" cities that have a population of at least 250,000 people and are not as popular among tourists.

Almost always, second-tier cities will have girls who are not used to meeting foreigners, meaning that they will see you as more exotic and attractive. Second-tier cities also tend to have a higher percentage of girls in university. Other advantages are cheaper costs, a more compact center that makes logistics easier, and greater comfort for longer stays. The downsides of second-tier cities are a quieter nightlife and a lower standard of English. I've experimented with both first-tier and second-tier cities and prefer the latter, because the girls are more receptive, younger, and less worn out by foreign cock.

For your first international trip, I recommend you visit one first-tier and one second-tier city, staying in each for five to seven days. If you cannot do a vacation of at least ten days, stick to only one city. Unless a place has a strong one-night stand culture, such as Scandinavia and other Western countries, you will likely need a date or two to seal the deal. This is particularly true if you're not skilled at getting one-night stands. Another reason I rarely stay in a city for shorter than a week is that its character from Sunday through Wednesday can differ completely from Thursday through Saturday.

The strategy for a general tourist is completely different to yours. The tourist will pick as many cities as his energy allows, focus on visiting historical sights, and take hundreds of photos of buildings and landscapes. This is exactly how I did my first trips abroad, and it's no surprise that I never got laid. Love tourism is different in that you need extra time in any one location for luck to work in your favor. This means getting familiar with the city and being ready to go on dates. If you jump around every few days, you will decrease your odds of success.

Pipelining

Chat with an experienced love tourist and he will tell you about pipelining, a tactic where you use the internet to line up girls to meet before you set foot in the country. Internet game in your own country may be unsavory, but with foreign girls it's sometimes a necessary evil to ensure a trip's success, especially if you're traveling for less than two weeks.

A close sibling of pipelining is "sampling," where you gauge the responsiveness of a representative sample of girls in different cities. On an app such as Tinder, I may view a certain number of girls in multiple cities and count how many matches I get from each one. On a dating site, I may message a certain number of girls in a city and see how many phone numbers I can get. If you encounter a *noticeably* higher response rate in one city compared with another, and not just a small difference that can be explained by statistical variance, you could have a potential gold mine on your hands.

Beware that sampling girls online doesn't always translate into real-life interest, so use it as only one way of helping you decide where to go. Your main determinant when choosing a place is how strongly you want to go there, because nothing beats inner motivation when it comes to predicting success.

Foreign girls can be found on a number of sites including Facebook, VK, Badoo, Tagged, Tinder, Couchsurfing, language exchange sites, and local dating sites. Research which sites are popular in the country you're going to and apply a basic internet game program where you upload a handful of solid photos that show you as fun, adventurousness, exotic, and social.

I'm not a fan of chatting online so I keep things basic and let my photos do much of the talking. If a girl likes how I look, she'll respond to mediocre messages, especially since I'm foreign, but if she doesn't like how I look, she won't respond to even the best game. My main formula is showing that I'm a foreign guy who is a virgin to her city to tap into her nurturing instinct to help. Here are two basic openers I use:

> "Hello. You look like you lived in the USA or England for a while because of your style." She will share her experience in the countries I mentioned.

> "You like [stated interest in her profile]? I wouldn't have imagined someone from Hungary liking that." She will explain why she likes it.

After the ice is broken, immediately highlight your foreigner status to gauge her receptiveness. Even if you don't get far with a girl romantically, use the information she gives you to speculate whether a particular city will be good for you.

"I'm from Washington DC and coming to your city. What's your favorite restaurant where I can try the best Polish food?"

"Do you have a favorite place in Rio that someone new should visit?"

"What is the most fun thing to do in your city?"

Your initial chat won't be that different from a day game opener where you ask for help. Usually, internet game in the West involves extreme humor and cockiness to separate yourself from the hundreds of other men who have contacted her in the past week (or day), but when I use internet game abroad I want to see if basic game will be effective. Having to use hardcore game abroad means that the experience won't be that much different from my home city, which takes away from the point of traveling for better women in the first place.

If a girl is responsive, she'll likely ask for your backstory of why you're visiting or what you do. You can play the tourist angle or hint that you're developing long-term ties to her country. The sluttier a girl, the more she won't mind banging a tourist for a few days, but it helps to plant the seed that you may stay a while so she has a reason to invest in you. Weave a story where it's not obvious you'll bang her and then immediately leave the country.

"I'm doing a work project in Ukraine. I plan to come and go often. And you?"

"I'm traveling to Mexico because I plan to move there. I'm not sure which city to pick. And how about you?"

"Me and a friend are looking for the best city in Thailand to start our business."

"I've heard a lot of good things about your city so I want to come for a week of partying and fun. If I like it, I'll stay for longer."

One way to proceed with the chat is to inquire about her city or culture:

"Should I get ready for any big surprises? I heard most cities in your country don't have internet."

"Are there any weird things I should know about your country before I come?"

"Is there anything about your country that you like the most?"

If she asks you questions or seems genuinely interested, go for the date:

"Well you seem cool. Let's meet when I arrive so you can show me that place."

"Well you seem fun. How about we meet at that bar you mentioned for a drink?"

I have a few stock lines I throw out that can bring a girl out of her shell:

"You're the first Colombian girl I've heard of that likes [insert stated interest]."

"You seem shy. Are all Estonian girls like that?"

"People warned me that Brazilian girls are very serious. Is that true?"

I'll be the first to admit that my internet and text game is on the dry side, but I feel this is justified with foreign girls because their poor English will not enable them to understand sarcasm or humor. Nonetheless, you can add spice to your game if you feel she is throwing out humor, especially if you're using a site that is more geared towards hook-ups.

Be mindful of your reply times and don't use more emoticons or exclamation marks than her. If you want to hit her with jokes, whether in a conversation or as an opener, keep them on the corny side so that she'll understand.

> "What do you call a cow with no legs? … Ground beef."

> "What do you call a boomerang that doesn't come back? … A stick."

Many men I know prepare for their trip by messaging hundreds of girls online for the goal of having three or more dates lined up before they land. To save time, they often do multiple dates a day to screen for girls who are most likely to come through for a bang. In addition to dates from pipelining, they also supplement with day and night game upon arriving.

Personally, I don't pipeline for dates, because girls so regularly misrepresent themselves online that I'll get stuck with a mediocre-looking internet date while a large number of hotter girls are walking around. Instead, I may use sampling to test both the attractiveness of girls in a particular city and their responsiveness towards my appearance. As long as you understand that sampling is exactly that—a sample—and not a guarantee of how things are on the ground, you will arrive in any city fully prepared to put in the work required to succeed.

The Trip

Many men screw up their logistics before they even land by booking hostels or shared apartments that don't allow them to bring girls back. You can hope that a girl has her own place, but why take the risk to save a few bucks? You don't want to cockblock your mission in any way, because I promise that you'll have enough obstacles to deal with after you land. I try my best to book a private apartment that is 0.7 miles (1.1 kilometers) or less from the area where I think I'll be going out at night or taking girls on dates. The closer, the better.

Besides pipelining, sampling, or having optimal lodging logistics, be prepared to leave your ego at home. You should make the decision to abstain from bitching out girls, calling out cockblockers, or getting into beefs with men who give you minor disrespect. Your time is too limited to take your eyes off the prize. Focus on your goal by keeping activities unrelated to women, such as sightseeing, to a minimum. If you want to be a general tourist, by all means do so, but if you have sexual or intimate goals, you must act like it. Also refrain from masturbating before the trip. You want your balls to be full and ready to explode. The only time you should masturbate on your trip is to relieve debilitating testicular pain.

The first thing you should do when you arrive is buy a prepaid SIM card from either a mobile shop or a reseller in a convenience store. You will almost certainly have to communicate with girls during your trip, so don't limit yourself by having an international number that is too expensive for girls to text and that makes it seem as if you won't be staying for long. Nothing screams "tourist" to a local girl than a man who doesn't have a local number. The second thing you should do is buy a bottle of wine or liquor to use as your excuse for inviting girls to your place.

Start the trip by running game that has worked for you in your home country. Gradually make adjustments with each approach as you learn the local patterns. When you're abroad, you don't want to *learn* game—you want to *adapt* your existing game to the local girls.

Be ready to approach like a dog. Ten approaches a day is the absolute minimum to strive for. Since nightlife can be hit-or-miss, make a real effort with day game, at least initially until the nightlife proves that it can supply you with girls. The problem with day game, however, is that it has a slow lead time if you don't get the same-day bang. It usually requires at least one date to get sex, but often two, which means that it's not particularly useful if you'll be in a city for less than a week. You should still do day game because you may get lucky and your approaches can lead to valuable intelligence about where to go at night.

Including pipelining in your game can enable you to employ multiple forms of attack if you will be in a city for a limited amount of time. Since this can be exhausting, many men take a break from everything else in their life so they can dedicate all their energy to a trip.

If you'll be in a city for a very short period, like a weekend, forget about dating and focus predominately on getting one-night stands through night game. This means you must select for obvious sluts while having extra high energy to stay out all night in the clubs until there are no girls left to approach. If girls you approach are skeptical because you're alone, approach men with indirect openers and become their instant "friend" by buying rounds of drinks.

Early Game

Day game is easy when you're a tourist and have authentic questions about how to get around and find things. If a girl is interested in the fact that you're foreign, she's more likely to show early interest, especially if you use the "Where I come from" bait (for example, "Where I come from, the supermarkets are huge and take hours to go through, but here I can only find tiny supermarkets"). In some cases, your mere existence is bait enough that you only need to maintain a light conversation. This applies to night game as well, where you should use openers that are void of cockiness or arrogance.

One opener modification is to make it obvious that it's your first time in the country. For example, let's say you want to ask a girl for the best espresso. Your modified opener would be, "Excuse me, do you know where I can find a good café? I just arrived to the country and don't know any good places." If a girl likes the idea of meeting a man who is a virgin to her country, which many do, she'll be excited to be the first to tell you everything you need to know.

Imagine you had the chance to show an African villager, who has never seen a big city, the sights and sounds of New York City. You'd greatly enjoy his reaction to seeing modern civilization for the first time. Girls you meet will also love seeing your reaction to new things in her country, which is why it's not a bad idea to make it appear that you're a virgin tourist even when you're not.

Being a weathered expat who has seen and done it all, and who even speaks the language, may bring value to a girl who wants a serious relationship, but for casual sex and excitement, it's better to sell her the idea that you're completely new to the country. I don't recommend outright lying, because that will bite you in the ass if you end up developing a relationship with the girl, but don't be afraid of coming across as lost or confused.

Use the most basic openers in your repertoire until you can establish what the general level of English is. If the level appears high, you can use any opener you want and be confident that you'll be understood. In other cases, you may run into a wall of poor English in cities that never see tourists or lack a large university population. You won't have time during a short trip to become fluent in a foreign language, so your mission in environments lacking English is to find an English-speaker. Use an opener of "Do you speak English?" until you find a girl you can communicate with. It won't be fun to pass up on pretty girls to find an average one who speaks English, but such an experience may motivate you to learn the language if you want to re-visit the country in the future.

An important component of international game is having a good backstory for girls who aren't slutty. If a girl is slutty, she will not care that you are leaving in a matter of days. In fact, she'll prefer it! When I was in Iceland, girls lost interest when they found out I was staying relatively long-term, because they wanted to sleep with me once and never see me again. The opposite occurred in a place like Ukraine, where sluts are much harder to find and girls are more interested in what they can get from a man over an extended period.

A backstory of "I'm here to have fun" will help you to get laid in Iceland, but it will hurt your chances in Ukraine. A backstory of "I just started a new job with a multinational company" will hurt you in Iceland while helping you in Ukraine. The more traditional the country, the more permanent your backstory should be. If you're in a country that is not full of sluts, have a backstory that you're there for work, business, or family. Keep it as vague as possible. If she asks for specifics, deflect.

Her: "So why are you here?"

Me: "For work."

Her: "What kind of work?"

Me: "I work for a company that buys commercial real estate."

Her: "What kind of real estate?"

Me: "Why do you want to know? It's not important. What do you do?"

Many men use a backstory that they are starting a business, often tourist-related. Some of the backstories I've heard are quite inventive, from "working with a government defense contractor" to "taking care of my sick grandmother." Provide just enough detail to satisfy the girl, but not so much that she can research it on her own, and definitely don't allow her to interrogate you.

Since I'm not a fan of lying, try to base your backstory on the truth. I write for a living, which includes travel writing, so it's easy for me to share a backstory about a tourist or internet business that could be regarded as mostly true.

The simplest backstory is "I live here." When she asks why, you can give her a standard response (work, business) or a humorous answer ("I ask myself that every day"), or you can deflect by asking her why she lives in the city. Another option is the romance backstory, where you say you fell in love with a local girl, moved in with her, broke up, but decided to stay. You only need to provide enough information to satisfy her for the moment. If you overcompensate by giving too much detail, she may get suspicious.

If you're staying in a city for only a few days, give a neutral backstory that is focused on fun but hints at something long term. This will allow a girl to rationalize that she didn't sleep with a man who only wanted to pump and dump her.

Her: "So why are you here?"

Me: "I heard a lot of good things about this city, so I wanted to visit."

Her: "So you're not staying for long?"

Me: "I like it so much that I'm already planning to come back in two months. I'm looking to start a business here with a friend."

This type of backstory hedges your bets. It won't score high value in a girl's eyes, but at least the interaction is likely to proceed and she'll consider sleeping with you. A similar option is to say you came only for a short vacation but have fallen in love with the city and are not sure what to do. This sets the stage for a "romantic" narrative where she convinces you to stay longer.

If you won't have much time in a city, and need to pull a bang out of your hat, use a purely fun backstory to screen for the most promiscuous girls. You'll find that a lot of girls will quickly exit a conversation if you jokingly say you're in her city for "sex and drugs," but the ones who don't will be up for fast sex. Experiment with different types of backstories to see which one selects for the type of girl you want.

Late Game

When it comes to scheduling dates, you won't have much

time to play out the seduction, so you'll have to move faster than in your home city. When I fail to venue change a girl back to my place, I ask her out on a date for the *following* evening: "So how about we grab a drink tomorrow night? I found a bar nearby that we can check out." If she says she's busy and doesn't counter-offer with a day she's free, she's not a good prospect. Get her number only when it's clear she's sincere about meeting for a date within one or two days. If a girl is going to take more than one date to have sex with you, and you won't be in her city for more than two weeks, you have to move fast, even if you may appear slightly needy for doing so.

Once you get her out on a date, and things settle in for a long conversation, remind yourself that she is out with you because she is unsatisfied with the local men, is curious about what a foreign man is like, and desires that which is exotic. She wants a man who opens her up to new experiences and treats her differently from what she's used to. Your conversation should therefore be an opportunity to highlight the differences between your two countries through stories, anecdotes, and general observations. Talk about your foods, customs, and habits. Describe what the men and women in your country are like. Describe your best cities. Give her opportunities to make comparisons. There shouldn't be much awkward downtime when talking to foreign girls because you'll have so much to talk about.

There are a few specific conversation pieces you can use. The first is to ask her what other countries she has been to, followed by what countries she would like to live in (if she's out on a date with you, it's a near guarantee that she likes the idea of travel).

Second, ask her how the locals date. Let her describe the process and how the local men behave so you can identify what she likes and dislikes. Since she's going out with you, she's already disenchanted with the local men, and may insult them.

The third conversation piece is to ask her whether she's known anyone from your country before, and what she thinks of them. Insist that you won't be offended by her honest opinion. If you're American, she will likely say that your fellow citizens are obese and ignorant of world affairs (both true).

One of my favorite routines is letting a foreign girl know that sex is fast in my country, implying that I won't judge her for putting out quickly. Do the routine towards the end of the night when you're getting ready to venue change to your place.

> "In America, we have sex first and then get to know the person afterwards. The word 'slut' is used more like a joke. We believe in equality, so everything a man can do, a girl should be able to do too. Now whether that's true or not, it's what we were taught, so things usually go really fast. If we were in America, we would have already had sex multiple times."

This technique is not effective on a traditional girl who requires you to make a major commitment before sex, but it does allow a girl with slutty inclinations to proceed without shame.

If you make a mistake and offend a foreign girl at any point during a conversation, use the fact that you're from a different country as an excuse.

> "That's a common thing/idea/saying in America. When people here do different things than I'm used to, I keep an open mind instead of criticizing. Cultures are different."

In essence, you condemn her for being culturally narrow, which no girl wants to be. You can use this excuse only once or twice, most commonly when you cross the line on cockiness. Western girls require larger amounts of cockiness than foreign girls, so you've likely internalized a cocky attitude that could cause you trouble abroad.

Since foreign girls are less likely to live alone, focus on going back to your place to seal the deal by inviting her for a drink or some other reason. If you want to experience sex at the same speed as you do in the West, it's better to hit girls with your fun backstory so you don't accidentally bring home a traditional girl who has rigid rules on not having sex with a man until a certain amount of time has passed. When I take a short trip, my goal is to get a taste of the easiest girls in a country to help me decide if

I should return for longer.

The last piece of advice I want to give you is to beware of maintaining a long-distance relationship with a girl you haven't had sex with. It will happen that you run out of time and have to leave before having sex with a girl. You may then attempt to maintain the relationship when you get home, and perhaps even promise to fly her to your city. This is dangerous because you're putting her on a huge pedestal. She will feel that you're lacking options to chase after her even though she hasn't slept with you. There's no harm in pinging her periodically if you think you'll return to her city (under the guise of "business" or "seeing friends," so she doesn't think she's the only reason you're coming), but you should be careful about pursuing a romance with a girl who hasn't made a sexual investment in you. It's often a trap.

Appendix Summary

The rising popularity of love tourism is a sign that Western women are declining more rapidly compared to their foreign counterparts, but understand that foreign women are still women. They also want to become independent of men by choosing a career over family and be showered with attention from male suitors via the internet.

I expect international game to get harder as time goes on, but there will always be a niche for you somewhere in the world. If it's not a first- or second-tier city, it may be a third-tier city that is barely on the map. As long as a man desires sex and love, there is a path for him to achieve his goals in the most efficient manner possible.

The only major downside of experiencing success abroad is that you'll find it harder—if not impossible—to be satisfied again with your own women. Now that you've had greener grass, your life may become a waiting game of saving money so that you can hit the road once more. There is the option of seeking out foreign girls in your country, such as in salsa clubs or other international venues, but that experience simply can't match being an exotic piece of meat in a foreign land. For many men, their first steps as a love tourist will put them on a path that will lead to a major life change, just like it did for me.

Other books written by Roosh...

30 Bangs: The Shaping Of One Man's Game From Patient Mouse To Rabid Wolf

'A fun-quick read about Roosh's adventures with many women. I laughed at his analogies and thoroughly enjoyed this read.'

30 Bangs details how Roosh made romance with 30 different women while consciously using various game methods and techniques. The purpose of this book is to show by example so that you can duplicate the behaviors, moves, and lines that led to his romantic success. The short stories contained in this brief memoir include...

The Giraffe. Roosh's first Latina romance that eventually sent him packing to South America for more.

The Freckles. A lay-up where all he needed to do was not mess up.

The Train. A group romance attempt that didn't quite make it for everyone involved.

30 Bangs contains straight-forward reports about meeting women. As you make your way through each story, you'll be able to see how Roosh's skill at sealing the deal became more effective. His hope for men who read this book is to realize what is possible when it comes to fast romance.

'There's some great techniques on display here over a variety of approaches, that include both day and night game, as well as domestic (US) and international game.'

'This book was on the short side but definitely entertaining. The stories were captivating and I finished this book within a day.'

A Dead Bat In Paraguay: One Man's Peculiar Journey Through South America

'The honesty of the book shines through very brightly. The book is fearless.'

A Dead Bat In Paraguay is a true adventure story about a 28-year-old man who decided that the best way he could deal with his existential crisis was to sell his possessions, quit his professional career as a scientist, and hop on a one-way flight to Quito, Ecuador in order to visit every country in South America.

He sincerely believed the trip would put him on a track towards a more fulfilling life of excitement, intrigue, and exotic women, away from his soulless corporate job in a Washington D.C. suburb.

Instead, he humorously falls from one country to the next, striking out repeatedly with the local women, getting robbed, having dreams that became reality, self-diagnosing himself with a host of diseases, and suffering repeated bouts of stomach illness that made marathon bus rides superhuman feats of bodily strength.

Along the journey he chronicles the friendships, the women, and the struggles, including one fateful night in Paraguay that he thought would lead to his end.

'This is a really fun entertaining book, with a self-deprecating sense of humor. Imagine a young Larry David before he was famous, broke and traveling through South America.'

'It's one of the most honest and straightforward examples of what it's really like to travel by one's lonesome while a young single guy.'

'A extremely enjoyable book. Roosh writes in a deadpan straightforward way which is easy to get into.'

Free Speech Isn't Free: How 90 Men Stood Up Against The Globalist Establishment -- And Won

'His brutally honest and courageous writing does not fail to hold the reader's attention and keep the pages turning.'

Free speech may be your right, but unless you fight for it, you'll lose it. That is the message of Free Speech Isn't Free, which chronicles how organizing a lecture tour for masculine men inserted Roosh into an unexpected free speech fight spanning several continents, putting both him and his family in danger from the globalist establishment and their mob of deranged social justice warriors.

After becoming activated by mass-scale media distortions and mayoral denouncements, the SJW mob in Canada rose up against Roosh and his followers to halt his tour. Roosh refused to cancel and set out to hold the lectures in secret.

He shares how he fought back against the mob while trying to come to terms with the globalist agenda that they're controlled by. The well-informed men he met throughout the tour were critical in sharing hidden knowledge that put the agenda's puzzle pieces into place.

Even after the lecture, when Roosh tried to conduct happy hour meetings for his followers, a bigger worldwide outrage befell him, leading to the doxing of his family and threats to burn their house to the ground. Free Speech Isn't Free shares that story for the first time in a special epilogue, and what was going through the mind of a man who was the number one target for a 1984-inspired "two minutes of hate" that took place worldwide.

'When Roosh recounts his experience in Montreal, Toronto, and the Meetup Outrage, strap in your seat belts. You're in for quite a ride.'

How far will you go if the establishment attacks you for what you believe in? Are you ready to defend yourself if they come after your reputation, your job, and your family?

Free Speech Isn't Free shows what one man did when powerful groups tried to silence him, along with everything he learned during the most momentous months of his life that will help others be able to identify and defend against attacks within their own lives.

Bonuses included are the transcript of the "dangerous" speech that started it all, The State Of Man, and an important new article explaining how to keep yourself safe from social justice attacks.

'This is classic red pill reading.'

'A chronicle of a modern brave success and victory for free speech.'

'The chapters on Montreal and Toronto paint a grim picture of Canada. It truly seems like an Orwellian nightmare to someone who is awake to the reality of their social engineering.'

Poosy Paradise: The Obsessive Hunt For A Land With Easy And Beautiful Women

'Roosh takes us on a wild ride through the truths often left-unsaid.'

Roosh's search for girl paradise led him to a grisly city in Eastern Romania that had a plentiful supply of beautiful girls. It's a place that no sane man would voluntarily live in had it not contained the best fruit of what the human female species can offer.

After blanketing Romanian television and newspapers as the "famous American sex writer" and a "world Don Juan," Roosh was determined to leverage the temporary fame with his existing game to experience nonstop pleasure with the world's most beautiful women. The result was not exactly what he expected.

'A truly captivating account of a man's journey with many lessons learned and fleeting moments of happiness. The ultimate holy trail quest that is fated to fail as success would lead to the biggest loss a man could ever have: his sense of purpose.'

'Whereas many dudes like to exaggerate things to the positive in

the extreme, Roosh is not afraid to detail the bad and the good even at the cost of making himself look worse. It really resonates as reality and truth of what it's really like, moreso than anything else I've ever read by anyone else, anywhere, ever.'

'At first glance, it's a thoroughly engaging memoir about life alone in the hunt for 'poosy paradise', but it also provides a lot of inner and outer game advice.'

Bang Ukraine: How To Sleep With Ukrainian Women In Ukraine

'His methodology is damn accurate.'

Bang Ukraine is a travel guide that teaches you how to meet Ukrainian women while in Ukraine. Here's what you'll find inside...

-A deep analysis of the culture

-How you can hack the backwards Ukrainian mentality to find romance

-The type of guy who would do best with Ukrainian women

-The 3 types of Ukrainian girls, and the one you should go for in order to obtain intimacy

-The 3 types of men that a Ukrainian girl wants to experience, and how to be the one that gets romance the fastest

-How to develop a solid backstory so she doesn't think you're a sex tourist

-A detailed breakdown on how to pick up during the day, including opening strategy, conversation tips, pitfalls to avoid, and how to best answer their common questions about your visit

-How to have a conversation with a Ukrainian girl who possesses bad English, with over a dozen topics and ideas to be used both for when you meet her and on dates

-Three date strategy for completing the seduction, with specific venue suggestions, tips, and moves

-What to do when a Ukrainian girl tries to extract resources from you in a long-term relationship

Bang Ukraine aims to be a must-read guide for any Western man who wants to make romance with Ukrainian women while visiting Ukraine.

'This is the journey of a man who goes into a country and tries to figure out how it works. It is a beautiful work and very few people are daring enough to do something like this.'

'A very enjoyable, easy read, packed with tons of information to help future travelers. Would highly recommend to all readers. It's amazing that for 10 or 20 dollars, you can gain access to inside knowledge that would cost you many weeks, and thousands of dollars to acquire on your own.'

Bang Poland: How To Make Love With Polish Girls In Poland

'For anyone considering a visit, this book is a must. It will save you many hours of research, frustration, effort.'

Bang Poland is a travel guide that teaches you how to seduce Polish women while in Poland. Here's what you'll find inside...

-A breakdown of the best Polish city to visit for securing romance (hint: it's not Krakow or Warsaw)

-A detailed breakdown of the three types of Polish girls

-The type of guys that Polish girls are obsessed with, and how you'll do far better if you can pull off their look

-The one quality that Polish girls desire above all others, and the one that turns them off

-My favorite opener to use on Polish girls

-A detailed breakdown on how to pick up during the day, including opening strategy, conversation tips, pitfalls to avoid, and how to best answer their common questions about your visit

-How to date a Polish girl

-5 short stories that offer additional insight and information to Polish culture, including interesting examples of seducing Polish women

Bang Poland aims to be a must-read guide for any Western man who wants to seduce Polish women while visiting wonderful Poland.

'An unblinking, matter-of-fact view of Polish women, culture, and certain cities in Poland.'

'The book is more of a "how to" guide, but it is well written and very entertaining. It's obvious that the writer has actually been there and 'bang'd that'. He has advice and insight that only a seasoned traveler would know.'

For more of my writing, visit my blog:

http://www.rooshv.com

CPSIA information can be obtained
at www.ICGtesting.com
Printed in the USA
LVHW021027101118
596660LV00002B/523

9 781732 865402